americans

Also by Desmond Wilcox

TEN WHO DARED

americans

DESMOND WILCOX

DELACORTE PRESS / NEW YORK

DESIGN: *Giorgetta Bell McRee*

PRODUCTION: *Martha Schwerin*

EDITOR: *Betty Kelly*

PRINTING: *A. Hoen & Co.*

BINDING: *Economy Bookbinding Corporation*

Photographs on pages 17, 42, 45, 76, 97, 98, 121, 149, 219, 220, 261, 276, and 327 from the Bettmann Archive
Photographs on pages 10, 16, 77, 117, 159, 189, 238, and 308 from Culver Pictures
Photographs on pages 25, 36 (bottom), 56, 57, 200 (bottom), 246, 252, 258, 268, 279, 296, and 317 by Desmond Wilcox
All other photographs by Paul Hyman, © 1977 BBC-TV and Time-Life Films

Published by
Delacorte Press
1 Dag Hammarskjold Plaza
New York, N.Y. 10017

Library of Congress Cataloging in Publication Data

Wilcox, Desmond.
Americans.

Bibliography: p.
1. United States—Social conditions—1960–
2. United States—Biography. 3. National characteristics, American. I. Title.
HN59.W47   309.1'73'092   77–28016

ISBN 0–440–00108–0

For Esther

FOREWORD

Cowboys really do wear stetsons and throw lariats; Indians really do say, "How"; District Attorneys do cry out, "I object"; Film Stars still think, "It's all too wonderful"; Generals lead "for God and country"; Big Businessmen talk of that "good old get-up-and-go" spirit. It's all true; fact, not fiction.

Nearly twenty-five years ago I came to American shores, steaming past the Statue of Liberty, as a brand-new foreign correspondent. I was ready and eager to report, for British newspaper readers, all the exciting affairs and events of the richest country the world has ever known. I arrived— as most visitors for the first time probably do—filled with a whole set of preconceived ideas about America and Americans, molded and formed by what I had read and, particularly, by what I had seen on movie and television screens. It is hardly surprising then that I felt I already knew, very well, the archetypal American characters who had been presented to the outside world against colorful landscapes so frequently that they had become, not archetypes, but—stereotypes.

In the years since then, while going about the business of reporting this rich and open society, I have often thought of bringing together a personal collection of American archetypes. This book is that collection. The people in it are men and women—archetypes—that I personally would wish to remember with affection and a sense of celebration. They were not chosen (for both the television series and the book) because they fit into a careful sociological pattern or design. They are not meant to represent a balanced arrangement of geography, income, race, or sex. But they are, for me, the larger than life characters with whom I grew up. And I was delighted to discover that they are still real today.

Cowboys and Indians; Preachers and Generals; Businessmen and Southern Gentlemen; Film Stars and Private Eyes; District Attorneys and Schoolteachers; Trade Union Leaders and Sports Heroes; even the occupants of the White House have all become the stuff of fiction. But they provide too, I find to my personal delight, the facts of life. And in this book I have been able to explore, much further than in my television series, the historical beginnings and the rich backgrounds against which these American characters exist.

New York 1977

ACKNOWLEDGMENTS

I would like to acknowledge, with deep gratitude, the immense help I received from the whole production team of the television series *Americans;* in particular Adam Clapham, the executive producer; producers Jeremy Bennett, John Bird, James Kenelm Clarke, Ivor Dunkerton, and Ian Sharp; the researchers Tristan Allsop, Sally Evans, and Sally Hardcastle; Marcus Cunliffe for historical advice and June Leech for all the historical research; as well as the producers' assistants and all the film crews and film editors who made it a pleasure to work on the series. And Lorna Dodd and Connie Blease, without whom the book would never have been written.

D.W.

CONTENTS

americans

THE COMPANY PRESIDENT
PETE ESTES

He leaned back in his executive chair in the president's suite and gazed at the map of the world with its scattering of colored pins and flags. In Brazil it was early morning; in Britain the middle of the evening; in Australia it was just before dawn. But, however uncomfortable the hour around the world, he knew his top executives would be in their offices, waiting for him. He punched a button on the loudspeaker phone to start the routine weekly overseas conference of General Motors. In Detroit, Pete Estes' time, it was just after lunch.

In the richest country the world has ever known, it is certain that more people would rather be president of a giant corporation like General Motors than President of the United States. To succeed in business is to succeed as an American, in what has been called the business civilization. And in the business world, people are fond of quoting Calvin Coolidge: "The business of America is business." Another favorite is attributed to Charles E. Wilson, then president of General Motors and later Secretary of Defense under Eisenhower: "What's good for General Motors is good for the country." But, in fact, Coolidge was underquoted, and Wilson was misquoted. Coolidge went on to say: "The ideal of America is idealism," and Charlie Wilson (he was known as "Engine Charlie"), testifying before a Senate Committee, which was considering whether to confirm his appointment, actually said: "What is good for our country is good for General Motors and vice versa."

No business in America is bigger, fiercer, or more competitive than the motor industry. The car and the truck have played an essential part in the history and development of America. Today it is almost impossible to imagine an American without a car—and the motor industry tries to en-

Estes starts early.

sure that Americans never imagine themselves without a *new* car. Within the motor industry, the colossus to beat them all is General Motors, the second largest corporation in the world. (Exxon is the largest.) If nations were measured by wealth, General Motors would be the sixth nation on earth, a "corporation state" wealthy enough to stand alongside the great powers. So perhaps it is little wonder that surveys show that more boys in school, teenagers in high school, and young men in college would rather make it to the company president's office than the President's Oval Office in the White House. The president who rules over GM has achieved the corporation man's most spectacular dream, the pinnacle of business success. And if he does it from humble beginnings, as even today he still might, then he has achieved it in the best of all the American traditions.

Elliott Marantette Estes made it that way, all the way, from small-town beginnings and the factory floor to the executive suite. These days he earns a million dollars a year as boss of 800,000 employees. Still firmly in the center of the American business tradition, he'd like every one of them to know him personally, as "Pete."

He rules from Detroit. Detroit is Motor City, it always has been. Here they started by building horse-drawn carriages and wagons, and even built some of the wagons which rolled westward and opened up America. In time, the wagonmakers became auto engineers and now the city turns out 10,000 vehicles a day. The freeways that slice and quarter Detroit join Ford with Chrysler, and Cadillac with Chevrolet, and Oldsmobile with Pontiac, and American Motors with Dodge. The people of Detroit see nothing ugly about the business of cars and trucks and roads in Detroit. It has always been, and it seems likely it always will be, their whole life. Years ago the center of the city died and was left, abandoned to poverty and to crime, a ghetto in the middle of a ring of roaring car plants and soaring glass-walled office blocks. There have been attempts to solve the problem of the center of Detroit by creating an architectural renaissance. It is possible that the latest may succeed but, effectively, Detroit has for decades been a ring-shaped city, a wheel without a hub.

There is no single minute in the twenty-four hours of every day, and the seven days of every week, when the production lines in the city aren't spewing out new cars. While executives sleep and the new-car buyers haven't wakened, an army of American working men and women—the troglodytes of the twentieth century—hammer and blast to supply 200 million people of the most motorized country in the world with new cars they've yet to be persuaded they need. And of all the companies and all the conglomerates, General Motors is a giant among giants; a global conglomerate of hundreds of companies making and selling a range of products, spreading far beyond the auto industry into the business and family life of the world, from ships and trains to refrigerators, freezers, and air conditioners.

For the president of General Motors the day begins at six A.M., or even earlier, with a swim—except in winter. By six-thirty or six forty-five he's been collected by the most polished and best maintained executive Cadillac on the road. His chauffeur is an ex-cop, who was trained as a bodyguard and who, in true Motor City tradition, packs a significant bulge under his arm. Pete Estes starts his working day in the car, on the way in to his office. He knows that for more than seventy years General Motors has stayed in front of the most cut-throat competition in the business world and he knows, too, that it is his job to keep them out in front. He's paid to succeed, he doesn't think about failure; perhaps he doesn't dare to. His father was a small-town bank clerk in Mendon, Michigan. Pete Estes came into General Motors as a management trainee, after graduating from the company's own university, The General Motors Institute. Every morning when he reaches the downtown headquarters, he walks through the lobbies lined with the preserved and polished trucks and cars which are the reminders of his company's history. Today three-quarters of a million employees are affected by every decision he makes. His own time is worth nearly ten dollars a minute, and he says he doesn't think about that, but you would have to get up early in the morning to be at work before him. And if you weren't at work soon after him, he would probably notice it and do something about it.

Although General Motors is considered a good company, a fair, even paternalistic, company, it is still part of the American business pattern and the driving General Motors motivation is to succeed and beat competition. They are not interested in employees who don't feel that. Pete Estes' own philosophy is straightforward. "You have to win every day and you musn't be satisfied unless you do. It is this competitiveness in our industry which, I think, makes for this intense feeling in car workers. We have to tell ourselves that we're building the best car in the world, and we have to believe it. Of course I tell it to myself. I do believe it, too. I really do, I'm quite convinced of it." Pete Estes' identification with the spirit of competitiveness is so intense that if you are talking to him about the motor industry and mention the names of competitive corporations such as Ford or American Motors, Chrysler or (heresy of heresies) Volkswagen, he will clench his fists and tighten his lips. He himself cannot say the word "Ford." Instead he invents, quite naturally and easily, a score of euphemisms and semantic tricks to refer to his biggest competitor without speaking the name.

A dip a day keeps the doctor away.

Safe inside the inner councils of General Motors executive committees, he confesses that he will use the word, but he is completely conditioned against saying "Ford" in public. "I know it may seem silly to many people," he told me, "but I've always been like that and most of the top men in this industry are like that. Even within General Motors it is difficult for the leaders not to put one hundred percent of themselves and their loyalties into the product they are working with. When I transferred from Oldsmobile to Pontiac I found that I could never mention Oldsmobile, although when I had been working for Oldsmobile I couldn't have brought myself to mention Pontiac. People outside really don't understand our industry. If you talked to our competitors, you would find the same kind of feeling there. Perhaps it is particularly a characteristic of the auto business, more, for instance, than electronics, aviation, or shipping. After all, to be successful in a free marketplace, in our economy, and with our product, you have to have that kind of attitude.

"I know that our competitors have the same plant, the same equipment, the same tools, and the same machinery as we have, so the difference between winning and losing in this business has as much to do with the people as it has to do with machinery. And I think that our people in General Motors may just be a little more dedicated than the others; I like to think so, anyway. I've always said that when you go to work in the morning you must look in the mirror and tell yourself, 'I'm a General Motors man,' and when you come home at night you've got to think about it and tell yourself, 'I'm still a General Motors man.' And I'm the boss, but I still look in the mirror every morning and I say, 'You're the guy that can get this thing done.' That's one of my theories. It's one of the things I try and make all my people do, look in the mirror in the morning and say to themselves, 'Right there, in that mirror, there's someone that's more responsible than anyone else for the success of General Motors.' Then I myself always go on—and I'd like my men to go on—and say, 'What am I going to do today? I didn't do anything yesterday that was worth a damn, so what am I gonna do today?' This kind of philosophy applies right down to the man on the production line, putting the hub caps on. He's got to do his job right too, just the same as the board of directors and his managers—and me."

If Pete Estes arrives at an airport to rent a car and there isn't a General Motors model, then, as a last resort, he will drive a competitor's car. "I would really feel myself to be in a terrible situation, but if it was the only way of getting where I needed to go, then I would," he said. "But, all the time I was driving it, I would be looking for things that were wrong with it—or even things that were good about it. Then I'd make sure that, when I got back to our company, we took note of where the competition was weak—and also where it was good. And in the meantime I'd be calling up the rental company all the time and asking them why they weren't stocking more General Motors' cars. So, it would disturb me to drive a competitor's car, but I would get around that by trying to make something useful out of it, for both me and General Motors. I guess that all sounds almost like a public relations man talking, but you can't work for General Motors unless you believe in the product, and if you believe in the product you've got to believe in it the way I've described. I guess it's the same for our competitors, possibly that they behave in exactly the same way." He still couldn't bring himself to speak the word "Ford."

It is perhaps this kind of dedication that has helped take Pete Estes from his small-town beginnings to the very top. He was born in Mendon in southwestern Michigan in 1916, in the old Wakeman Hotel, which his grandparents owned, "in the second story left-hand front room, the same room my mother was born in." He told me, "My father worked in a bank in Mendon, a small bank. There were only 535 people in the whole town. From there we moved to Constantine when I was about ten years old. Constantine is another little town, only 1200 people, but my father finally worked up to chief cashier in the bank and he was pretty much running the Constantine branch. We had an automobile in those days, it was a big red Flying Cloud, and we had plumbing in the house after I was about ten years old; prior to that we just went out into the backyard. I wouldn't say we were rich, but we were middle class in a small town. I had a strict moral upbringing, my mother was a Catholic, my father was a Protestant, and so they joined a church somewhere in between those two and we went every Sunday."

He remembers an early attraction to machines and machinery. "In high school at fourteen, I really became infatuated with automobiles and that's the first time I remember getting into real trouble with my parents. They went away for a weekend and I was left to stay with my younger sister. Now I wasn't supposed to drive a car, but the fact is I put a lot of miles on it that one weekend and I really got interested in it. I think it was the beginning of my infatuation with moving things. But boy, I really got into trouble with my father for driving it. I remember, too, being interested in the threshing machines and the steam engines on my uncle's farm. But in those days I don't think there was too much thought given by my parents to the possibility that I would be an engineer. I think my dad was like most fathers and would have liked me to follow in his footsteps and go into the banking business, but I really didn't fancy that, and while I wanted to be tactful with my father, I wanted somehow to make it on my own and not through my father's connections. At that time too I had a great respect for physical labor—I enjoyed sports and athletics at school—and I felt I wanted to do something that was more manly than running a bank. So, when the time came to leave high school, I just wanted to get out and start

work; I didn't think about college, I didn't think about university, I looked around for something to do.

"There was a creamery in town and everybody who worked in the creamery had a house and a motor car and a happy-looking wife. So, I said to myself, it's got to be a good job and I got a job in that creamery. It wasn't a very difficult job and it was mostly physical labor, so soon I looked around and wondered whether or not I was going to get to be the boss of the creamery one day. But soon after I'd joined, the minimum wage law came through in about 1932—remember Franklin D. Roosevelt was President at the time.

"By then I was making a dollar a day and all of a sudden, because of the minimum wage law, I found myself making forty cents an hour, and the boss who had been making five dollars a day before that, he was still making five dollars a day. So I thought, what was the point of working for twenty years to climb from three dollars twenty cents a day to five dollars a day, just to take all that extra responsibility. So I reckoned the creamery wasn't for me. When I'd been at school we'd all been vocation-tested for the kind of job we ought to do and my form had come back saying that I ought to be a civil engineer, so I started to look around for that and see if there was anything that I could do in that line—I'd been in the creamery about a year by then. I'd just about made up my mind to sign up at Michigan State University as a civil engineering student, when I got a note from a cousin of mine in Pontiac, Michigan, who worked in General Motors Truck and Coach, and he said to me, 'What about General Motors Institute?' So I went up there and knocked on the door and enrolled. I'd saved about a thousand dollars and I felt independent enough, even though my dad would liked to have helped, to use it to go to college. I knew, too, that when you'd finished the course at General Motors Institute you were pretty certain of a job with General Motors. Remember, we'd just come through the Great Depression and my dad's bank had even been locked up for three years, and he'd had a terrible time getting along and had lost practically everything he had and everything he had saved, so I was very much more concerned in those days about security than perhaps any youngster would be these days."

It was at General Motors Institute that Elliott Marantette Estes (Marantette is his mother's maiden name) became known as "Pete." On his first day of practical work in the school machine shop, an instructor asked his name. After he was told it, he responded simply: "We'll call you Pete." Four months after joining the Institute, Estes also got a job at the research laboratories, working in the experimental shop. Through four years at

He shows off an electric car.

General Motors Institute and two at the University of Cincinnati where he earned a degree in mechanical engineering, Estes divided his time between the classroom and General Motors Research Laboratories. After graduating he went to work for General Motors. He himself believes that his first big break came in 1947 when he was promoted from senior research engineer to motor development engineer on the Oldsmobile team concerned with the new high-compression rocket V-8 engine. By 1961 he'd been elected one of the General Motors vice presidents and general manager of Pontiac. He was the youngest general manager of any of General Motors' five car divisions.

Pete Estes was obviously a comer—it even says so in his official press biography. *The New York Times* thought so too and in 1964 they wrote: "Elliott Marantette Estes, Automotives Management Rookie of the Year, has not only survived the General Motors jinx but is a front runner for Man of the Year honors in the hotly competitive industry." Translated, it marked Estes down for top promotion, pointed him out as an ambitious man to be watched—a man most likely to succeed. I asked him when he personally first considered the idea of becoming the big boss, president. But he insists: "I never did have that idea, I never really set my sights right at the very top, I always looked just toward the next job ahead. I just did my job as best I could and any time I was picked out for promotion I was pleased. It never entered my mind that I would be president of General Motors [he is the fifteenth]. I started to believe that it might be possible just before I actually got it, a year or two before. Then I started reading that maybe I was a candidate and by that time it seemed likely that I could get it, but it wasn't the most important thing in my life; ambition has never been a driving influence with me. When I was chief engineer at Pontiac, I reckon I had the greatest job in General Motors; I was going to make Pontiac the best car that General Motors ever had. About that time, I thought, 'Maybe I'll become general manager if something happens to the boss above me,' but it never became the only thing I wanted to do; my ambition was always to get closer to the product."

The history of "the product" began before the turn of the century in 1897, when Mr. R.E. Olds built his first successful Oldsmobile. Five years later Henry M. Leyland founded Cadillac and in 1903 the Buick Motor Company was formed from a predecessor firm established by David Buick. In 1907 Edward M. Murphy organized the Oakland Motor Car Company in Pontiac, Michigan. Eventually, these four firms became the nucleus of General Motors, following its incorporation by W.C. "Billy" Durant in September, 1908. Durant was really the creator of General Motors, an entrepreneur in the archetypal American mold.

Durant started, as many American successes do, inauspiciously. His father was a bank clerk, as was Pete Estes' father. But Durant's father was

Old Cadillac factory.

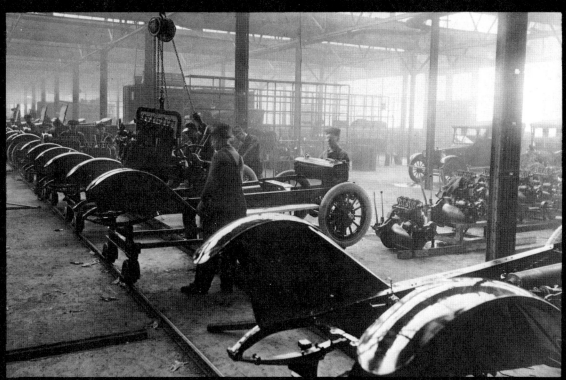

Old production line.

also a drunkard and a gambler. When Billy was seven his parents parted, but his mother had money from her own family and was not destitute. Billy did well at school and, at one time, the family thought he might become a lawyer or even a preacher. But just before his seventeenth birthday he dropped out of high school, went to work in a lumber yard for seventy-five cents a day. He made extra money by clerking at nights in a downtown drugstore. During the seven years after he dropped out of high school, Billy sold lumber, groceries, patent medicines, cigars, and real estate, making it to respectability at the age of twenty-four by becoming a partner in an insurance agency. He was therefore a very small-time businessman on the day he hitched a ride in a two-wheeled road cart and became dramatically impressed by the easiness and comfort of the ride. That same day he dashed off to Coldwater, Michigan, 120 miles from his home town of Flint, and asked the manufacturers of the cart for a share in their business. To his surprise, they wanted to sell it all and for fifteen hundred —borrowed—dollars he and a friend bought the whole operation. Together they organized the Flint Road and Cart Company, but once their purchases from Coldwater had been shipped over they found they only had two road carts to sell. So, using them as show pieces and himself as salesman, Durant toured the county fairs and won orders for six hundred carts; he also won a blue ribbon in a fair competition giving his company the slogan, "The Famous Blue Ribbon Line." The company was not even able to fill all the orders but had to contract out to another carriage factory, and on September 28th, 1886, The Flint Road Cart Company was formally set up with capital of two thousand dollars and an agreement with the factory to build 1,200 carts for twelve and a half dollars each, designed to be sold at twenty-five dollars each.

The cart was such a success that in its first year the Flint Road Cart Company became manufacturers, as well as wholesalers, and their total sales came to four thousand dollars. The company soon developed its own sophisticated assembly line and Durant said of it later, "We started out as assemblers with no advantage over our competitors. We paid about the same price for everything we purchased. We realized that we were making no progress and would not do so unless and until we manufactured practically every important part we used. We made a study into the methods employed by the concern supplying us, the savings that could be effected by operating the plants at capacity without interruption and with practically no selling or advertising expense. Having satisfied ourselves that we had solved our problem, we proceeded to purchase plants and the control of plants which made it possible for us to build up, from a standpoint of volume, the largest carriage company in the United States." By September, 1893, the Flint Road Cart Company had been incorporated with a capital of $150,000—seventy-five times the original two thousand dollars

Every day Estes walks by the history of GM.

which Durant's charm had won as a loan from a local bank. The name of the company was later changed to the Durant-Dort Carriage Company and by the turn of the century it had helped give Flint the name, "The Vehicle City." By 1906—the peak year for horse and carriage production —Durant was employing one thousand people in Flint and building up to 480 vehicles a day. The company had subsidiaries throughout America and in Flint alone produced 56,000 carriages in that one year.

But the horseless carriage was coming and Durant initially saw them as a nasty fad. "I thought it was terrible the way those noisy contraptions, especially the steam engines, shocked people and frightened horses," he is quoted as saying. "My cousin W.C. Orrell had one and I was mightily provoked with anyone who would drive around annoying people that way. I was not in the least bit interested in managing an automobile concern." But he was forced to take more interest in 1904 when Flint's title, "The Vehicle City," was endangered by the threat of the collapse of the Buick Motor Company. Billy Durant, known as a super salesman, already a millionaire at forty-two, was a natural man for the owners of Buick to appeal to. His loyalty to Flint and its interests was strong, so he listened. And after driving the Buick itself, he was won over by the performance of the automobile. He bought into the company and a few weeks later justified his super-salesman stature by going off to the New York Auto Show and returning with orders for 1,108 Buicks—and this at a time when the Buick company had been producing less than forty cars a year. By 1907 Billy Durant was producing 4,641 motor cars a year. He had already announced that he intended to be the world's largest producer of automobiles. In two years he had increased his production six times.

But the most historic year for the automobile industry was 1908—the year Henry Ford introduced the Model T. It was also the year that the General Motors Company was formed. And it was the year that Billy Durant met Albert Champion, who created the Champion spark plug and whose company became, as a result of another of the super salesman's conversions, General Motors' first subsidiary. It seems hard today to realize that when Billy Durant predicted that some day 500,000 automobiles would be built and sold in a single year, bankers thought he was mad. (In the first six months of 1977, General Motors built and sold throughout the world nearly five million motor cars, trucks, and coaches for $28.5 million.) Billy Durant always knew he was right. "I figured if I could acquire a few more companies like Buick, I would have control of the greatest industry in this country; a great opportunity—no time to lose—I must get busy." One interviewer at the time reported: "Durant sees—actually *sees*—ninety million people just aching to roll along the roads of this country in automobiles, and he wishes to fill that void." The incredulity of the reporter was more than matched by the accuracy of Billy Durant's vision of the future.

Durant moved on to control more and more of the motor industry in America. He bought the Oakland Motor Car Company in Pontiac, Michigan, eventually the Pontiac division of General Motors, and he bought Cadillac, which already had a name for quality. By the end of 1909 he had bought into or purchased twenty-two companies manufacturing cars or car parts, not all of them worth having but certainly all of them contributing to a solid base for his ambition to be the leader of the motor vehicle industry. He even at one time came close to buying out Ford for a mere eight million dollars, but he was unable to get bank approval for the loan of two million dollars he needed to clinch the sale.

By 1910, Durant was in trouble; the bankers were losing confidence in the automobile industry and General Motors seemed to justify their suspicions of reckless spending and lack of proper financial control. For the most part, the numerous General Motors subsidiaries had failed to settle down together easily and there was little effective control over their operation from the center. General Motors' sales increased from $29 million in 1909 to $49.4 million in 1910, but net profits rose to only $10.2 million —not enough to finance expansion and purchase supplies. General Motors was forced to borrow heavily and by the summer of 1910 its creditors were meeting to total up company debts. They found that Buick alone owed around seven million dollars. Reorganization and rationalization was forced on Durant—and the bankers took control of General Motors.

Almost immediately, however, Durant proceeded to build a new company—Chevrolet. After five years this new organization was producing 16,000 cars with net profits of $1.3 million. Then in 1915, the stock of General Motors suddenly started rising dramatically. Someone was buying and buying and buying—in great quantities. It was, in fact, Durant, and by May, 1916, Chevrolet had bought control of General Motors. The bankers had lost; Billy Durant was in charge again. Under his new rule the company was once again expanding and diversifying so that in three years his profits jumped from fifteen to sixty million dollars. By that time General Motors was on its way to becoming recognizable as the conglomerate that exists today. It had already bought Frigidaire, and formed its own finance house and construction companies to build homes for General Motors' workers. But central management was again weak, and it was about this time that the new era of Alfred P. Sloan, the father of today's General Motors, started. Sloan was an organization man and, while Durant still operated on a fiery, personal, charismatic basis as he had in the old days, General Motors was by now employing 86,000 men and women in a huge network of divisions and subsidiaries without a central base. They needed not fire and charisma, but organization and security. The day for Durant's kind of leadership was nearly over and the new messiah was to be Alfred Sloan. The company had become too big and too complicated to remain a one-man show. By the end of 1920, after General Motors' debts had once again risen to crisis levels, Durant was finally ousted from the Board. After a temporary period under Pierre du Pont, Alfred P. Sloan became president in 1923. It was he who oversaw the painstaking, detailed build-up and development of the complicated interrelated monolith that exists today.

GM execs vintage 1940. Alfred P. Sloan third from left.

Billy Durant, the fiery man who created General Motors, who became a millionaire, was no longer at the helm and had failed to build the empire he saw in his dreams of the future. He died broke.

It was Sloan who set about creating the system by which the chief executive of each of General Motors' operations, while allowed some autonomy, was nevertheless still subject to the control of a strong central organization. This has been described as a policy of decentralization, although in fact it actually seems more an attempt to rationalize the excessive decentralization of the Durant regime. The policy which was espoused by General Motors in the days of Sloan was the production of "a car for every purse and every purpose." Dollar sales between 1923 and 1925 increased by $37 million and produced a net income of $240 million for the three-year period. With this much cash in hand, Sloan proceeded in 1925 to a massive expansion of the company to put it on a world-wide basis. Among its purchases that year was the small manufacturing plant of Vauxhall in Britain.

The thirties were a period of stagnation for General Motors, as well as the rest of the country, but the corporation came out of the Depression better off than most—and the war years did it far from harm. Sloan, perhaps because of his experiences with Durant, had a deep prejudice against being in debt, so most of the company's expansion was financed out of profits. When Sloan resigned as president and chief executive in 1946 (he remained on as honorary chairman) he had created a solid and liquid business.

But it was only well after the war that the automobile market realized its full potential. Between 1946 and 1963 General Motors spent seven billion dollars on plant—nearly seven times the value of all its assets at the start of that period. Even then, consumer demand remained huge and, as Sloan put it, "Whatever the manufacturer could make, customers were waiting to purchase." In the fifties, as consumer purchasing power increased, the industry invented and developed new, and more expensive, packages to satisfy it. Accessories, luxuries, improvements, and innovations were piled on to the basic utilitarian unit to give the customers more

Postwar production—finishing touches on Chevrolets.

Estes is an avid gardener
in rare off hours.

Estes' second wife
was once his secretary.

for their money. Styling started to dominate the industry. "Indeed," said Sloan, "the rapid movement in styling in the late forties and fifties sometimes seems to many people to have become too extreme. New styling features were introduced that were far removed from utility, yet they were demonstrably effective in capturing public taste."

One of the more excessive captures made on public taste was achieved by the tail fin, which first appeared on the Cadillac in 1948. Although at first it was not easy to sell, it has since appeared on every major line of cars in one exaggerated form or another. The idea for the tail fin was born when the chief stylist of General Motors saw the tail fins on a World War II fighter plane and showed them to his designers.

Variety and choice became everything. In 1963, there were 429 different models of cars produced in the United States, 138 of them by General Motors alone. The then-president of General Motors, John Gordon, said: "Taking into account all the colors available and all the optional equipment and accessories that we now offer, we could in theory go through a whole year's production without making any two cars exactly alike."

To become the boss of that empire takes more than just talent and skill, ambition and luck; it also takes all the hours there are, all the energy you can find. It means sacrifices, particularly domestic sacrifices. "I think from a domestic point of view you have to put in far more than is really fair to domestic life," Estes told me. "That is, if you truly want to succeed. You have to put your job ahead of everything else, you have to reckon on being away from home for at least twelve hours a day and then to put more hours in on top of that. Your family must understand all this and realize that you don't love them any less if you're devoting that kind of time and single-mindedness to your job and your career."

Pete Estes' first wife (he met her when she was a nurse and he was at the General Motors Institute) died in 1965, a short time after they were divorced. Two years later he married his present wife, Connie, who had been his secretary. She knows and understands automobiles; she also knows the kind of dedication that is demanded from those who aspire to the top ranks of the auto industry.

Pete Estes has three sons and seven grandchildren. When his sons were little he didn't see as much of them as he wanted. "It's very difficult, when you're working twelve, fourteen hours a day, to keep a woman happy. You know, Connie isn't joking when she says that she thinks I've the words 'General Motors' tattooed across my chest and I can see her face sometimes when I come home late on Friday night and say I'm going to have to work Saturday and Sunday. That's when she calls me Elliott, not Pete."

The Esteses live in a long, white, single-story house with a very large "E," in wrought iron, on the wall above the front door. There are three acres of lawn and the garden runs down to a small stream. They are both keen gardeners and in spring and summer nearly all Estes' spare time is occupied with planting the tomatoes and protecting the geraniums.

It's only after some time with Connie that you may discover that her father's job in the auto industry was with the company that Pete Estes can't name out loud. He worked for Ford.

Car designers claim to be, and almost certainly are, the true artists of the auto industry. The General Motors breed live in modern buildings and landscaped splendor on the outskirts of Detroit, far removed from the Götterdämmerung atmosphere of the production lines. In the complex of thirty-six buildings which makes the research center they practice their craft. Estes calls frequently at the design center—long before most General Motors' office workers are at their desks—to inspect sketches, photographs, materials, cloths, pieces of chrome and steel, lengths of plastic and fur; all of which, when put together, will turn an engine and four wheels into high fashion. Designers not only try to predict, but also attempt to influence, the taste of the car-buying public. Deep in the most security-protected area of the design building they keep "the clay," a full scale wood and clay "mock up" of a new model. It is carved and sculpted as though for an art gallery, an artist's concept to be produced in millions —and then sold to a nation. They design three, or more, years ahead, but what they design is top secret; so secret that "the clay" made for any one division of General Motors is always kept secret from even the top executives of other divisions. What they fear most is a leak: a leak within the corporation—or even worse, a leak to the competition.

However, the president of General Motors is permitted to know the designs, colors, and shapes of all the models. He alone knows the secrets of Pontiac that are withheld even from Buick and Chevrolet; the dash board secrets of Cadillac that Oldsmobile may discover too late—and he takes mischievous pleasure in the knowledge. He believes it not only encourages internal competition in General Motors but is the best form of security. General Motors may manage to guard against industrial spies, but they cannot always guard against defection. Executives leave. Worse, they are sometimes tempted to leave to join Ford or Chrysler—or even Volkswagen. It is then that both security and corporate pride are damaged. Pete Estes will take a long look in his bathroom mirror on the day he discovers a defector. Recently one of his top men did leave—to join Volkswagen. It was a time of trauma in the boardroom of General Motors. He told me: "That's when I really did look in the mirror and say, 'Where did we fail? Where did we let that man down? Where did we go wrong?' If we can't find the answer to that question, then we're going to lose more good men and that isn't what General Motors is about—we have to hang onto them."

The internal combustion engine helped develop America and pioneer the world, but its days are as numbered as the supply of fuel oil. Meanwhile research goes on to find a replacement for the gasoline engine. Pete Estes personally supervises the development of many prototypes, most of them so "way out" and experimental that they can never become the car of the future, but may provide information which will help develop it. On Sunday morning the driveway of his home is often filled with experimental cars brought to him by senior engineers from the research divisions. And

Estes visits the designers.

engineer Estes neglects the planting of this year's crop of tomatoes in order to take Connie for a noisy drive around the block in, for instance, a gas turbine car, virtually an aircraft engine in a car body. Fuel consumption and other problems make it an unlikely runner for the freeways of the future, but it is an impressive test-bed for many devices and systems that may yet take over from those we know.

In the design center, I was with Estes when he drove an electric car, a sort of sophisticated motorized phone booth, looking like a cross between a golf cart and a milk delivery cart, in which he whipped us around in a demonstration figure-eight on battery power. He believes that the electric car might well be the car of the future. He thinks that just one major breakthrough in battery technology, to enable the batteries to be made of lighter material and to store more power, is all that is needed for it to become a mass-production possibility. He agrees that there might, at first, be some resistance from the machismo-minded male motorist, reluctant to part with throbbing symbols in exchange for a smooth silence designed to travel modestly between home and work and take his wife between home and the stores.

Few motorists realize the expenditure involved in this kind of research. Pete Estes told me: "We have more than 2,000 engineers, scientists, and technicians working full time on emission control alone. In the past six years we've spent $1.5 billion dollars on engineering research, for emissions and on testing and tooling facilities. Despite our efforts neither General Motors, nor anyone else in the motor industry, has been able to develop an emission-control system which can meet the requirements that are now on the books for 1978. Our people have developed two different control systems which will meet a number of the requirements most of the time. But we've only done it on an experimental basis, in the laboratory —and not on the thousands of engines that General Motors builds. We have been able to run one car 20,000 miles on this system. It's still running, but that is only one car and it's tremendously expensive. It depends on fuel injection which, on any production line car, would price it out of the market. I'd hate to have to put that kind of cost on to every automobile we make. So in one area of research we cannot even meet the standards that are being laid upon us in Washington, by Congress.

"That is because Washington doesn't understand what we're capable of doing. We're going flat out, and spending as much money as there is, and we still cannot design or invent what they want. It's one of the major problems facing the motor industry today, the impossible standards that are being set by a demanding and unknowledgeable political leadership. Even the Environmental Protection Agency itself agrees that the tighter 1978 emissions standards that we're trying so hard to achieve are probably unnecessary, and in any case should be postponed. There's no argument that our objective has to be clean air, but the nation's air quality standard should be based on sound scientific data. Even the EPA scientists have been quoted as saying, 'We're making multi-billion dollar decisions about controlling air pollution on a twenty-five percent data basis.' The nation can no longer afford such luxuries. It is imperative to reassess those standards on a basis of sound, adequate scientific information. It's imperative because Congress has now added fuel economy standards to the existing emissions standards for our industry. And as you probably know, emission standards and fuel economy standards work in conflict with one another. When you get fuel consumption down the emission levels tend to go up and vice versa. The only thing that goes up, and stays up, in a case like this, is the cost. That is the cost to the nation, the auto industry —and our customers."

Pete Estes is fiercely critical of Congress and the demands it places on the auto industry: "When the marketplace can't get the job done (and I'm talking about emissions and safety), then we must have regulatory controls. That is because no one wants to accomplish it for himself, he always wants his neighbor to do it. You don't want to clean up your car and you don't want to lose fuel economy to clean up the air, but you sure want your neighbor to do so; so that has to be regulated by law. But in areas where the good old marketplace is effective (and now I'm talking about the availability of energy and natural gas, the price of natural gas and oil, the fuel economy of our vehicles and how good-looking they have to be), then the marketplace will also tell you whether you've done the job right or wrong. I believe freedom in this country is based on the fact that we are the outstanding marketplace society in the world. Now I ask you, are we going to throw up all this for a bunch of lousy legislative practices? I think it's wrong. At the last count that I made, there was just one engineer in Congress—and now they're trying to tell us how to design a car. This is a serious situation."

It is, however, a serious situation that was brought about by the motor industry itself. Locked in a euphoric and profitable honeymoon with the car-buying public of America, it had roared ahead, unchecked and undeterred—until November, 1965. It was then that a young Washington lawyer published a book called *Unsafe at Any Speed*. Ralph Nader became a household name, and a national consumer champion almost overnight, by taking on the whole of the American auto industry—and General Motors in particular. The book went so far as to say: "General Motors is symbolic of almost everything that's wrong with life in the United States today." Nader focused on one of General Motors' most publicized cars, the Chevrolet Corvair. And the man in charge of the Chevrolet division at that time was Pete Estes. General Motors reacted by trying to discover something disreputable in Nader's private life. They were discovered doing it and a Senate investigations' committee under Senator Abraham Ribicoff, and including Senator Bobby Kennedy, sternly sent for James Roche, the president of General Motors at that time, the General Motors lawyers and the private investigators who'd been digging into Nader's life. The committee was unimpressed by the explanations given by the private detectives and only slightly mollified by the fulsome and complete apology offered on behalf of General Motors by the president, James Roche. (Subsequently Nader successfully sued General Motors and received $425,000 in damages.)

A new era had dawned for the motor industry, an era of caution and response to public criticism. The words consumer, protection, environment, and public accountability became part of the necessary programming for the ever-rolling production lines in Detroit. Pete Estes is cautious about revealing the exact degree of his knowledge or involvement with that infamous "counter investigation" mounted by private detectives on the instructions of General Motors lawyers into the life of Nader. But he does concede that the Nader confrontation was a time when General Motors blotted its copybook. "I guess as long as we have people in General Motors who are pressing on to succeed, then we're going to make mistakes and we're going to need constructive criticism to be sure we are taking everything into consideration. And it's true that some of what Mr. Nader talked to us about—and presented to the consumers—was constructive. But, for me, I'd say that seventy percent was destructive rather than constructive, and that more than overruled benefits that we received from Mr. Nader. I don't think we need the kind of help that Mr. Nader offers us in our business. But then you are bound to feel that that's a prejudiced reply, aren't you?"

He smiled with the rueful expression of a survivor. "It was quite a time, the Nader time," he told me. "I guess now I have the feeling that in order to be a really rounded General Motors' man you have to run into some pretty severe criticism and you have to stumble and, possibly, make a big mistake in order to be really seasoned for the long pull in our industry. Our industry is so cyclical that every three or four years we're either tremendously high or tremendously low, and to get out of our own obsession with that cycle you occasionally need a rap on the head and certainly the Nader experience was that for me. Now, was it a mistake to put detectives in on Nader? I don't know that, even now, I would regard that as a mistake. Perhaps the mistake was to apologize at the Senate investigation for having done it. I think it's all still open to some question. Anyway, it's all past history now."

Past history or not, it is clear that Pete Estes would still like to fight that last round with Nader again. And mistake or not, the arrival of Nader, and the events that followed, changed the pattern for the whole auto industry. For instance, General Motors' proving ground, suddenly, became even more important than it had been in the past. Here they could not only test and research car behavior and safety but, much more to the point, they could also loudly tell the public they were doing it. General Motors poured millions into the proving ground and today it's become an essential and dramatic part of the manufacturing process. On its miles of tracks and its water splashes, hills, skid pans, and crash simulators, cars, buses and trucks are tested to what may seem absurd lengths—until you consider the "absurd" things that happen to the ordinary motorist at the wheel of his car.

Humans fail more often than cars, and research engineers have discovered the only really safe speed for any driver is—zero. So the most successful research is always aimed at protecting the people behind the wheel from themselves and each other. To do this General Motors makes dummies, model human beings created to behave like stupid people. Each

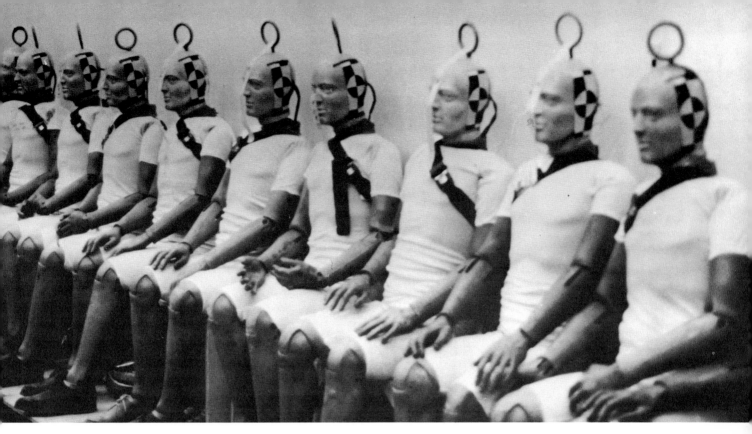

Each dummy costs $35,000.

dummy can cost as much as $35,000 and the hundreds that are kept in the proving ground add up to more than one million dollars: whole families, even busloads, of mechanical joints and electronic nerves designed to register hurt without feeling pain, designed to help men fight off the monstrous possibilities of dying on the roads. But how much protection do you need, how much protection does your wife or child need? The 50,000 who die and the four million who are injured on American roads every year provide all the incentive they need at the proving ground. It may be excellent publicity to have the motoring population of America know that such a place exists, but the engineers and scientists who work there see their aim and purpose as more vital than just public relations.

Pete Estes still believes that the amount of safety you can build into a car is regulated by the amount the public will accept. "Too much legislation, in our opinion, produces too many difficulties and doesn't solve the problem. But I guess we're never going to persuade Congress to give up. The motor industry has become a tremendously good political football. We welcome constructive criticism. I know that can produce hollow laughter in some places, but it's true. But when we get Congress compromising on things they don't know about like what the fuel economy average on General Motors cars ought to be in 1985, it's ridiculous even to discuss it. There aren't enough facts available for anyone to make any kind of guess, let alone a law. Here is Congress telling us that we must have twenty-seven and a half miles to every gallon of gasoline in 1985. But the whole energy bill is ridiculous, it's a disaster. Perhaps it's our own fault; everybody kept asking for an energy policy in the United States and we probably should have kept quiet. Now we're worse off than we were without an energy policy."

The motor industry is frequently criticized for policies of planned obsolescence, for only thriving as an industry by selling the customer a new car, which he probably can't afford, before the one he owns is worn out. Planned obsolescence is not unique to the auto industry, but Estes is at his fiercest on this point: "What's actually happening in the United States is the envy of the world. Our transportation system in the United States is based on the fact that we, as an industry, have been able to build a product which the customer wants badly enough to buy it when he has a car only two and a half years old, not a worn-out car, but a car that's still got plenty of life in it. We have developed a system in which every one of our cars is owned by three and a half customers, on the average, during the ten-year life of that car. You can purchase four-wheeled transportation in the United States for anything from $20,000 to five hundred dollars today. Nowhere else in the world can you obtain freedom and mobility at this kind of price and with this kind of variety. Now all this is based on the fact that we do the kind of job that we should do and we improve our product enough so that our customers come back to buy, not just because of sales pressure or advertising pressure, but from need or want or desire, or because of price or fuel economy or appearance or comfort or prestige —you name it, there are many incentives. The customer knows that his old car will go on to someone else, and after that, on to someone else and on to someone else again. He buys a new car because he wants to; I don't think that he feels manipulated.

"But if we had a system in which we went on making the same car, without improving it or changing it or altering its color or its design, and we sold it to a customer and we knew he was going to drive it for ten years, the whole life of that car, then that would be a catastrophe. It would be a catastrophe for the very person that we're most concerned about, the fellow who can't afford to buy a new car. He still wants the freedom to own a car and to be able to change it, but he can't afford a new car because he's at the end of the income line. But at least at the end of that system he can still change his car. It means that, for five hundred dollars, he can be on the road alongside the man with the Cadillac or the Rolls-Royce. This is all part of the greatest mass transit system in the world. No one in the world today will pay what it actually costs to ride in a bus; you know that and I know it. To ride in a bus these days you have to be subsidized by the city and the cities are going broke."

For the men and women on the remorseless production lines, it may seem easier to comprehend the practice and philosophy of mass transport economics, and to care about them, when you are in top management. But Pete Estes thinks they should know—and believe too. So, from time to time, he has his own form of presidential walkabout. He went, when I was with him, to the Cadillac production line. How many workers actually were impressed by his handshakes, his jokes and his "keep it up" urgings, is hard to say. Most of them had to ask me who "the guy with the handshake" was. The production line workers are there for the money; they'll accept the conditions as long as the pay is right. Pete Estes believes that they identify more with and are closer to the product than that. He'll invite you to ask them. When you do, you find not aggression or resentment but, rather, a dulled and apathetic acceptance of the monotonous and grinding routine of a production line.

There are a surprising number of women workers. Traditionally the American auto industry always has employed women, even before World War II, and during the war it became a necessity to replace men who had gone to fight. Many of the women are supporting families. Nobody that I spoke to believed that the job they were doing took longer than twenty minutes to learn and most of them believed that five minutes was quite enough. At first, they agreed, the job was painfully boring, but after a while you filled your mind with anything other than thoughts of work, became robotized, automated, part of the "line." The unions negotiate fiercely for more pay, sickness and insurance benefits, and better working conditions. When I was there, the take-home pay for most people on the production line averaged between six and eight dollars an hour after deductions and at that time 27,000 workers, who had been "laid off" because of a fall in production demand, were waiting to get back on the line.

Estes knows that working on the line is the least demanding and the least dignified job in the auto industry. But he told me: "I would like you to know that working conditions in our plant have improved considerably over the past twenty to thirty years. We have air conditioning, we have incentive schemes, we do everything we can to keep our employees happy and to make them identify with the products they're building. We also try and encourage the man on the production line to reach for promotion, become more senior, climb through the ranks. We also have the required percentage of minority and women employees in our organization. Not only do we have the relevant organizations looking over our shoulders, we also have the Government on this matter." They do not have many senior executives who are women—and none on the Board. "It's a problem, I agree," said Estes. "But we are trying to remedy it with more women in our training schools and on management courses, so that I think in the future we may even see women managers in our plants. It may be a little way off, but I think it will happen."

The mandatory retirement age at General Motors is sixty-five. Pete Estes will reach it in 1981. It's a reasonable guess that, at that time, he will still be as energetic and as enthusiastic about his work as he is today. How does he face a future without work? "I'm not worried about it, I'm actually looking forward to it. I can't see myself slowing down, but there are so many things I've always wanted to do over the years that I don't think it will be a problem for a long time ahead. I love to read, read books, but I've never had time to read things apart from research reports and things like that. I like to hunt a little, I like to fish and play golf. And there's nothing I like better than driving a car, nothing I would like to do more than get into a motor car tomorrow and just set out all the way to the West Coast. I like to travel, I'm interested in other countries and I want to spend more time in them than I can as president of General Motors. Retirement will give me a chance to do all that."

But Pete Estes, sitting at home contemplating retirement with equanimity, even energy, is still, for the present, the man in charge of three-quarters of a million employees, and the motoring habits of a nation. And he knows one thing for sure. He knows all about the continuous and remorseless production lines. He knows that each new model is headed, eventually, for the scrapyard, even before it rolls off the "line." Pete Estes, too, is on a production line. He knows there'll be another president of General Motors. And then another. And another. All his working life he has understood that. It is the first principle of the auto industry.

The production line.

THE SCHOOLTEACHER

GERRI FEEMSTER

She doesn't live in the ghetto but that is where she comes each day —to Harlem. She is black and beautiful and determined—and she may eventually be beaten, beaten by the system, the prejudice, beaten by the fact that New York City is going broke, and she is part of the city and could be crushed in the process.

Gerri Feemster is twenty-five, a southern girl, the kind of vivacious black girl you see in *Ebony* advertisements and on television commercials. Her "natural" is natural, and she smiles a lot. She's slim and shapely and her Afro earrings are big and aggressive. She carries them well. She's a teacher.

Gerri Feemster always wanted to be a teacher. She was born and brought up in Rock Hill, South Carolina. Her mother was one of thirteen children in a black sharecropping family. Her father is a truck driver. Both Gerri's parents had only the most rudimentary education, but they knew the value of education. Few black people didn't. It was often the only way out, the only chance of escape from poverty and oppression.

Gerri used to play "teacher" as a child. She was a bright girl. She was also a lucky girl. She went to a school where there were teachers who encouraged her and took time to help her.

In elementary school there was a tough lady principal who pushed her to do better. In high school there was a psychology teacher, Willie Cain, who managed to pass on to his pupils—and Gerri in particular—his own belief in the value of education—and being an educator. At college in Rock Hill, and later at the university in Atlanta, she remained lucky in her teachers. They were dedicated and persuasive. They convinced Gerri.

"They were all exactly the kind of teachers I would like to have been myself,'' she told me. ''But down in the South I couldn't be sure how well I would be able to do once I left. It is true that a really dedicated teacher will always find the chance to teach and influence bright pupils. And in the South discipline is firm. You really can control a class and pass on ideas. So I guess I knew that in the South, even with all its disadvantages for people like me, I could teach, and even teach well.

''But in a ghetto school it's different. There's too much against you. I don't know if I will ever be able to look at a pupil, as some of my teachers must have looked at me, and know that I'm helping to inspire a teacher of the future. And I don't know if this city will even let me try.''

Gerri had already been laid off once, and then temporarily reinstated, when I first met her. Her future was uncertain and her chance of surviving New York City's latest wave of sweeping education budget cuts looked slim.

At the time we spoke, she was teaching in Benjamin Franklin High School as part of a special education project. Trying to teach those who had been told they were unteachable, trying to control those who had been classified as unmanageable, even labeled impossible. She had a master's degree in French and she wanted to teach French. But there were no openings for French teachers when she came north to New York. So for three years she went into the general teaching side of a New York City junior high school. Then came the first wave of budget cuts, and Gerri was axed. For three months she received no salary and used up her savings. Eventually she managed to get a job with the Special Education Department.

Her degree in French still didn't help much, but being black probably did. For her success—and her survival—she had to depend upon being good at assessing difficult kids. So I asked her to assess herself: ''I believe I am friendly and outgoing and I think of myself as being gregarious because I have a circle of friends that I enjoy, and I think they enjoy me. I relate well to people in general, and I try not to find fault with them, because I believe that everybody is an individual and entitled to do their own thing. So I try not to make judgments. But I have to say that I have recently become very cautious. There was a time when I was flippant and very trusting and I thought that New York would be a place where I wouldn't have to worry about tripping over the prejudices and the hatreds that I'd lived with all my life in the South.

''In the South I was brought up in a predominantly black neighborhood. I went to school with blacks until I went to college. Then at college I met whites and began to learn what the system was all about. But at least in the South there was no subtlety, no deceit. Everything was out in the open, out front.

''You knew that you lived in a neighborhood that was across the tracks.

And you knew the color of the people who lived on the other side of the tracks.

"And it wasn't black.

"But if a white person was friendly, they meant it. You could at least trust in the fact that their attitude was exactly what they showed you.

"Up here in New York I guess I thought it was all going to be much more liberal and understanding. I was wrong. People here will talk to you in one way to your face and another behind your back. They'll spread rumors and lies about you. Not all of them do this, just some of them. But because, on the surface, they all behave in a friendly, smiling fashion, you can't tell which are the ones who mean it and which are the ones who will behave differently behind your back. So you become hostile inside. You may look confident and trusting, but you become very, very cautious."

But—for the moment—Gerri is still a young, good-looking New York girl with friends and a full life. She drives a car. She lives in her own neatly furnished apartment in Queens. She has a regular boyfriend and is a very independent girl.

And this is *really* why she left South Carolina. It is, of course, why a million small-town girls leave home for the big city: to escape domestic restrictions, to search for glamor—and find independence. It is also a way of leaving behind disapproving parental glances.

It has its own special ingredients, this kind of independence, for girls like Gerri. Discos. Shopping in Bloomingdale's. Weekend trips to the country. But that kind of life costs money. Independence in New York City isn't cheap. Teaching has never been a highly paid career, and Gerri wasn't what is known as an "established" teacher. She was still employed only on a temporary basis. Every time there were staff cuts older and more experienced teachers with priority over the newcomers were "grandfathered" into the remaining posts. Every time that happened it was a threat to Gerri's independence—even to her survival. When I met her she was earning $350 a week. Even by New York standards that is enough. But only just enough.

"I think every girl sort of longs for the sophisticated life. I know I did. At home it's all sleepy and friendly and everybody knows everybody else." She thought about that and giggled. "Perhaps that's the trouble. You just can't ever imagine being able to do something and not have it known about by the whole town and all your family. So New York becomes an image which represents escape from all that. Not that, down south, life isn't warm and friendly and loving. But like all warm and friendly and loving things, it's also clinging. And you need to get away.

"In addition, I *had* to come here. I actually had a thirst for it. I had to come to the big city to see if I could make it. I used to say to my friends, 'If you can make it in New York, you can make it anywhere.' "

Gerri: a smart apartment,
shopping with friends,
and dancing in the evenings.

Benjamin Franklin High.

The schools of New York City have always been tough and the schools of Harlem are tougher than most. And in Harlem, Benjamin Franklin High rates among the toughest. In it there are three thousand pupils—all of them black or Puerto Rican. In it there are less than one hundred teachers, most of them white and all of them ready for trouble. The school that houses them all is guarded and barricaded. Learning in Benjamin Franklin High is something that takes place under siege conditions.

Most New Yorkers have seen the school where Gerri teaches, although they probably haven't noticed it. It is on East River Drive, at 116th Street, overlooking the route that takes millions of commuters in and out of the city every day. It was constructed shortly before the last world war, and looks something like a Greek edifice. Built as a monument to educational ambition in a part of the city where these days both education and ambition are hard to find, today it is essentially a place where life has become a daily battleground between apathy and violence, dedication and hope.

It takes a special kind of knowledge to survive in the ghetto, and the kids who go to Benjamin Franklin High have it. It takes a special kind of attitude to want to teach those kids the way out—and Gerri has it.

Reaching such pupils was a challenge. But the real challenge was trying to put knowledge into the heads of youngsters who were more interested in mastering the tricks of survival.

New York was cutting back on its education program. Teachers were being fired and laid off. And the pupils knew it and resented it. It affected their attitude. Gerri said: "You know, with the budget cuts and with everything else that's happening in New York, a type of debauchery has grown up in the schools, a type of demoralization, and I think it's spread to teachers as well as families and parents. And now the students just don't care. You can tell students, 'Hey, I'm going to fail you if you don't come to class, if you don't do this, you don't do that,' and they tell you, 'I don't care, I'm not concerned about that.' And if you try to explain, 'Hey, this grade is going to be on your record years from now when you go for a job and you look back to this, this grade will be here for misconduct, for academic failure or for whatever it is.' They just don't care. They really *do not* care. And if you say, 'Well, I'm going to call your mother,' they say, 'Call my mother, I don't care.' Well, to me this is impossible; I become very frustrated. I really become incensed because I was never exposed to this kind of thing before, and it was a very difficult adjustment for me to make."

But she coped—for three years. For three years she believed she was a successful teacher. She was certainly a dedicated teacher. Then she was laid off. The cuts had caught up with her.

Luckily, her dedication and enthusiasm had caught the eye of Frank Quiroga, the man in charge of New York's special education project. It is a program designed to help the disturbed and the difficult and the drop-outs. It tries to reach the youngsters who have quit, or been kicked out of, the main stream, students who, if this project couldn't save them, were destined to become part of the statistics of educational failure in New York City.

At that time the special education project was responsible for forty-five thousand children in New York City, gathering together a range of ages and abilities in loose, noisy teaching groups and then attempting to re-awaken their interest, stimulate their desire to learn—and pull them back into the system.

Gerri's youth and her black skin encouraged Frank Quiroga to "smuggle" her into the project. There was no established post, but he found a way to "fiddle" her into special education as a temporary; to "hide" her position. So he sent her to Benjamin Franklin High.

Gerri knew the risks. Teachers have been beaten up, knifed, even raped in ghetto schools. And in schools like Benjamin Franklin, the security guards have become essential—as necessary to teaching as chalk and blackboards. They wait at every door, keeping kids who've come in from going out, and those who've somehow got out from coming back. During and between classes they patrol the corridors and hallways, walkie-talkies in their hands, always ready for trouble in an institution that must sometimes seem more like San Quentin than school.

In Benjamin Franklin the special education project has two teachers and one lay helper. Gerri was given a class of twelve kids between the ages of fourteen and eighteen, rejects from the mainstream of teaching. After a year she felt she was winning. She knew she had their confidence. Soon, she felt, she could keep their attention, perhaps even challenge their enthusiasm.

• The personal histories of her group make horrific case reading, a cross-section of social workers' clichés: children who had backgrounds of parental drunkenness, broken homes, prostitution, crime, drugs, violence. All these were just the everyday circumstances of the schoolchildren in Gerri's charge.

When I visited Gerri in her class, the atmosphere, to an outsider, seemed disturbingly free of discipline. Pupils wandered around—even in and out—at will. With her "helper," Mike, she moved between individual kids, or little groups of them, engaged on different projects she had set them.

And all of this was punctuated by the slamming of the self-locking classroom door as kids just got up and walked out, or thundered on the door to be let back in.

In regular classes this is not allowed. The students are given a cardboard sign to carry in the corridors during lesson time if they have the teacher's permission to go to the lavatory. The sign is in case the security guards stop them. But Gerri's students roam almost at will, almost, it seems, with the freedom of licensed bandits. All the staff in the school and the guards seem to know that these kids are nearly written off—if they fail at this there is no second chance.

An inspired teacher.

But Gerri is a disciplinarian. She believes in discipline, she was brought up with it. And she admits that the new teaching atmosphere was a strain at first: "This was a big adjustment. It really was quite an adjustment from the outset, but still I think I've maintained some of my feelings and some of my beliefs because I find I can be gentle—but firm. It has to be a certain firmness, you know, that shows that I mean what I say, that I'm not just jiving around.

"I really try to impress upon them the fact that without education you have nothing, you have no life goals, nothing to look forward to. I tell them: 'There's going to come a time when you're going to get tired of just hanging out, there has to be more to life than just hanging out. Look at some of your friends.'

"It's something that you have to continue to reiterate because initially it's not accepted. They'll reply: 'I don't care, it doesn't make any difference.' But if it's reiterated day after day after day, then it becomes a part of what they think. It becomes part of what they begin to believe. I think it's effective only if you're very, very persuasive and you're determined to register. Slowly but surely I've begun to see it register a little. They've become more concerned about how many credits they have, when they're going to graduate, what they're going to do when they leave here. That type of thing is a far cry from what it was at the outset of the year."

These are the words of a teacher—a good teacher. Gerri Feemster stands at the end of a long tradition; she is part of an American educational pattern that, in spite of failures, is still the envy of much of the rest of the world. In many ways the problems at Benjamin Franklin High School reflect the problems of cities in crises, rather than a failure of the American educational system as a whole. Education in America has always been more than just a fine thing; it has been an essential thing. The teacher has been one of the most respected members of any American community, ever since the days of early New England settlers when she was known as "the schoolmarm" or "the school lady."

That early Puritan society was a literate one, a society that believed that all children should be able to read the Bible and follow religious services. By 1647 the rulers of Massachusetts clearly felt that the previous *ad hoc* arrangements for school ladies or schoolmarms were inadequate and they passed a law directing the officials of each township to ensure that all children should be taught to read. Later this law was amended and became a direct instruction for towns of fifty people or more to appoint "a teacher of reading and writing," and for every town of one hundred people to provide "a Latin school to prepare youths for the University." This became, in fact, the establishment of the first basis of schools, funded from town taxes.

In those days schools stressed reading and writing—and discipline. The basis of much of the education of young children in schools toward the end of the seventeenth century was the famous New England primer, a collection of religious verses designed to stress the fallibility of man and his need to be aware of sin. While Latin and Greek were also acceptable for older children, such subjects as mathematics and geography were not thought necessary.

In other parts of the country the development of education was less formalized. And then, as now, the people of the South resented the imposition of authority from outside, regarding schooling as a private matter. In the richer families children were taught at home, mainly by tutors imported from the North, or even from Europe. The poorer plantation owners banded together to set up what became known as the "Old Field Schools." In them, their children were taught the catechism and the "A.B.C.'s" by poorly paid and often not very well informed "teachers."

But as people started to move toward new frontiers and to push west, education became even less formalized. In those small isolated communities the backbone of the education system was the "dame school" run by a woman, usually in her own home, who was paid a minimal fee for her labors. The pastor was very often pressed into service as a part-time schoolmaster, his church building doubling as a learning institution. Of necessity, it seems, the pattern of the West was bound to follow lines similar to those of the first New England settlers.

The development of a more widely based system of education was moving ahead, however. New England, of course, led with the establishment of colleges—Harvard dates from as early as 1636. But it was in Philadelphia that it was first suggested that it might be worthwhile to teach subjects other than reading, writing, and Latin, providing information as a basis for pursuits other than Bible-reading or classical knowledge. In 1749 Benjamin Franklin opened a new era of education by producing a pamphlet proposing the establishment of an academy that would teach a wide range of subjects. Students at the academy, he proposed, would be presented with "those things that would be likely to be most useful and ornamental; regard being had for several professions for which they are intended." The Philadelphia Academy opened in 1751 and significantly widened the concept of schooling in America. At that time, incidentally, the population of Philadelphia was just over eleven thousand. Then, it is estimated, there were fifteen teachers at work in the city, serving a total of more than twenty-five hundred children.

It wasn't until the next century that the first public high school was set up—inevitably, in Boston. After that, the public school system started to develop fast. By 1890 there were 3,526 public high schools in the United States, and in 1900, there were 6,005. In those early days maintenance of the public school system was always a problem for city and state governments. The poor were to be educated, but it had to be done cheaply. So they developed a particular system of pupil teaching. In one room the teacher would be placed in charge of classes varying in size from two hundred to as many as one thousand pupils, but each "line" of students would be monitored by one of the brighter members of the class. So, very often the children were taught to read and write by their peers.

By then, Harriet Beecher Stowe—herself a teacher—had written *Uncle Tom's Cabin*, and Gerri's grandparents were scratching out a living as sharecroppers. Slavery was ended. Poverty and oppression were not. Education, at least, had become the right of everyone, although everyone didn't always get it.

Harriet Beecher Stowe.

But whatever the system—dame school, church school, academy or free school—literacy rates were extremely high, even in remote areas. At the turn of the century immigrants were pouring into the United States, all with an overwhelming desire to learn a new language and to see to it that their children could take full advantage of the New World. It is interesting that, often, within one generation, the children of new immigrants would have been provided with enough information to become the teachers of the following group of newcomers. So, the Irish taught the Jews, and the Italians. And they, in turn, became the teachers of the Spaniards and others. And so it went. Education was recognized from the beginning as the fast route to the middle-class establishment, to money-making, to security, and to success. This above all is the lesson that Gerri Feemster is trying to teach in the ghetto.

However, teaching itself remained a rather informally organized profession for some time. What were called normal schools did have classes in teaching, but it wasn't until after the Civil War that colleges began to introduce lectures in the "arts of teaching."

As in the days of the dame school, it was a woman-dominated profession, teaching being one of three occupations that were regarded as suitable for the respectable female—marriage and charity work being the other two. Not only was the teacher a highly respected member of every community, she was also expected to set an example of religious morality to the rest. Included in her contract was a ban on the consumption of alcohol and tobacco.

By the early part of the twentieth century a huge network of publicly financed schools had been established throughout the United States. But, judging by statistics, the dame school was still the backbone of the system. In 1930, out of a total of 250,000 elementary schools, 150,000 were run by just one teacher. Today the single-teacher school has almost disappeared. At the last count, in 1973, only 1,500 single-teacher schools remained in the United States. And at the time of that count there were 90,000 schools in the country (elementary, junior high, and high) servicing a school population in the United States of around 6 million. During that same period expenditure on education went from $3 billion to $90 billion. And it is estimated that by 1975 the United States was spending $110 billion on educating its children through school and college. Of this huge sum of money, nearly $60 billion was spent on children in elementary and secondary schools. Schools like Benjamin Franklin High.

At that time, too, in 1975, Gerri Feemster was one of nearly 2.5 million teachers in the United States. The national pupil/teacher ratio was a comforting 19:1. So it would seem then—and did to Gerri—that at the end of two hundred years of education history both teaching and being taught were in good shape.

But that was before American cities started going broke. And no city went broke quite as fast, quite as spectacularly, as New York City.

In New York City there are more than 1 million school-age children and nearly a thousand schools. Even before the crisis struck, the New York City public educational program had a tough job. There were, then, 60,000 teachers in the city, which maintained the pupil/teacher ratio at more or less the national average. And there were 665 security guards; which nobody bothered to compare with a national average, because everybody knew that it took that number, in New York, just to allow the process of teaching to happen.

But New York's Mayor Beame faced crisis and, as part of his commitment to wipe $500 million from New York's accumulated deficit, he authorized the dismissal of 14,000 teachers. Fourteen thousand—a small military division or a small town. All teachers. Nearly one quarter of all teachers in New York City: fired.

What's more, Mayor Beame announced further plans which would force the Board of Education to cut even more teachers. They were to cut, too, security guards, lay helpers, the special education project, and a whole multitude of other services and support facilities. Overnight a good education in New York became a favor—it was no longer a right. Overnight the pupil/teacher ratio went from nearly 20:1 to 40:1. And overnight the pain of these cuts was felt most severely where the strain had already been most difficult—in Harlem, the ghetto.

At Benjamin Franklin High School the cuts wiped out more than one third of the teaching force and nearly half the security guards. The cuts also sponged away the enthusiasm and drive, the spirit of a school that was just getting back on its feet when it was knocked flat on its back.

The principal at Benjamin Franklin High is Melvin Taylor. He is unusual. He is black.

There are not enough black teachers in New York schools and certainly there are not enough black teachers in the New York ghetto schools. Since the education cuts, their numbers have dropped from 15 to 8 percent.

If it is difficult to find enough black teachers, it is harder still to find black principals, and really quite remarkable to find a black principal like Melvin Taylor. He's from Harlem. He was brought up just a few blocks from the school, in the heart of the ghetto. He was one of five children —three of whom managed to live past youth. The other two became drug addicts and died in their early thirties. It's a familiar pattern, part of the ghetto. It wouldn't shock a policeman or a social worker or a journalist.

But Melvin Taylor was determined to beat the pattern. And he put his faith in education as the way out. Then, after he himself made it, he was

A one-room schoolhouse in Montana, 1893.

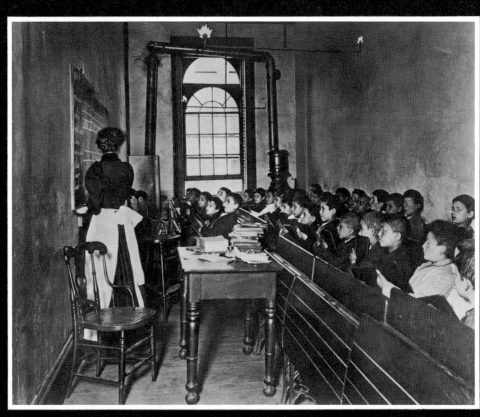
Lower East Side, New York, schoolhouse in 1886.

Melvin Taylor, school principal.

determined to teach other children in the ghetto the same route out. He felt he owed it to his dead brother and sister.

So the day he was appointed—not without some considerable opposition—principal of Benjamin Franklin High, where all the students were either black or brown and every one of them was from the ghetto, he believed he could begin to justify his faith.

By then, the civil rights movement appeared to have made real and worthwhile change at least possible. Ways seemed to be opening up for young blacks in the professions and industry. Money was available to educate ghetto children. Melvin Taylor believed he needed only five years to recruit the right kind of teacher, create the right sort of atmosphere, and turn Benjamin Franklin High into a good—maybe even a very good —school. Nineteen seventy-six was the year by which his school would have taken positive shape and begun positively to meet the needs of its pupils. But 1976 was, instead, the year New York City went broke.

Now Melvin Taylor can no longer see himself as principal of a great school. Indeed, he fears that Benjamin Franklin will soon hardly be any kind of school at all. "After the last round of cuts it'll be hopeless to pretend that my job here will be worth anything," he told me. "All I'm doing now is holding the fabric of the institution together—just. Nothing more. I didn't go into teaching to end up that way. But the real tragedy is what's happening to the staff. I haven't just lost a number of teachers,

I've lost the young ones, the black ones, the ones who had that extra feeling for their job."

Melvin Taylor knows all too well why it happens. He knows, too, that the kind of knowledge, the style of education, that is most likely to equip the youngsters for survival in the ghetto is called being "streetwise." He himself has that knowledge and will never lose it. "I learned a lot from the street. My survival sense comes from the street, not from anything I've learned from books, not anything I've learned in school.

"I think that one thing that doesn't ever come out very fully is that survival in the ghetto is, in itself, an education. But, then, it depends on what one does with that education which makes it either valuable or not valuable. There is a great deal of sense to what happens in the ghetto on a day-to-day basis. It's a very pragmatic kind of existence. It's a day-to-day kind of existence. People don't have the luxury of planning ten, fifteen, twenty years from now; you plan two or three days at a time.

"But you have to last—to survive—those two or three days."

Melvin Taylor isn't streetwise for nothing. "I won't believe that we've really lost the battle. I just can't let myself. I have to believe that we can somehow reshift and reform. I have to think that somehow we can take a different approach. It may take longer. It may be harder. But it can be done. I have to tell myself that. I have to tell myself we're going to win the battle somehow."

But the big, reassuring, intelligent black man in the principal's office cannot do it all on his own, cannot infuse everybody around him with the same dedication that he feels himself. For all his hopes and urgings, the teachers who work under him are frequently only able to observe that standards are falling, violence is increasing—and there is the threat of a return to the days of apathy and chaos.

In the corridors of Benjamin Franklin it is easy for teachers to feel frightened and the youngsters know it. They even know that the Teachers' Union has demanded more guards to protect staff in schools. All this only serves to increase the tension and reinforce the menace. Particularly since not only has the city authority failed to provide more guards, but education budget cuts have, in fact, *reduced* the number of guards.

The staff knows that in the corridors what a stranger may regard as just high spirits can in fact all too easily turn into visciousness and violence. It may be a place where kids "act" tough, but it is an act that can explode into real violence.

The Teachers' Union representative told me of a recent attack on a young woman teacher. It wasn't the first. He fears it won't be the last.

Gerri says: "Speaking from a female point of view, I don't have any problems with the troublemakers. They might curse and say things that

A tough school.

are offensive at first, but I ignore it. It's not so much that I'm black and female, it's just the way I am. Why can't we all do this? It's not so much what you are or the color of your skin, even if you're white. I think that you can make that adjustment. But you have to go back to *their* heritage and understand that. If you're white you have to understand what makes them tick, how it is for them to be black. Those of us that are black probably already do understand that."

But many of the kids at Benjamin Franklin High—too many of them—spend most of their time "copping out" on the school handball court. Little or no attempt is made to round them up or force them into class. And it is these kids that represent the biggest challenge to Gerri. Actually,

From the windows of a tenement.

they are hardly kids, they are men and women now, who have somehow bypassed the fun of teenage, lost the freshness of adolescence.

Certainly, they are not innocent youngsters who have come, trustingly, to school, looking for love, leadership, and an education. Why should they be? Life outside teaches them to misuse love, to mistrust leadership—and to reject education.

On the handball court I found a scene that resembled something from *West Side Story.* The students were friendly and interested enough to crowd around me and talk, even argue.

One girl, Peggy, told me: "You don't actually drop out, you just come here to have fun. Come on, man. It gets boring at school. Like, you go to school every day, you get bored."

She's nineteen. She's attractive, even sophisticated. Away from Benjamin Franklin High School she could be an office worker, a shop girl, or a mother. She's still trying to get enough credits to leave school. She says: "Why do you think I've been here for so long? When I first came into the school you only needed thirty credits to get out. And now you need thirty-eight. And I've only got something like twenty-eight. So I'm going to be here for ever." Whose fault is that? "The teacher's fault. Well, I suppose it's my fault *and* the teacher's.

"Listen to this. There are about forty kids in one classroom, right, there's about forty of them. When the teacher comes around to you you start talking and you start telling her what's happening and maybe the teacher just begins to get your attention and then the bell rings and it's over and you never get to learn anything.

"It's not a tough job being a teacher. Some teachers have told us, man, that whether we do well or not in school they still get paid for it. They just sit down and they get paid for it. They just write on the board. They don't even explain some of the things they give to us, you know. They say they're getting paid for it anyway, so what the hell. They don't care whether we learn or not."

Peggy knows that in a few years time she will probably be married, may even have children. So what kind of school will she want her children to go to?

"I'm not going to let them go to a school like this. My kids aren't going to go to this kind of school. They're going to go to a real hip-type school, they ain't going to go to no shit like this, man."

It was the only time she became really passionate when speaking to me, the only time she used the language of the streets to reinforce the lesson of the streets. And already, it seems, she sees herself as a write-off—but hopes, at least, that she may one day save her own children from the same fate. But rejecting education this way is a particular product of the ghetto and this situation is not representative of education in the U.S. in general.

On Sundays, in Harlem, Gerri walks the streets near the school and visits, when they'll let her in, the parents of the children she teaches. Sam Felder, one of her most disruptive and difficult youngsters, lives, I suppose, in better circumstances than many. It could even be said that his tenement is only average; average overcrowded, average broken down, average rat-infested.

Sam's mother came from the South too and struggles these days, without the husband who walked out on her, to bring up her boys in a jungle of violence and hopelessness. She knows her children are already labeled with that urban social worker's tag: "problem." She's a calm and jolly black woman who feels slightly hopeless and welcomes a visit from Gerri. From the windows of her tenement she and her children can watch molestings and drunkenness.

It is perhaps hardly surprising that her three boys will fight among themselves with all the viciousness of the slums. And she has almost given up trying to separate them.

"At one time I used to get me a stick. Because I figured that it's what they needed. Certainly it was no good trying to hit them with my hands because they're much too big for me. You know, they're taller than I am now. So I used to have to hit them with a stick, and I used to say to them, 'All right, you're going to clear up the mess that you've made in here. This is where you live. When you tear up the place in here then you'll have no place to live and you'll have to go out in the street and live. So why tear up where you have to live?' But it doesn't seem to get through to them."

She remembers her own childhood, a childhood that must have quite closely resembled Gerri's. "I was born in the country, you know, and you had to be in the house before the sun went down or else you got a whipping. When the sun went into the trees then you had to be in the house, otherwise that was trouble.

"You can't do that here. You can't tell the boys that here. You're in the streets here. The first thing they're going to tell you is, 'It's not like it used to be, Ma. We didn't come up in your time, Ma. This is this time, Ma. This is Harlem, Ma. This isn't your time, Ma.'

"At school, too, we had to behave there, or the teacher would give us a whipping and then when you got home somehow or other the teacher would have got in contact with your parents and then you'd get another beating. That meant that you had two whippings coming that day. But that doesn't work here. They're not frightened of that. They've got everything going on in the schools. Just everything. It's just like the teacher isn't there. And I think a lot of it is down to the parents. Because I figure if you teach your kids how to obey at home, then they won't go too far wrong when they go to school."

But being from the South, and being black, the one big gap in Gerri's

own education has been the lack of close contact with white people. Although it hasn't been a gap she's ever felt the need to fill.

She's a pretty girl and in a city with a liberal reputation she causes many men's heads to turn, many an eye to roll her way. She hasn't been without offers, but she doesn't care to date white men. She says it is because she hasn't thought about it very much.

"I don't go out of my way to limit myself to black Americans as friends, but it just so happens that most of my friends and associates are black. This is the way it's always been. If I come into contact I get on with them all right; although I'm always just a little suspicious, I will rise to the occasion. I actually feel that I can fit wherever I am. So I don't have white boyfriends. But I do know some that are nice and that I like, and if I found my black friends weren't enough to make me happy, then I might have reached earlier for white friendship. You've got to remember that I was brought up in the South and all my environs were limited. I was in a black neighborhood. I went to school with blacks. It was only at college that I began to meet whites. And then that was in the South. And frequently everything was what you would call 'out front.' That means you could tell if they didn't like you because they didn't bother to disguise it. So you retreated, inside yourself. Black was safe."

Gerri has a boyfriend, Fred Bostick. He's with an insurance firm. She's known him since they met at college in Atlanta. Both of them decided to come north together, and now it's a matter of argument as to who persuaded whom. I believe that Fred followed Gerri to New York. But they're happy to say it was something they agreed to together.

There's no doubt that Fred wants to marry Gerri and there's no doubt that he asks her frequently. But she's only twenty-five, enjoying her independence, and she keeps saying no. But she does mean maybe, or at least, please ask again. So they're together all the time.

He was with her on the day she was sent for by Frank Quiroga, the leader of the special education project, and he waited in a nearby restaurant while Gerri talked to Quiroga in the midtown headquarters of the project. Quiroga told her that the latest educational cuts had forced his hand and now there was no longer any way that he could "hide" Gerri's job. The inevitable had happened. Gerri was fired.

He told her that somebody else would have to be "grandfathered" in, an older teacher made redundant somewhere else in New York City. Gerri's confidence seemed to desert her. For just a moment there were tears in her eyes as she told Frank Quiroga: "I don't understand why they have this tendency to destroy people who really want to help the kids. I

Gerri visits students' homes.

Gerri and Fred—coffee and a crisis.

just don't understand it. People can sit around for fifteen years or more, you know, and that's all they need for tenure. But it doesn't mean that they are the best teachers. It doesn't mean that they are best for the kids. All they have to do is sit around, and take the money, and keep on taking the money. Just pay in the checks and stay in the system. I don't understand a system that has no room for merit—or enthusiasm. And what I am really questioning now is what effect all this is going to have on the kids. Never mind how I feel. And I feel pretty bad, you know. These kids have enough problems as it is without having someone come in bungling around making a mess of things. So I think there is going to be a lot of trouble next year—for the kids."

The word *roots* has, perhaps, become a cliché. But roots are what Gerri has and roots are what she turns to in crisis. Gerri Feemster went home —to mother.

Rock Hill, South Carolina. To most eyes it seems to have charm and atmosphere, the sort of friendly rundown warmth that is often associated with happy childhood memories. Thirty thousand people *do* live happily here. It is where Gerri first decided she wanted to be a teacher. And it is from here that she set out to succeed as one.

Her mother, Mrs. Maggie Feemster, was as strong and as comforting as mothers always are—and always will be. She told me: "I'm resigned to it, for her. I have said to her, 'Maybe it was best, you know.' I pray for her and I pray for all my children. Maybe she has to go into another field. Maybe all those years of wanting to be a teacher and of being a teacher has been what God wanted for her. Maybe it's good for her. Maybe it's good that they've cut back on teachers. Maybe it is time for her to get into another field. She could just wind up gray-haired, exhausted, and all worn out by giving herself to other people.

"So maybe Gerri Feemster will be able to think more about Gerri Feemster. It isn't her fault that it is that way around. It is not her selfishness. They've done this to her."

That Sunday in Rock Hill, Gerri went to church, the local Baptist church. There the preacher, once a military padre, welcomed her as a returning—and successful—member of his congregation. He even specially adapted his sermon to include glowing comparisons between teaching and the Christian ministry. When he thundered from the pulpit: "Christ was a teacher and teaching is the most noble and beautiful profession of all," he may have speculated on the effect his words were having on Gerri Feemster. Five pews from the front, sitting alongside her mother and brother, Gerri wept.

Later, in a smart black silk dress and broad-brimmed hat, she walked among the flowering dogwoods and the azaleas in the park where she had spent many of her happy days as a teenager, a place where she had always before found calm and a capacity to reflect.

She speculated on whether she would marry Fred. "I suppose I will one day. We have been through many years together. He's lovely, he's marvelous, he wants me—and I suppose I know I'm going to say yes. But somehow I don't want to say yes when I'm at the bottom, when I've failed. I'd like to feel that I was giving something up in order to marry him. As it is right now, I would feel that he would be rescuing me, saving me from disaster. Maybe there's another job for me. Maybe I'll do well in public relations—even television—but I don't suppose there's any place in teaching. At least not in New York, not yet.

Home with mother in Rock Hill.

"But I'm determined to make it. Coming home and talking with my mother, and being with my family, going to church, just walking here in the park, has made me feel very much better about it. And I don't look at things as quite as impossible as before. Here in Rock Hill are my roots, and just being here and feeling part of this place again gives me the same old motivation that I had when I was young, the same old drive to get back out of here. And try again. And try to win and hold on.

"I really do believe that you're only a failure if you allow yourself to fail. I mustn't think of myself as a failure. I am in the business of proving that nothing can stop me. If you think who I am, what color I am, where I come

She faces the future.

from, then you must know that nothing can stop me. I must succeed. I really must—mustn't I?"

Gerri Feemster is still trying. But now she is becoming bitter. She has tried to get into public relations—and failed. She has tried television—and failed. There is still no room in teaching. She's been working in shops, trying to hang on to that independence, that desire not to be beaten. She thinks frequently of those kids she used to teach at Benjamin Franklin High. And sometimes she wonders if they think of her, and miss her—as she misses them.

THE DISTRICT ATTORNEY
FRED COX

John D'Angelis sat, neglected on a bench in the basement corridor beneath the court. A fat man. His flabbiness seeming looser now than it had in court. He was dressed in a cheap gray sweatshirt, baggy trousers, scuffed shoes—and handcuffs.

He was sorry for himself. His big brown eyes filled with tears. He had some right to feel self-pity. He was facing four years in jail.

The sheriff's officers and the policemen in the radio room alongside the bench went noisily about their business, ignoring him. The prison superintendent, in an office farther down the corridor, was loudly arranging transport to the county jail. D'Angelis pinched nervously at the fold of skin between his thumb and forefinger. Every time he did, the shining steel handcuffs jangled a little. It seemed as if nobody cared about him now. Certainly nobody seemed to notice him now. But only minutes before, in court, he had been the center of everyone's attention when they found him guilty and passed sentence—exactly on the lines recommended by the district attorney.

John D'Angelis, thirty-five years old, had been arrested and brought in —extradited—from another state, Massachusetts, to the superior court in Ossipee, Carroll County, New Hampshire. He'd been charged with fraud —bouncing checks. Twice before he had failed to surrender bail and appear in court to face trial—and District Attorney Fred Cox was a hard man, with a reputation for demanding harsh sentences—and getting them.

John D'Angelis was thinking of Cox now, and not kindly. He told me: "When I came up with my lawyer to surrender to the court, this time, Fred Cox was here. I suppose he's got his job to do and I suppose he does it

59

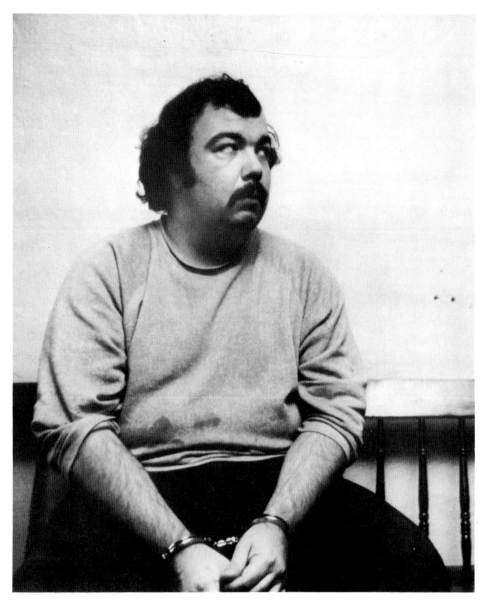

John D'Angelis has been brought in . . .

well. They keep reelecting him, so he must. But he doesn't have to behave as if he really enjoys it so much. I mean enjoys hearing people like me in trouble. When we were here he kept saying, 'Oh, you'll be going away for a few years, you'll be behind bars before all this is over.' Well, he was right. I hope it makes him feel good. I feel pretty bad about it. And I feel worse because Fred Cox feels good about it.''

D'Angelis' lawyer, in court, pleaded eloquently for a light, merciful sentence. He described his client's heart condition, his difficult family circumstances, the fact that he had "kicked" a drug habit and that he now felt truly remorseful—eager to repay the money and repair his position as a good citizen. The judge listened impassively, and then followed the recommendations of Fred Cox, the district attorney (in Carroll County they call him county attorney, but it's the same thing). They were harsh recommendations. The total sum involved was only $1,000. It will cost the taxpayer many times that amount to keep the accused in prison, but John D'Angelis committed a crime against property, never treated lightly in any court.

And Fred Cox, the people's prosecutor, was moved neither by pleas in mitigation nor urgings for mercy. He told me: "My understanding of this type of person is that he is the kind of guy that the rest of the people in this county should be well free of." He stood pugnaciously on the steps outside the court. The Stars and Stripes moved gently in the breeze behind him. "The only way I know to be free of people like John D'Angelis is to lock them up. We don't have a colony like Australia, or Georgia for that matter, so that we can do as the English did in the old days and ship thieves out. So the only alternative we have is to lock them up. Was I moved by what his counsel said about trying to make amends? Trying to make a new life? Being ill and having a wife who was ill, and all that? Well, I've heard that story too many times before. Everybody facing the kind of recommendations that I made there in court will find all kinds of excuses, suddenly, for not facing punishment. Has this guy got a heart condition? Well, he is only thirty-five years old, and I know he's heavy-set, but I don't think that he has any more heart problems than I do—and I'm ten years older than him and I weigh as much as he does." I pointed out to Fred Cox that he wasn't facing four years in jail. "That's why I don't have a heart condition," he said.

"Since I've been district attorney here, more people have been incarcerated, on a per capita basis, in our state prison, than in any other county in the state. Further, more people have spent time in our county jail than at any time in the past. And that *is* something that gives me pride. It means that I am doing the job I am paid to do, the job I was elected to do."

If you ask Fred Cox, as I asked him, what gives him the most satisfaction, the most pride, in being district attorney, he will answer: "When the foreman of the jury stands up, after they have all deliberated, and the clerk says, 'Mr. Foreman, have you reached a verdict?' and the foreman says, 'Yes, sir, we have.' 'What is your verdict, guilty or not guilty?' And then you hang in midair for a minute or two—just hang there—and the foreman says, 'Guilty as charged, your honor.' It gives you more than a bit of satisfaction, having won a case, having won it as the public prosecutor, the county attorney."

If that, for Fred Cox, district attorney, is the best part of his job, what then is the worst part? "When the foreman of the jury gets up and says, 'Not guilty, your honor.' That's the worst part—for me," he says.

The peaceful New England countryside of Carroll County, New Hampshire, is hardly the setting in which you would expect to find the sharp-edged abrasive kind of district attorney that we have been conditioned to expect by the television dramas and the movies. But, nevertheless, Fred Cox can, and sometimes does, demand hard labor, a life sentence—or even the death penalty. He is in charge of seventeen different police forces, all the prosecutions for the county, supervises police investigations wherever they take place, and is there to advise selectmen, counselors, and town authorities. He likes the job and he's had it for eight years. Every two years he has been reelected by the citizens of the county who, clearly, feel that he is the man for them.

He's overweight, drinks too much, smokes too much, swears too much, loses his temper far too often, and has a reputation for being abrasive, which he denies—abrasively. He loves his children, and his wife—and likes to cook as a hobby. In Carroll County, he is the boss, the big fish in a small pond. That's the way he likes it, that's the way he planned it. And that's the way he'd like to keep it.

Carroll County is twelve hundred square miles of the most striking part of the New Hampshire mountains. Half a million tourists pour through the county every year. They come in winter for the skiing and the hunting, and in summer for the swimming and fishing, and in the fall for the autumn leaves—or "foliage," as it is called. In this part of the United States an accident of acid chemistry in the soil produces, each and every year, one of the wonders of the New World. In Carroll County, New Hampshire, the America of the Norman Rockwell *Saturday Evening Post* covers lives on.

The people are dour New Englanders. Tourism brings most of them a very good income, but one gets the distinct impression that they would like to find a way to keep the money—and manage without the people. The small pretty white-boarded towns of Conway, Ossipee, Wolfeboro, and the mountains, the lakes, and the rivers which draw tourists from all over the world are a familiar background for Fred Cox, county attorney, and, at forty-six, lawyer, fisherman, hunter, family man—and politician.

His father was a Boston-Irish coal merchant, and his brother still carries on the family business. Fred was studying to be a doctor at college and switched to law after seeing a movie in which Frank Sinatra, playing a medical student, joked about doing the same. When he qualified he chose Carroll County to practice in because there were fewer lawyers in the whole state than in his parents' hometown of Lowell. He said: "When I was coming toward the end of my third year in law school, I looked in the Lowell County phone book and there were in excess of four hundred lawyers in the city of Lowell. I did a little questioning, a little research, and I discovered that there were less than four hundred lawyers in the entire state of New Hampshire. I decided that I would rather be a big fish in a small pond than a small fish in a big pond. So, in 1953 I started practicing on my own in Carroll County. Now, in those days the county attorney made only $3,000 a year. But I decided to run for the job. I liked the idea of being county attorney; I liked the idea of all that useful experience in court. And, in addition, I actually liked the idea of serving the county, and the state, and the whole legal purpose of the United States, in the kind of way that a district attorney does.

"And since a steady income of $3,000 a year would at least pay the rent for an office, and if I had a reasonable private legal practice going alongside it, there were obvious practical advantages to being county attorney. So I ran for office. I ran against the fellow who is now our probate judge —and lost. He was running for a sixth term, if I remember rightly, but the next time around he decided not to run and I ran against a fellow from Conway. Conway is the biggest town in our county—and the fellow got elected. That was the second time I was beaten.

"I didn't like it, I wasn't used to it, but I was getting to understand it. The local fellow in Conway, I worked out, would pick up almost automatically one third of the votes in the entire county. So I didn't run the next time, and the fourth time I ran because he wasn't running—and I had no opposition. So that's how I came to be county attorney. Not necessarily because I was the most overwhelmingly popular man in the county, but because I worked out what was a good time to run and get elected."

In Fred Cox's county there are no large squads of detectives, no highly trained policemen, supported by scientific and forensic experts. Some of the policemen and deputy sheriffs in his area even have other jobs. The deputy sheriff, who runs the village store in Ossipee, knows most of the people in Ossipee not just because he is deputy sheriff but because they are the customers in his store. As far as Fred Cox is concerned, this "moonlighting" doesn't necessarily make his police forces the most professional investigation agencies in the country. But it's his job to see that they are at least as good as they can be.

The job of district attorney in a small place like Carroll County is not only to supervise the police cases when they come to court, but also to supervise the police investigation when a crime is committed. Since Fred Cox came to office there's been a standing order for all police forces in the county that as soon as a serious crime is reported to any radio room

New England in the fall—
one of the wonders of the New World.

63

Fred Cox shall be notified—whatever the time of day or night—so that he can take over the investigation in his own way.

He was at home with his wife, Ellen, and his three children when one telephone call came through. Violence had come to the picturesque town of Conway. A young girl, walking home, had been badly beaten up by a masked man who tried to rape her. Conway has its own small police force, but they're not used to this kind of frightening crime. Nevertheless, they had to deal with it, try to solve it. They sent for Fred Cox. I went with him.

He wasn't pleased with what he found. The girl had been attacked only two hundred yards from the police station. But it had taken the police more than half an hour to turn out in anything like orderly form. Eventually, they had sent for bloodhounds. The dogs led them on a trail from the site of the attack to a nearby apartment house, but at the door of the apartment house the police chief himself had stopped them from going in. He was heavily conscious of the laws and ordinances within the county that might have made life difficult if he had gone in. But had the police gone in they might have discovered the attacker, or so an irritated Fred Cox believed.

He used the rough edge of his tongue on Conway's twelve-man police force. The police chief, a small intelligent likeable man, looked only slightly uncomfortable beneath the castigation. It was quite clear that he was used to it. Fred told me: "I don't think this investigation is going at all well. I think there are many things left undone by the police force and I think that they should have moved faster. But I suppose you've got to remember that the local police here are neither very well paid nor very well trained. Most of their training comes from experience rather than having been sent to any kind of police school. Chief Maclean, the police chief here, actually did recently go to school, but it was, I think, for just three weeks. Now, I would argue that he should have been trained before he even became a police officer—and particularly before he became a police chief. I know that they don't like me shouting and bawling at them and I know that they think that I'm aggressive and ill-tempered and foul-mouthed. But it's my job to see that if they get a suspect for a crime—and they charge that suspect—then the evidence they give me to take into court to prosecute that suspect is at least worth a damn when it comes to pushing back against a defense counsel."

Fred Cox interviewed the attacked girl in the hospital and spoke to people in houses along the road. The girl had been walking home from work, late, but on a main highway which ran past an empty lot, fairly thick with bushes and trees. A man in a black rubber gas mask and rubber gloves, wielding a black baseball bat, leaped out on her and dragged her into the bushes. The gas-mask disguise must have added an element of

Police Chief Maclean.

macabre horror to a terrifying situation. He hit the girl over the head with the baseball bat. She started to bleed and fell down but did not lose consciousness. He stood over her, and when he told her to take her clothes off, she remembered that it was best to appear, at least, to cooperate. She asked him if he was going to take his own clothes off; if he had a blanket on which they could lie; she appeared to reach for the zipper of her jeans —and he stepped back, thinking perhaps he'd won, and dropped the baseball bat. Wounded, bleeding, dazed, she struggled to her feet and ran to the road, seventy-five yards away. It was a well-lit road, the main route through Conway. Once in it the girl waved frantically and flagged down a passing car. The woman driver saw her blood-stained face and distressed state, rolled up the window—and drove off. The girl ran to another car, one going in the opposite direction. It too slowed down, and then the driver saw the state she was in—and sped away, nearly knocking her over. The girl then ran, staggered, the one hundred fifty yards to Conway police station. Her attacker got away.

The girl's assailant left behind the black-painted baseball bat, the gas mask, a pair of rubber gloves, all of them blood-stained. On Fred Cox's instructions the detectives and uniformed police of Conway went to local stores trying to discover if the gas mask or the gloves or the baseball bat had originated locally. They hadn't. And there wasn't much else the police could do—except worry.

And Fred Cox worries, too. What he worries about most is that the assailant may have been a local man. And a local man could do it again. A visitor, a tourist, would be far less likely to return. But Conway police, and Fred Cox, were aware of the problems that would arise if the assailant had been a local man. Then, they would have to find him. Or wait for him to do it again.

And with that threat, that possibility, hanging over them all Fred Cox pushed, and shoved, and harassed the local police. They weren't surprised, they were well used to it. So why does he do it? "I'll tell you why. I shout and push because when you've told a police officer how to do something twenty times and then on the twenty-first time he still does it wrong, then you do begin to shout, you begin to push, you begin to harass. And who but a saint would not? You have to do it. Some people say I blow my stack. Some people say I'm foul-mouthed. Some people say I'm abrasive. Well, maybe I am. But you get frustrated, you get mad, you get angry, when you find that what you know needs doing isn't being done. If I lose my temper with a police officer, if I bawl out the police chief in front of his men, if I call them all kinds of sons-of-bitches, then that is only because I am trying to make them do *their* job as policemen, so that I can do *my* job as Attorney."

Alan Maclean, the Conway police chief, knows that however well he tries to do his best, his best will not often be good enough for Fred Cox. He runs his police force in a small shabby bungalow building off the main street of Conway. It is not much of a place, nor much of a police force, to deal with the increased problems of crime that tourism has brought to Carroll County. He told me: "I don't always approve of the way Fred Cox expresses himself. I find that he really does go overboard and I've told him sometimes that the only really strong objection that I have for him is the way he talks. He is so abrasive and very, very rude. But he isn't always like this. And that's the problem. Sometimes he can be the nicest fellow in the world and we get on together and, maybe over a couple of drinks, he may pat me on the back and tell me what a terrific police department we've got here. Mind you, this has only happened once."

If Fred Cox, county attorney, makes reluctant supporters out of the policemen he castigates, there is no doubt that he makes enemies in the court. One local lawyer told me: "Fred does go hard on people at times and that means he makes enemies. He rubs people the wrong way. He rubs them really very hard indeed. And in this part of the country people have long memories. But the fact is that they are all fair-minded people and at the end of the day everybody remembers that Fred Cox did his job, won the case, put the criminals away. And that's what they want."

The superior court judge who followed so exactly Fred Cox's recommendations in court told me: "Fred Cox is one of our better prosecutors in court. He has as many supporters as he does critics. As a judge, I would rather assess a prosecutor from his critics than from his friends. If his critics say that he is harsh but just, demanding but accurate, tough but honest, then I am better pleased, better served. And, I think, so are the people of the county—and the best interests of justice."

But there's a rival for the job of district attorney in Carroll County, another lawyer, Bill Shea, for years Fred's most vigorous opponent in court. Bill Shea's opposition to Fred Cox has a personal, red-blooded, feuding chemistry about it. He has even changed his political party in order to run for office on an opposing platform. Shea's campaign focuses on education for youngsters, a manifesto concerned with crime prevention, but mostly he is out to collect anti-Cox voters. Shea's wife will not even speak to Fred Cox when they meet—as they do, frequently, in a small place like Carroll County. Bill Shea is, himself, a histrionic advocate, a man who likes to gesture and display in the local courts. He, like Fred, enjoys the theatrical aspects of advocacy. But why does he want so passionately to unseat Fred Cox politically? He told me: "I believe that you can get more cooperation from the law-enforcement agencies if you do not constantly take their skins off in public. Abrasive is hardly the word for Fred Cox. I wish there were a word in the dictionary to describe his behavior toward the people who must serve under him. One of the examples that comes to mind is the way he treats the elected sheriff of this county, Grant Floyd. At one time there was a case in court that was not very well or correctly prepared, and I saw Mr. Cox say things to Grant Floyd that I wouldn't say to my worst enemy. I was surprised at Floyd's reaction. He was amazingly calm and unruffled by all this. But Floyd is like Fred Cox; he, too, is elected. He, therefore, has the confidence of the people. He's an elected official just the same as Fred Cox, and yet he submitted to this tirade against him, and I think that what Fred Cox has done to the officials of this county, elected or appointed, is to instill in them a kind of fear which allows them to go on listening to his bellowing, his harassing, and his shoving at them. Just because they are not just as well equipped as he is professionally, or don't have the same level of intelligence as he does, is not enough reason—in my opinion—for them to lie down under his kind of behavior. I don't believe he can get proper cooperation from officials of this county with an attitude that I regard as malignant."

Bill Shea is not alone in feeling that Fred Cox is too much of a good thing. But somehow the voters of Carroll County clearly want a man who is in charge, determined to remain in charge; a man who is, also, determined to punish the wrongdoer and pursue the criminal.

Fred Cox is, himself, a peaceful and trusting man. He doesn't lock his doors at night. And the men he prosecutes in court, or the policemen he bawls out for inefficiency, may find the domestic Fred Cox a difficult man to recognize. But there are similarities. He is still in charge, wherever he is. His three children, Jane, Martha, and Anne—"Bananas" to the rest of the family—love him without fearing him; but there is no doubt that they respect not only him but his parental authority. His wife, Ellen, knows that while Fred may be her partner, for the children at least, he is always the boss.

Ellen is active in the social life of the village, belongs to flower-arranging groups, the Red Cross, and the Ladies' Fire Brigade Auxiliary; she is also a local "supply" teacher at the high school. Her own college graduation certificate hangs over the ironing board. When you notice this and point it out to her, she denies that it is a victory for chauvinism, a surrender of Women's Lib. She says that she put it over the ironing board deliberately, so maybe Women's Lib isn't dead in Ossipee, Carroll County.

Ellen's a good mother, attentive, intelligent, and imaginative. And, perhaps surprisingly to the crooks and policemen, Fred is a good father who cuts out paper dolls and teaches his children to fish, to ski, to grow beans in the garden—and be kind to the dog. Fred cooks with the kind of flamboyance that those he prosecutes in court would at least recognize. He says he finds it difficult to cook without wearing a tall chef's hat, and when the children help him they also have to wear chef's hats. He keeps a small steel file box in the kitchen with several hundred of his favorite recipes in it. They are clearly and easily indexed—rather like the "Method of Operation" index you will find in any good detective's room. But these will lead you easily to a recipe for tomatoes stuffed with spinach, or veal chops cooked in pastry.

When I asked Fred about his own upbringing, about his childhood, about the early moralities and rules in his life as a youngster, he told me: "My mother used to keep an eighteen-inch ruler behind the stove. Now, when I was a small kid I don't ever recall my father laying a hand on me —except once. Then I did something wrong—I forget quite what it was —and I was upstairs and he called me down because of it, and I came down

Bill Shea, Fred's opponent in and out of court.

Fred and wife, Ellen—he calls her "Charlie."

He loves to cook with the family—he's still in charge.

A nice place for his kids.

the stairs, and my father was waiting at the bottom of them. When I got to a point on the stairs where I was level with him he brought his hand up and slapped me across the face—hard. 'That,' he told me, 'is for what you've done. Don't forget it now.' And then he went away. And I went to school. I came home from school that afternoon with the mumps and I recall my father coming home from a day's work, later, and my mother saying, 'Look what you did to him! Look at his face, it's all swollen up, that's where you slapped his face.' And my father was really taken in by this. For a while he thought that the one time he had slapped me had produced that. Later my mother had to reveal that it really was the mumps. Nevertheless, I don't recall my father ever slapping me again.

"But what all that was about is that my father had instilled in me a respect for property, a respect for other people's rights, a respect for rules and order. So even to this day that respect is what motivates me as a lawyer. I think the system under which we live has to produce a reasonable deterrent to crime. We have an increased population, particularly a floating population, coming to this county. There is an increase in crime in the country as a whole and that includes travelers through Carroll County; some will be the kind of visitors who bring their crime to us. I resent them, I resent their lawlessness, I resent their attitude to crime. It isn't wrong

He also has a private practice.

of me to do so, I'm sure it isn't wrong of me to do so. And, at least, the people who elect me to office agree with me.

"I believe that there is too much softness is society today. I believe that there are too many people who go on saying, of the criminal, 'Give him a second chance,' until he is getting a tenth and eleventh chance. And he knows it. And he takes advantage. I think an awareness of right and wrong, an awareness of what is a crime, what is good and bad, should be instilled in a person from the age of five. I don't believe that we have to look at men at the age of eighteen or twenty or twenty-five and think, well, maybe he doesn't understand what is wrong. He understands all right. He just wants us to *feel* that he doesn't understand. I feel that we have to cut through all that—and sentence him, sentence him hard; in such a way that anybody else who may feel as he does can see how we feel too, and stay out of our lives—for good."

Fred Cox also has a private practice as an attorney. He has an office, with an associate, Timothy Sullivan, in the picturesque town of Wolfeboro on the edge of Lake Winnipesaukee. There he advises on matters of property, purchase, business disputes, divorce and marital arrangements. He will not, if you go to him for such a purpose, defend you against a criminal charge. He hardly could. He is more likely to prosecute you.

Fred Cox is a member of the District Attorney's Association of America. There are 2,700 district attorneys in America today. It is a job that in definition and practice is almost unique. It is certainly not a role which came to America with those first settlers from England. It is a job that grew up—as American law did—with the country.

The early settlers, from 1607 onward, had little need of law—and little taste for English law. England was a country most of them had left, resentfully, for legal reasons. What disputes there were in those early groups were settled mostly by the preachers and mainly in a religious manner. Lawyers among the settlers passed on their knowledge as it was required. But by about 1700 the need for more expert legal knowledge was felt. A number of students, mainly those who could afford to do so, returned to London, to the Inns of Court, in order to study law. Others stayed in America and apprenticed themselves to existing lawyers. Thus in the early colonies there were barristers in the style of England, who had been trained in England, and barristers trained in America by those who, in their turn, had been trained in England. But those trained in America, it was ruled, had to practice in court for four years first as attorneys, and then as counselors, before being accepted as barristers by the court. The word *attorney* had arrived.

The profession flowered in the eighteenth century and reached its peak at the time of the American Revolution. Twenty-five of the fifty-six signatories of the Declaration of Independence were lawyers.

After independence all things English, not unnaturally, were out of favor. Many Loyalist lawyers returned to England or ceased to practice, perhaps involuntarily. And the students of law, Americans now, and no longer British settlers, stopped going to London. With none being called to the bar in London, and without an equivalent of the bar in America, the term *barrister* died out. The lawyers in America from that day on were known as counselors or attorneys. The term *solicitor,* common, even vital, in British law, never came into general use.

But the new American lawyers continued to use, albeit reluctantly, English law books. They had none of their own. William Blackstone's commentaries were preeminent in every lawyer's library in the early days after the Revolution—although they were usually accompanied by an

Typical American courtroom of the nineteenth century.

American supplement by Tucker. Later Thomas Jefferson, before he became President, instituted, in 1779, the first chair of law in an American university—at William and Mary College in Williamsburg, Virginia. Litchfield Law School, Connecticut, was the first of its kind and was open for approximately fifty years from 1784 to 1833. From this school came twenty-eight United States senators, eleven members of Congress, thirty-four state and three United States Supreme Court justices, fourteen state governors, three Vice-Presidents and six members of the Cabinet.

The celebrated Harvard Law School started in 1817 and, after a shaky beginning and several setbacks, set standards that were widely followed. The school has had some part in the education of 25 percent of all law teachers in the United States.

One of the complications—some would say one of the strengths—of law in America today is that from the very beginning there have been multiple legal systems. Each state has its own legislation, enacts its own laws, and runs its own courts. But the United States, or federal, legislature also enacts its own laws, and federal law may overrule state law, although not always without a struggle. Once America was independent it was obliged to set up a central unifying legal system. The new federal system was based

Courthouse in Lowell, Massachusetts—
more lawyers in his hometown than in the whole state of New Hampshire

on the English assize courts set up under Edward I. Then, to save everyone traveling to London to the King's justices, the King's justices went to various parts of the country, at certain times, on regular circuits. So America decided to do the same and divided itself into three circuits—east, middle and southern. The first circuit court sat in New York on April 14, 1790. And from then on the American federal legal show was on the road—literally. Some went by coach, most on horseback.

Judges and lawyers covered hundreds of saddle-sore miles each year. Justice Pinckney Charleston started out early each morning and consulted with lawyers and clients en route. If he was given an opinion, he would write it down as "given on circuit," since he had no books with him to refer to. "Horseback Opinion" it came to be called. And some of the judges of the time were rough. An Iowa justice of the peace, berated in court by a rowdy for not ordering meals for the prisoners in the cells, personally clubbed the man senseless; and then had himself duly charged with assault and battery—and acquitted.

In later years young Abraham Lincoln rode the circuit in Illinois—an unmatched opportunity for a budding politician to feel the pulse of the public. Andrew Jackson's Presidency in the 1830s ushered in the era of the common man. Excellent in many ways, it was in fact disastrous for the legal profession. Always highly suspicious of authority or any sign of privilege, many Americans resented the power and prestige of lawyers. And they proved it at election time. In one state after another laws were introduced reducing the qualifications for admittance to the bar—almost to a point of absurdity. And, in 1832, Mississippi was the first state to elect, rather than appoint, a judge.

But lawyers, and particularly federal and state lawyers, were still not respected. As late as 1890 a judge of the New Hampshire Supreme Court, not himself a lawyer, is reported to have said. "Gentlemen, you have heard what has been said in this case by the lawyers, the rascals! . . . They talk of law. Why, gentlemen, it is not law that we want, but justice! They would govern us by the common law of England. Commonsense is a much safer guide . . . a clear head and an honest head is worth more than all the law out of Coke and Blackstone, books that I have never read—and never will."

Dean Roscoe Pound of Harvard said: "The harm that this deprofessionalizing of the law did to the law, to legal procedure, to the ethics of practice and to forensic conduct has outlived the era in which it took place and still presents problems to promoters and administrators of justice."

But most states have by now adopted the standards of the American Bar Association for determining qualifications of persons who can be considered for admission to the bar. Almost all now require a college degree before a student can be admitted to study law. Students, therefore, are usually of a high academic level. They tend to come from middle- to upper-middle-class homes, and there is a high proportion of Jews and Catholics among them. At the present time there are about fifty-four thousand students in American law classes, and about ten thousand are being admitted to the bar each year.

America has become a law-conscious nation. There are now proportionally about two and a half times more lawyers in the United States than there are in the United Kingdom. And lawyers themselves constantly debate whether this is a reflection of more crime in America than in Great Britain; or because laws in America are more complex and differ greatly from area to area, needing more interpretation; or because the lawyers in America are less efficient than their British counterparts.

And legal officials are still, mostly, elected. In country areas the district attorney is usually elected to serve on a part-time basis, combining his work as a county or district prosecutor with a private practice. This is how Fred started; it was all Carroll County needed when he was first elected.

In big cities the district attorney frequently heads a staff of assistant district attorneys, and even then they are all overworked. Criminal lawyers are seldom rich lawyers. And lawyers who enter criminal practice on the public payroll are certainly *never* going to be rich. But one day they may become judges or politicians or successful private lawyers—or just older and wiser for having served in public office. And that is why many of them do it. But the reputation of the district attorney hasn't always been that of an upright public defender. And the image of corrupt, or downright stupid, D.A.'s, manipulated by political pressures, hasn't been just the invention of Hollywood scriptwriters. It was bound to have been based in fact. There have been too many cases, too well documented, too well-known throughout the nation, of district attorneys serving the whim of gang bosses and crooked politicians. And those who were honest, those who struggled on low budgets and small salaries to clean up corruption or root out crooks, were hardly helped by the image of the D.A. shown on the movie screen. When the defense lawyers were Spencer Tracy or Jimmy Stewart or Dana Andrews, everybody knew that the D.A. was bound to be crooked or stupid—and probably both. Certainly, he was bound to lose—to everyone's delight.

Of course, the reputation of criminal lawyers, either prosecutors or defenders, has never been that high, and Carl Sandburg's "The People, Yes" contains this joke. *Question:* "Have you a criminal lawyer in this burg?" *Answer:* "We think so, but we haven't been able to prove it on him."

But district attorneys do have considerable power. If they are successful they can become rich. Fred Cox can only be regarded as successful. But

A hard campaign.

he doesn't want to be rich, or famous, or even go on to bigger political jobs.

On the face of it, it is impossible to consider Fred Cox a retiring or diffident person. "Hail fellow, well met" would be an understatement for his own particular brand of back-slapping noisy bonhomie. And yet there is a reluctance in him, a private diffidence and lack of push, in this the most aggressive of men. He doesn't like electioneering.

At election time he will see that he has the necessary number of bumper stickers, tree posters, and give away handbills printed. He will attend official lunches and the occasional dinner. He will, if pressed, make a speech. But he's far less effective at making election speeches than he is when addressing a jury. I was with him at election time when he visited the County Fair at Sandwich, an annual event anticipated with pleasure by

Fred votes—for himself.

farmers and their families all year. It is a nice time in a nice place, and usually an occasion when Fred and Ellen and the children enjoy themselves. On this year clearly he did not. He felt obliged to seek out and shake hands with all his friends—and then ask them how they were going to vote. He seemed only able to do it by teasing and joking, suggesting that they look up the obituary columns on election day and vote twice in his favor.

And yet he believes in the system in which powerful and influential public figures must also be political figures, elected by voters on the basis of a party ticket or political persuasiveness rather than selected by their peers for professional merit. He told me: "I find it a basic element of American society, essential and also beautiful. Anyone who has public responsibility should answer to the public. I don't care who he is, whether he is the President of the United States or one of our local selectmen. I answer to the public, and if the public don't like the way that I'm doing my job, then they can vote for somebody else—and I'll be out of a job. I think that that is essential. I feel, somehow, protected by serving within that system. It doesn't make me feel uneasy; it doesn't unsettle me. To have my job, to have these powers, to have this amount of influence and control, would be too much if I were not accountable to the public at election time.

As county attorney, Fred Cox also has to advise his county officials on their legal rights—in disputes about rights of way, land ownership, frontage rights on local lakes, bylaws relating to tourist control, traffic ordinances, and so on. He also has a quasi-judicial role in relation to the county jail. The County Jail and House of Correction holds up to forty prisoners, some awaiting trial, some serving sentences. It may not be San Quentin but it isn't a holiday home, either. The discipline is strict, but the regime fair. Nevertheless, when I was there, the men in the jail had complained about the food. They thought it was monotonous and insufficient. Fred Cox, as district attorney, had to be called in to assess the merit of their complaint. He ordered the prison superintendent and the probation officer to conduct a full inquiry—then he visited the jail to listen to their findings. The prison superintendent argued passionately that the prisoners were better fed in prison than they ever were at home—where, he insisted, they lived mostly on Coca-Cola and potato chips. In prison they had the delights of creamed cod and boiled asparagus and nearly all put on weight and left healthier. Fred Cox listened patiently for about five minutes and then ruled: "The whole thing is just a crock . . ." a judgment

---

A complaint in the jail.

that must be reckoned as brief and to the point as any of those given by the circuit-riding judges of the early days.

Fred also frequently attends the county jail whenever a prisoner has been extradited from outside the county and is brought in to await trial. He supervises while the men are searched, stripped of their possessions, fingerprinted, photographed, and then locked up—innocent until proven guilty.

Fred's political rival, Bill Shea, was, like Fred, a Republican. Not a bad thing to be in a solid Republican county. While Bill Shea wants to be county attorney, in the primaries, on two occasions, he has failed to beat Fred as the Republican candidate for the job. So Bill Shea switched parties, changed his ticket, in order to be able to run against Fred. It was a gesture that was naturally bound to cost him the majority of votes, but he felt it at least allowed him an opportunity to demonstrate his opposition —and air his opinions about Fred Cox.

Bill Shea told me: "Frankly, I am a law-enforcement man, as much as Fred Cox is. But if I was county attorney I'd probably be what they call a 'real' law and order man as supposed to a 'hard' law and order man like Fred Cox. You see, the way that I look at things, almost everyone is entitled to a first mistake. And I'm particularly concerned with the way young people are being dealt with in the courts in our county. I believe that they are more or less entitled to go wrong once. Now, don't get me wrong, we are not talking about crimes of violence, not talking about rape or robbery or murder at gunpoint or knife point. These are things that we must deal with as severely as possible. But we are talking about crimes against property, like burglary when nobody is occupying a particular structure, crimes where no particular violence is involved. With this kind of crime, particularly where the offenders are young, we have a chance to rehabilitate the offenders and give them a chance to try again. Most criminal convictions in this county are of people under the age of twenty-five. And I think that we have to rehabilitate them, not lock them up and put them in jail. And that's what Fred Cox does—just locks them up. That's his legal philosophy in a nutshell. Shut the door."

But Fred Cox has his own opinions about Bill Shea: "If Bill Shea was running for county attorney, unopposed, I would decline to vote, and the reason that I would do that is because I don't think that he would be a very good county attorney. I think he's soft in the center, impetuous, he loses his cool and he has a temper that he displays in the courtroom. And that's the point. I have a bad temper, but never, never in the courtroom. The

---

A pause in court.

courtroom is a place to keep your cool, and that isn't what Bill Shea does."

With all this, Fred's wife, Ellen, sometimes finds the burden of a political job, which always comes home with its holder, almost too much. The phone calls in the middle of the night, the sheriffs, the deputies, the policemen who tramp constantly through her home seeking the district attorney—hardly the life she thought she was getting when she met and married a young country lawyer with a practise in Wolfeboro on Lake Winnipesaukee. In fact, when he first decided that he wanted to run as county attorney for Carroll County he talked it over with Ellen and she was against it. "I was a hundred percent against it. I didn't even vote for him the first time. His own practice was going along great and I thought that was plenty. Plenty of work and plenty of complications in our life, quite enough. I couldn't see the necessity for him to become county attorney. He argued that it would be a useful job to do and that it might grow into something bigger and better in time.

"But once he was elected, and I saw how much he enjoyed the work, then I resigned myself to the fact that he would probably be county attorney, term after term after term. And that's exactly the way it has been. Somehow I always knew that he was the kind of man that people would go on reelecting. Eventually, I hope that he will retire and even cut down on his own private legal practice. But I can't see him ever retiring permanently. He needs to feel involved with what's going on, particularly with what's going on legally. But he's a good husband, and a good father to the children, and we've had a great marriage and I've enjoyed every moment of it. And I intend to go on enjoying it. And I am sure Fred does too."

On election day the voters of Carroll County turned out in force. In this particular election they were choosing a President, senators, congressmen, state and county representatives; they were also voting on various state referendums as well as choosing a number of local officials—and the county attorney. The voting paper looked nearly as complicated as a legal examination. But the voters didn't appear to be disturbed and the county attorney didn't appear to worry.

On election night, as the votes were counted and the results started to come in, nearly everybody gathered in the kitchen at Fred's house— everybody, that is, on his side. By midnight the result was clear. Fred was the winner by about three votes to every two. When he heard over the telephone from the local radio station that he'd sealed it for certain by winning back from Bill Shea a town he'd lost to him at the last election, there were whoops of glee from Fred and his supporters. Fred chortled untactfully to the radio station: "I wonder whose kid got out of jail."

The next day was quiet and peaceful. The New England foliage looked as beautiful as it always does, the white houses glowed in the autumn sunshine—and the superior court in Ossipee was in session. Fred Cox, once again district attorney for Carroll County, addressed the jury: "Ladies and gentlemen of the jury, my name is Fred Cox and I am the county attorney . . ."

THE PLANTATION OWNER
ANDREW GAY

The sugar was burning. Andrew Gay, plantation owner, steadied his horse; the animal was fretting and dancing a little in the smoke, as he turned from the flames and pointed his way home to the Great House. He was doing exactly as his father did before him, and *his* father before him, and *his* father before him. On the banks of the Mississippi, in Louisiana, the Gay family has always planted, and always harvested, in grand style.

As the horse picked his way between the blackened and smoking furrows, the cane reduced now and readied for the mill, the faces of the black workers turned toward Gay. He waved to them, greeted them, remembered their names, remembered to ask after their families, and to joke with them, as he always did. It has always been like this for him, for his father, for his grandfather, for his great-grandfather and for all the Gays who have farmed and lived this way on the St. Louis Plantation.

The St. Louis Plantation House stands solidly and grandly beside the Mississippi in Plaquemine, Louisiana, seventy miles north of New Orleans. It is an elegantly pillared antebellum plantation home. And, unlike most of the plantation homes still standing in the South, the St. Louis House has been the home of one old Southern family for more than a century now. It has hardly changed since it was built by slaves a hundred and twenty years ago for Edward Gay, sugar planter and Southern Gentleman. All along the banks of the Mississippi these graceful plantation homes still stand as a reminder of an elegant, romantic, and doomed period of American history.

The St. Louis House, however, remained, even after the tragedy of the Civil War, as the home of the Gay family and the center of a 5,000-acre sugar plantation. But then, as now, the house also stood as a symbol of something else. Andrew Gay and the rest of his family are determined to keep alive what they regard as the best of their heritage: a Southern style, characterized by gentle manners and fair dealing, a way of life which they feel is often misunderstood these days by other Americans and by the rest of the world.

Locked in twentieth-century competition with local chemical plants, "agribusiness" tycoons and cheap food produced abroad; pressured by the price of hired help, the demands of unions, the resolutions of Congress, and many other demands for change, Andrew Gay and his family are determined that their plantation and their way of life shall not soon be "gone with the wind."

It is, of course, a way of life that was based on slavery. Indeed, not only was the plantation house built by slaves, but the plantation was created with their labor. The affluence of the Gay family is an inheritance from those days. Does Andrew Gay, 120 years after the Civil War, feel any sense of family responsibility or guilt? "No, I certainly don't," he told me. "The situation that existed at that time was certainly not of my doing or making. I feel now that it is part of history, something that is passed, and gone, and over. I think it probably is to be regretted and I think there were wicked and terrible things done in those days. But I think the Civil War was the most terrible of those things. I think we, in the South, and my family in particular, paid the price for all that. In any case, it is in the past. We cannot go on being guilty for what was in the past."

Today on the St. Louis Plantation there are ten black families working a little under 5,000 acres of sugar. But when the plantation was first built, it needed several hundred slaves to run the same acreage. The relics of those old slave days, the slave shacks, are not hard to find. Many are still occupied today by black workers. The older, more ramshackle shacks are usually the homes of retired workers, allowed to stay on rent-free, paying only for electricity and gas, raising a few chickens, a little corn, and doing odd jobs.

The bell which used to summon them to start the day still stands. And the very shape of the plantation is a reminder of its early history, a thin slice stretching back from the river frontage just exactly the distance that a team of mules could haul a full load in a day. To stretch the plantation farther from the Mississippi banks would have made it unworkable for both slaves and mules. For obvious reasons both had to be "in" at night. The pattern of sugar plantations on both banks of the lower reaches of the Mississippi is a repetitive geography of slices, each one touching the river. There, on the banks of the river, they invariably built the plantation home. On top of each home they would build the "belvedere," a small railed observation platform (in richer families it would have a roof to keep the sun off) from which a black child would keep watch daily for the unscheduled arrival of the river boats. Then stores would be purchased, produce would be loaded, passengers would embark or arrive.

As the plantation families grew in size and the daughters married, or the sons set up on their own, more plantations were required—and more plantation homes were built. These days a tourist to New Orleans may book a fascinating guided tour of the plantation houses of the Mississippi. The style of the houses is varied and was determined partly by the pocket-book of the owner, the size of his family, the artistic taste of his wife—and whether or not he employed an architect. The St. Louis House, for instance, is almost uncharacteristically elegant for this region, with much of the pillared and wrought-iron-balconied grace found in the houses of the old quarter of New Orleans.

Andrew Gay loves the house and knows its history well. He took me around himself. "The house was built by my great-grandfather," he told me. "His name was Edward J. Gay and he built it in 1858, just prior to the Civil War. He was a merchant and had lived in St. Louis, Missouri, and traveled quite extensively by the steamboats up and down the Mississippi river between St. Louis and New Orleans. It was in New Orleans that he met a Miss Lavinia Hynes and in due course he married her and came here to manage the property that belonged to her father. At that time there was another house called the St. Louis House, and it was in front of this site up closer to the banks of the river. But we're on a curve in the river and on the encroaching side of the bank, so eventually the house had to be demolished because the river was about to move in on it over the levee. It was then that he built this house. It must have taken hundreds, perhaps even thousands, of slaves to construct it. It's very beautiful, very large, and was clearly designed to be not only the focus of his own elegant and graceful life but of an elegant and gay social life for the whole area.

"He lived here for quite a number of years and when he passed away his son, Andrew H. Gay, moved in and operated the plantation and then my father later came to live here and run the plantation, and there are five children in father and mother's family and all of them, with the exception of one, were born right here in this house. The Gay family has raised sugar here since about the early 1800s. That was about the time when Étienne de Boré discovered how to crystallize sugar juices and thus make it a very profitable crop. Before that they raised indigo quite extensively on this property. Now, since I've been managing this place we have raised, in addition to sugar cane, rice, and soya bean and beef cattle and at one time we even had a pretty elaborate dairy operation going on here.

"I myself was born in this house and I lived here until I was about fifteen years old, when I went off to school, and then to high school and on to college. After college I served in the armed forces for about five years

during World War II and when I got out of the service at the end of the war I came back here to work and help manage the plantation. I hadn't meant to—I didn't really think that it was part of my job or what I wanted to do—but my father wanted me to come up here and sort some things out, so I agreed to do it, just for a day or two. I've stayed ever since.

"I was married by the time I came out of the army and we lived in this big house for several months but it was very difficult, it was cold in the winter and it was a huge place and we didn't have servants. Remember that this was a house that was built to be filled with people and also staffed by many servants. Just after World War II, that wasn't a condition anybody could enjoy unless they had very much more money than a poor plantation owner.

"Now, when I was a child, I remember the house being full of people, guests, and servants. We had a woman who came in six days a week just to do the washing of the linen and clothes and the pressing of all the garments. That was her only job. She would just wash the linen and iron the clothes. Then there was a cook that came early in the morning and stayed until dark, preparing at least three meals a day, and she would have helpers in the kitchen. Then there was the downstairs maid who kept the downstairs part in order. And there was an upstairs maid for the upstairs portion of the house. Then there was a yard man who just looked after the garden and the yard around the house. And there was a man who attended to the family cows which were kept purely for family use, for our own butter and milk, and he also did gardening. Then there would be help from special field hands, and from time to time special carpenters and plumbers and craftsmen would come and work in the house. If we were entertaining guests in the house, then of course we would need other servants to help out. So there was usually a kind of butler figure in the house, in charge of it all. It may sound an awful lot, it may even sound indulgent and spoiled. But to run a large house like this didn't cost a lot comparatively speaking, and it did give a great deal of employment to people who otherwise wouldn't have had any."

These days the St. Louis House is shared on a carefully managed rotation basis by all the members of the Gay family. Most of the Gay family, therefore, only see their heritage when they visit the house for a weekend or for the "family meeting," which has become the governing council of the several companies that now run the Gay plantation and the St. Louis House. But it is the house which has, in fact, become the focus of all that the family believes in, the symbol of their desire to maintain and keep alive a Southern tradition, a Southern style. There is still a great deal of squab-

Cane is shipped to the mill.

bling, and some of it not at all gentle, about just how that style should be translated into furniture and furnishings; and that is apart from all the arguments about whose turn it is, on what weekend, to occupy the house with friends and relatives. But, by and large, it works out and it does mean that the house is constantly occupied, filled with life, with laughter, with the sound of children playing, and with the servants busy preparing meals. These days the "help" works alongside the younger members of the Gay family, all of them pitching in together to make the traditional mint juleps or the Baton Rouge and Creole dishes.

Andrew Gay and his wife now live in a beautiful home, still pillared, still Southern in style, built on the grounds of the St. Louis House from the bricks of the old "sugar house."

When the Second World War ended and she and Andrew moved to the plantation, Nancy Gay might still have enjoyed the chatelaine role of the Southern belle in the big house. But she didn't enjoy the lack of servants, the cold in the winter, the acres of floors to be polished, the difficulties of maintaining the old style in a house that had become too arthritic to make it easy. Tradition is not usually effortless.

The Southern tradition flowered, only briefly, in American history and its fine qualities, its gentle manners, its reliance on courtesy and honesty became, in the end, totally obscured by the resentment of its economic basis—slavery. The appalling and self-immolating events of the Civil War destroyed the remnants of Southern tradition. Long after the dreary and oppressive days of "reconstruction," generations after the carpet-baggers, there emerged, in some places and only for some people, a tentative second flowering of some of the more admirable aspects of Southern nature. It nearly didn't happen. It was obscured by rednecks, nearly lost in the conflict of integration battles, the noise of prejudice and the Klan.

But these days it is obvious that there has been a resurgence of belief in the Southern manner. The Gay family is not alone in believing that the strength of Southern business dealings is founded on an honesty which is the true inheritance of the South. And Andrew Gay is the first to point out, and to demonstrate in his own life, that it starts simply: between a man and woman. "That's certainly a great part of it," he told me. "I often see a man and his wife going out in an automobile and as they leave the house or a building one of them will go to one side of the car and the other will go to the opposite side. I still can't stop myself feeling shocked by that. It just wasn't the way I was brought up. I brought my children up to respect their parents and to show the same kind of courtesy to their mother as I do. They may disagree with me, they may argue with me. But they will always do it politely, they will never do it in company, they will always respect us as parents, and that, I think, is a strength in our family. The South has much to regret and Southern families have much in their past that was wrong and for which they were responsible. But this is something for which we were responsible that is good and should be kept and maintained. As I travel around the rest of the States I sometimes shudder at the casual, almost brutal, way men and women, children, and parents, behave toward each other.

"And I believe that we should maintain the same style of courtesy and manners in our business dealings. Not only should our word be our bond but we should show it to be so. Why should we be rude to competitors? Aggressive with people who want to do business with us? Whatever is wrong with a courteous manner? It needn't stop effective business and it isn't hypocritical. I believe that unless we keep that we will have lost, forever, the best that the South has to give to the world. We've overcome most of our troubles and we've shown that we can give not only a new economic strength to our own country but we can also restore style."

Andrew and Nancy Gay not only believe in the restoration of style, they believe also that the black population in the South would prefer it that way. Whether the idea, "together as Southerners," will ever really succeed, with the economic and other inequalities that persist between black and white, is unlikely—but not, perhaps, impossible. The white race may have at one time "owned" the other and has certainly exploited it since, but it is true to say that it took both to make the South. Between them, they created the plantations on which they *both* lived and on which they *both* depended.

The states that seceded and became the Confederacy at the time of the Civil War were Alabama, Arkansas, Florida, Georgia, Louisiana, Mississippi, North Carolina, South Carolina, Tennessee, Texas, Virginia, Oklahoma, and Kentucky, together making up "the South."

Today that is an area that comprises approximately twenty-eight percent of the continental United States and, at a census in 1960, contained about twenty-seven percent of the U.S. population. In the beginning the story of the South was much the same as the North; English settlers arrived on the East or Atlantic coast of America and bartered, or battled, with the Indians to wrest a living from the wilderness. They built homes, founded communities, tried not to feel too homesick and set to work to make a better life for themselves and for their children. But what distinguished the South from the North was the very thing that distinguishes North and South in most countries—climate and soil. The North was harsh and cold, the ground rocky and difficult. The South was warm— almost tropical—the land lush and opulent, with deep rivers giving easy access to the interior. It was, certainly in those days, an agricultural paradise. In the beginning, too, there were the aristocratic families, the famous First Families of Virginia, the FFV's. For the most part, the true aristocrats of England and Europe didn't emigrate and most of the settlers, even in the South, were from the merchant classes or the sons of country squires, or the younger sons of London gentry, who knew that they were never going to inherit land and houses at home and so pinned their hopes on the New World. That didn't stop them from developing a snobbishness and an aristocratic elitism to match, even exceed, anything they'd left behind in England. This snobbishness of the well-descended had its own store of jokes. A ferryboat captain was asked for a free ride by a Virginian. The captain asked if he was one of the FFV's, one of the First Families of Virginia. The man replied, "No, I can't exactly say that; rather one of the second families." "Jump aboard," said the captain. "I haven't met one of your sort before."

Cotton surpassed all other crops. Three-quarters of the nation of slaves worked in cotton. Half the total value of American exports was in cotton. America provided two-thirds of the world's production of cotton. From 1793 to the start of the Civil War in 1861, cotton production almost doubled every ten years. New Orleans became the center of the new South. Bought from France in 1803 as part of the Louisiana purchase, its many French and Catholic families were soon engulfed by the Anglo-Americans. Andrew Gay's family ancestors were among those who came to Louisiana in the "King Cotton" years to take advantage of the new prosperity—and to establish a dynasty for themselves. There never were all that many planters; in the 1860 census it was reckoned that out of a population of eight million in the South there were only 50,000, and of those only about three thousand owned more than one hundred slaves.

In those days a planter was defined as a man with at least twenty slaves. Fortunes were made and lost with the early crops; first of all Virginia tobacco, then rice in the Carolinas, then indigo, hemp, and cotton. Sugar came much later and it came from the Deep South. It was a boom time but it was short-lived. Andrew Gay's ancestors came to Plaquemine, Louisiana, in 1858 and Louisiana seceded from the Union and joined the Confederacy in 1861. In May, 1863, the Union occupied New Orleans and laid siege to upriver Vicksburg, capturing it in July, 1863. So the Gays' pioneering ancestor had just begun when the Civil War broke out and couldn't have owned slaves for more than five years. (The Emancipation Proclamation was issued in 1863.) But he did start the plantation and built the Great House. These days the St. Louis Plantation is one of the last working plantations still in the possession of the original family. In the old days, much was made of the elegant, aristocratic, and educated pattern of plantation life, but in fact the great libraries and the great intellects were fewer between and harder to find than the many middle-class autocracies and squirearchies maintained by slaves and run, harshly, for profit. The life that eventually was truly "gone with the wind" was a life that centered around parties and visiting, with dancing as the main social occupation for

Stevenson's cotton picker.

Slaves carrying cotton.

Greenwood plantation near St. Francesville, Louisiana.

men and women. The balls sometimes went on for days. For the men, cock
fighting, horseriding, and racing were the sports which raised their en-
thusiasms, and on which they gambled their fortunes. But the Southern
climate, the occasional Indian, and, not least of all, their hard drinking
habits killed them off at early ages. Then, as now, the women lasted longer
and many Southern ladies married many times. Three or four husbands,
for a Southern belle, was quite average. Women were in such short supply
that a widow would often receive a proposal on her way back from her
husband's funeral. But however languid the ladies and however indolent
the gentlemen, the plantation owners, to succeed, or even to survive, had
to be more than just well-mannered and well-bred. They had to be farmers, organizers, and administrators; they had to work hard as well as play

hard. They may have been addicted to dancing but they also had to know building construction, engineering, estate management, agricultural theory. Their women had to command large staffs and huge kitchens. Not only all the food but also all the raw materials of the plantations had to be manufactured and maintained within these self-contained societies. Throughout it all cotton was king and New Orleans was the biggest slave market in the world. There was no other way it could have boomed as it did. But economically even slavery was feeling the effects of inflation. Just before the Civil War the cost of a "prime field hand" on the New Orleans slave block was $1500—proportionately much more than the cost of a tractor after the Second World War.

Nearly 600,000 men were killed in the Civil War. The war may have ended slavery, but it didn't change much for the black people. Most of them had to stay on the plantations because there wasn't much else for them to do, and in the years since then the exploitation of black labor, the voting and the school integration riots have done little to improve the image of Southern ladies and gentlemen. Nevertheless, many black people still feel, just as strongly as many whites like the Gay family, that the old days were, in fact, good and that the rest of America still doesn't properly understand the loyalties and affections in the South.

On the St. Louis Plantation Martha was the cook. She is sixty-five now and lives in a little house just outside the plantation and is still the strongest voice in the Baptist church choir. She still works, too, in the Big House on special occasions. She told me: "When I first went to work for the Gay family in the big house I was paid sixty cents a day. But I wasn't working in the kitchen then. I was in the fields cutting cane and grinding it. Each day the mule cart would come around and pick us all up from the shacks —I lived on the plantation with my family then—and take us out into the fields to work. If there was no work in the fields, or the weather was bad, then you didn't get paid. And if you were sick, you didn't get paid. But still I loved being part of plantation life. I was raised on a plantation, I spent my childhood there, and I reckon it was my best life there.

"They were lovely people in those days, they would always put their head around the kitchen and say, 'Martha, that was the most marvelous meal.' My children played with their children. I do really think it was better in those days. I think there was love, you know, people just loved each other in those days. We were more together. I don't know what's wrong these days, but a whole lot has gone wrong. I know it's supposed to be a better world for black people and I know there's better education and better opportunities and we aren't pushed down like we used to be, but I still miss the old days. And people from the North, people like you, don't really understand the black and white situation, you don't realize there's been a lot more friendship between the blacks and the whites than most people know about. They just hear about all the troubles."

Andrew Gay's wife, Nancy, didn't know, as she sat beneath the portrait of one of her ancestors and spoke to me, that she was echoing, almost exactly, the sentiments of the family cook. She told me: "People don't realize how much friendship there's been between blacks and whites, they don't realize how fond we've all become of each other. They don't know how fond we are of those people who've worked for us. It seems a crying shame for all this disruption to come into our lives—and into the lives of the blacks. It's changed things for the black people and I think it's not helped them but made them worse. So many of them now are living on welfare and, I know I shouldn't say this and it will make me unpopular, but so many of them these days don't want to work.

"Now people outside don't understand all that, don't know the quality of friendship that there is between the blacks and the whites. Why, we are so fond of the ones we know, and they're just so good to us, and we just really love some of them because they have become like our friends, certainly they feel like part of the family. I know how I feel about the people who've helped me ever since I've lived here. The maid who helped me raise my children, for instance, she was the finest woman that I could ever have met and I think she helped make my children fine children. Her husband is now the pastor of the local church, and when my daughter, who lives in New York, comes home to Plaquemine, she goes out to see her every time and loves her just as though she were one of the family. When there were riots and troubles here during the time of the civil rights and integration demonstrations, it was a tragedy. You could see it in their eyes. They didn't like it any more than us. It made a barrier between us all."

Andrew Gay has a theory about it: "We've always had very close relations with the black people in our community here, and in the 1960s when there was trouble over the integration of schools and voter registration, it was because outsiders moved into this area. Now, I've been told that it was a mistake. They shouldn't, in fact, have come to Plaquemine in Ibberville parish. I'm told they intended to go to the *parish* of Plaquemine rather than the town of Plaquemine and that's down near the mouth of the Mississippi river, and that is the kind of target that they would have picked. I certainly wish they had picked it because what they did here has put a barrier between white and black. I remember before that time how we'd go down the street and say, 'Hello, Joe,' 'Hi, Mary,' to the people of the opposite race, and then during all this integration rioting you'd walk down the street and see a black person you knew and he'd pass you by, and you were like strangers. It was a very unnatural thing. It was certainly a very distasteful thing.

"The schools have been integrated completely here now, and I think the

people who came down from the North to do it, and promote it, didn't realize what it was going to be like. Anyway, they did it and they returned north, and now they're getting a taste of it themselves. For example, in Boston right now they're beginning to find out what can go wrong when you fully integrate schools. But the South generally speaking has accepted it. We fought it, we didn't like it, and when it was forced on us we resisted it. But now we've grown to accept it and we're beginning to get back to this feeling of friendship between the races and I think, looking ahead, this will continue to improve. The friendships on the plantation go across the black and white boundary. And I like to see it. It applies very much to my own family; I have two boys, Price and John, they both work here on the plantation, and they work alongside black workers."

When Andrew Gay says "we" he really does mean *we,* the whole Gay family: first cousins, second cousins, third cousins, fourth cousins, in-laws, and children. While Andrew Gay *is* the St. Louis Plantation, the man and the energy behind St. Louis House, he is, too, a salaried employee of the Gay family, the managing director of Gay enterprises and Gay corporations, obedient to, and ruled by, an almost overwhelmingly complicated family board structure stretching into nearly every one of the United States. Few managing directors can labor under the handicap of "helpful" relatives to quite the degree that Andrew Gay does. The family meets regularly—and seldom agrees. They don't agree about whether Andrew's running of the plantation is efficient; they never, ever agree about the handling of the Great House, about whose weekend should be on what date, about what color fabric should be used to re-cover the chaise longue or kidney-backed sofa. The arguments about the table-tennis table echoed for months; a row that split the family apart was about whether to have a swimming pool. The subject is now taboo at meetings, and the swimming pool is unlikely ever to be built.

Andrew Gay earns $25,000 a year and gets his house rent free. It's a small salary and yet he regards it as generous enough. He didn't always want to be in charge and what worries him most is who will take over when he's done. His two sons, Price and John, have been working on the plantation, with Price as his second in command, for some years. John is at Louisiana State University Agricultural College and doing well, working on the plantation during his vacations and weekends. Andrew hopes that eventually both Price and John will manage the plantation between them, sharing the responsibilities and sharing what profit there is, keeping alive the Gay name and the Gay business. They will have to cope, if they can, with the family meeting, which is the real problem. It has taken Andrew Gay, for all his diffidence of manner and a slight speech impediment, years to perfect the authoritarian manner with which he bullies the cousins, quiets the aunts, holds the brothers and uncles in check, and achieves what to many would seem impossible—getting through the family meeting in no more than one day. There is a small working committee, formed to manage the plantation and make working decisions without constantly referring to the whole family meeting. Without such a device it is unlikely that any decision would be made at all. Andrew's brother, Edward, plays a leading part on the committee. He's a lawyer practicing in New Orleans. He, too, is passionately concerned with the future of the plantation and he, too, believes in the resurrection and maintenance of a Southern style, not only in private life but also in business.

At the meetings the family fills the Big House. They arrive early and before the meeting there is Southern hospitality, Southern small talk, mint juleps, and lunch. Martha, once cook to the whole family, comes out of retirement to help serve the many dishes to the many guests and "Blue," who remembers only that his father came on the boats from Africa (which must mean that he was a slave), walks across the back yard of the Big House from his own shabby shack, in order once again to be butler. Blue isn't easy to understand; in fact, he's downright unintelligible, but this doesn't make him any less the favorite of the meeting. And once lunch and the meeting are finished both Blue and Martha sing spirituals with the family joining in and clapping hands in time.

Down the road from the St. Louis Plantation is a gigantic Dow Chemical plant. It occupies the plantation alongside, also once owned by the Gay family. That plantation house is occupied now by the manager of the chemical plant. He proudly showed me the extra window he'd cut into the drawing room in order, he explained, to see every retort, every vent, every gas escape, and every chemical process without doing more than swiveling in his chair. An impressive thought. The Dow plant represents the twentieth-century reminder that plantation life, and sugar as a crop, are both in danger in the future.

The Gay family is concerned about finding a way to cope with the problem of cheap imported sugar that undercuts the price of their own. They debate, should they get into another crop, like soya bean? But sugar as a crop is rotated over three years; the first year planted it grows tall, harvests well, and produces proportionately small quantities of sugar; the second year, the same cane, reharvested, looks scraggier but serves better when turned to sugar in the mill; after the third and last year, the ground is plowed and new cane planted. So starting another crop is not as easy as it might be for most farmers. Sugar farmers like Andrew Gay haven't made big profits since 1974, so the Gay family has been concerned for some years about diversifying. They now have the Gay Bowling Lanes and the Gay housing estate, largely lived in by industrial managers working in nearby chemical plants. And for years they've prospected for oil. At intervals they save enough money to bring in a rig and drill another hole. So

Josephine and the old shack where she still lives.

Blue, a devoted old servant whose father was brought from Africa.

far, every bore has proved dry. This is particularly unlucky as, on nearly every sugar plantation nearby, oil has been discovered somewhere. It is still possible that their turn will come, but until it does come, it means at least that they must, as a family, continue to face the challenge of maintaining the plantation much as it once was. It's mechanized now, of course, and is part of the local farmers' cooperative which uses the sugar mill, rather than their own sugar houses, as in the old days. There are fewer laborers and more machines these days but, nevertheless, growing sugar hasn't changed that much.

Andrew Gay still supervises both planting and harvesting operations on horseback. His father did it before him, and his father before him. But it isn't just a sentimental and archaic method of farming supervision. On horseback, he can pick his way from one giant harvester to another, from one trouble spot to another, with more facility than by truck, although he brings his horse to the fields in a truck and doesn't find the method inconsistent. He told me: "In the old days all the overseers and the plantation owners rode horses to do their jobs, and I still find that I can supervise the work of my men better from horseback; it's easier to pick your way over what they're doing and see if they've done it well. But our labor force is very much smaller than it used to be and we don't need so many men, either to harvest or to plant, these days. Mind you, there was one season when we had some very bad winds and they blew down all the sugar so that our machines couldn't harvest it. Then we had to import labor from Jamaica because they still know how to cut sugar cane by hand. We got a license from the government, we housed them in barracks, and everything was in order. They'd never been paid American wages before and they were more than pleased to come over and do the job, earn the money, and go home to their wives and families. But, I have to confess, it did seem strange at the time and it did cross my mind that we were employing, in our fields, scores of black laborers from Jamaica who were probably the descendants of slaves who had been shipped from Africa to the British West Indies to harvest the sugar there."

Nancy Gay is fair-haired, blue-eyed, open-faced, calm, always immaculately turned-out, a very modern Southern belle; certainly not the fluttering kind of Southern belle in need of strong masculine right arms, sal volatile, fans to hide behind, and with beaux lining up on the porch. Rather she is the true plantation wife, hostess, manager, accountant, cook, doctor, mission school teacher, housekeeper, and employer. But she wasn't always so; she came originally from the city. Andrew said: "Nancy is a city girl from New Orleans. I went to school at the university there and Nancy was a friend of my younger sister Gladys, and when I first met her I was seven or eight years older than she was and she was little more than a girl. But I did begin to notice her as the years went by and we began to

Harvesting the sugar.

Andrew Gay with
newly planted sugar.

Nancy at Les Etudients, the local cultural society.

The hostess at
the Bocage plantation.

date and eventually decided to get married, just after I'd gotten into the service in 1941. So when we came back from the war and left New Orleans to come and live up here, it was quite a surprise to me how well she made the transition to country girl. She's made many, many friends in this community right from the very beginning. She didn't know a soul when she came here, but now she plays bridge and belongs to lots of societies and ladies' clubs and has many acquaintances. She is truly a good wife for me, I couldn't have done any of this without her, and I certainly couldn't go on doing it without her."

Nancy describes those early days rather more harshly, although she looks back, now, with affection on the struggles just after the war. She remembers the difficulty of getting the plantation going, of coping with a young family and a huge antebellum home through which the wind whistled and the relatives roared. "I guess I was a little lonely at first," she told me. "But it all passed and now I think that living in the country is the grandest way of life there is. Mind you, at first when I was mistress of the Big House, I really couldn't get used to it, and I certainly couldn't cope with everybody descending on me all the time. Suddenly to open the door one morning and find not one, not two, not ten, not twelve, but twenty relatives on the doorstep saying, 'Hello, we're here for the weekend,' was just too much. I really felt that our life wasn't our own, so I was glad when we built our own house on the grounds."

How does she see her own role in relation to Andrew? "Well, I'm not a liberated woman, I suppose I'm just Andrew's slave." She laughed, a little nervously, before she realized that it wasn't such a bad joke at that. "Well, slave is really what I am. I'm at his beck and call all the time. But it's what I want. He has to have three meals a day, his home has to be maintained the way he wants it, and, when he comes home from work, he just loves to talk so I have to be here to listen to him. Now I don't consider that's subjugating myself to his masculinity, I just feel that it's a perfectly proper way of life. We have a wonderful time together, he's never been rude or cross with me in all our married life; in fact, he's never been anything other than a gentleman. And it's because he's a gentleman that he's always managed to make me feel like a lady, and there's something wonderful about that."

Andrew is not only the plantation owner, he's also a director of the local bank, a member of the Rotary, a director of the Soil Conservation Board, and a director of the American Sugar Cane League. He attends many local functions, business, charitable, and social. Nevertheless, virtually all his time is spent on the plantation. He starts at six-thirty every morning and works until seven or eight every night, particularly during sugar harvest time.

The profit on sugar in 1974 was almost embarrassing. Andrew is the first to admit it: "There is no doubt about it, 1974 was the year we made a pot of money. We were able to do many of the things that we wanted to, buy new equipment, new tools for the plantation, and a great deal of re-equipping." I remembered Andrew Gay's insistence that in good years they shared what profits they could with the workers on the plantation. I remembered, too, his regrets that the old plantation shacks were still in use and I wondered if 1974 might not have been the year in which, under a "sharing" policy, the housing could have been improved? Andrew Gay, clearly remembering a cumbersome and particularly quarrelsome family meeting, loyally responded: "Well, the members of the family have many ideas about how, and to what extent, dividends should be paid, as opposed to dividends being plowed back into the business. I've always wanted them to show recognition for the hard work of these people. But the members of the family wouldn't agree to building modern housing just for people who are retired. After all, these are old people and they're not going to be around forever; in fact they're not going to be around for very much longer, and unless we see a need for additional houses in order to take on more regular employees, I don't think the family would ever endorse tearing down those shacks and replacing them with modern housing—even if it was a very good year in 1974."

These days the laborers of the St. Louis Plantation must be skilled at many things: piloting their giant harvesting machine between the rows of cane or towing the heavy road trains of trailers to the sugar mill. They must also be adept at welding, bolting, and repairing the complicated machinery of the sugar plantation. But, in order to be a successful Southern plantation owner, Andrew Gay must not only compete as a modern farmer, he also works at being a Southern gentleman—and his wife at being a Southern lady. They belong to one of the older families of the South and that means social responsibilities—and in the South that means socializing.

Less than one hundred miles north of the St. Louis House is the Parlange Plantation, run by Lucy and Walter Parlange. They're good friends whom the Gays frequently visit. Their plantation house is lower built and more colonial in style; older, with an avenue of Southern oaks with dangling Spanish moss. Lucy Parlange presides over a house as crowded with antiques and mementos as the history of her own family. In rooms which are quite literally crammed with paintings, furniture, and art treasures, she gaily remembers the lady ancestor who saved the plantation house from destruction during the Civil War by entertaining, on alternate nights, the Union general from his camp five miles to the north, and the Confederate general from his camp five miles to the south. While she allowed troops from both sides to tear down the wooden structures in the plantation

Andrew Gay and Henry Brandon at the Parlange plantation.

grounds to use as firewood, she hid the family jewels in an alcove behind one of the mullioned window frames. The family, the house, and the tradition survived—and so did the jewels.

Her father, Henry Brandon, distantly related to the Churchill family of England, is in his late eighties and now past the age when discretion and tact are foremost in his mind. He has little doubt about what has been lost from the old days and little concern for the sensitivities of a new generation awkwardly reaching for peace between blacks and whites. He, noisily, regrets the passing of the old Bible and the old hymn book and the old ways. He uses phrases that bring a wince to his daughter's face. "Never walk behind a mule or trust a nigger with the corncrib keys," he told me. But for all that, he speaks with deep affection of the servants who cared for him when he was young and still do now that he is old.

The Parlange family was descended from the French. Many families in the lower Mississippi delta and in New Orleans are either of French or Spanish descent. It was considered necessary, if you were French and successful, before the Civil War, to travel frequently to Paris, only occasionally visiting the plantation or the New Orleans house. The Parlanges and the Gays are descended from families who had one thing in common

—plentiful labor to work on their plantations. The slaves gave the planters themselves leisure to live in a style which was based, either from experience or imagination, on the way of life of an English country squire—but in a warm and tropical land. The first plantation owners believed that all Southern gentlemen should be accomplished in riding, hunting, dancing, conversation, and manners. The Southern plantation owner should also have a practical knowledge of law, agriculture, and military science. But the indispensible ingredient of a gentleman's education was a knowledge of the ancient classics. Latin and Greek, therefore, became the most valued subjects taught by the private tutors in plantation homes and by the academies and colleges. Many planters sent their sons back to England to complete their education. So for many it became a life grander, by far, than that lived by the humble English squire.

In any case, not all managed to reach these high standards. Card playing, gambling, cock fighting, eating and drinking often to excess, wenching with black girls, all these were the more normal activities of many other Southern gentlemen. Wenching was so common that it was said, in Charlestown, that young men looked old before their time. Yellow fever and malaria were rife and Indian raids were not unknown. As late as 1850 life expectancy for whites was twenty-four and blacks twenty-two. It is perhaps little wonder then that many women outlived several husbands.

Andrew's brother Edward is a modern lawyer and does not find it inconsistent to regard the preservation of the St. Louis House, the plantation, its history (and all it represents) as a major purpose in his life. He told me: "Whether we are doing it on purpose or not I don't know, but we are quite clearly also preserving a certain Southern style and we are determined to make that style continue in the years to come. It is the style that I remember, as a child, existed in the Big House when my mother and father lived in it. Certainly it was something different from what prevailed in the rest of the country. It was a great place and time to be raised in. We kids got our education outside the public school system. Although some of us did go to public school, most of us never did. I, for instance, had tutors and was sent away to school after that. We had unlimited amounts of land to wander over to go hunting; we had horses to ride.

"My father and mother were gentle people in the best sense of the word and we were brought up to feel that the word 'gentleman' was an important word in the language, the same as the word 'lady.' Ladies, we knew, were protected by gentlemen. One of the things I recall reading, I think it was from Emerson, is that a gentleman is a person who can get along well with any other kind of person, a man able to conduct himself on even terms with any kind of person. I think that was one of the ambitions that was bred and trained into us; one of the things we knew was we all had to be gentlemen. Manners and courtesy were an integral and essential part of our upbringing. As a child I remember my mother using the word 'manners' more often almost than any other word in her vocabulary. Sometimes perhaps we got a little tired of it. She had one phrase when we weren't behaving too well; she would say to visitors to the house, 'Yes, they have manners, but the trouble is they are bad.' She always found a way to work the word 'manners' into conversation."

He thought, and added: "I'm not sure whether I can explain it properly, but there was a pride in those days, whether you were wealthy or not, in behaving in a certain way. It was and is a kind of Southern pride. It isn't to do with money. It may have begun with money, but it became a matter of responsibility, of caring and understanding. I think it exists today, and it must continue. There are many people in this community today who don't have any land or wealth but nevertheless are Southern ladies and gentlemen in the true sense of the words, and I've traveled all around this great United States and I know many people in the East and in the West who consider themselves ladies and gentlemen but I don't think they put as much emphasis on it, they don't put as much into being ladies and gentlemen as we do here."

Andrew Gay echoes that: "I'm glad to see the idea coming back into our society. Maybe it's got something to do with having a Southerner for a President and having Southern influences in Washington again. But I like to think that it's an idea that would have gained credence in any case. It is a good idea, the idea of self-control, not only toward friends but also to business colleagues. It means fairness, and honesty. These were things that were cherished in the past and we should continue to do so."

In *The Uncertain South* Charles O. Lerche Jr. wrote: "Being a Southerner today is a devastating experience, criticized by outsiders, misled by his own leadership; his cherished values repudiated and his long vaunted life pattern abruptly wrenched into alien forms, with even the fixed poles of his racial, political, and cultural systems drifting out of sight, he faces the world with a mixture of bewilderment, resentment, nostalgia, and hostility as his only defense, seasoned only irregularly by a dash of hope or anticipation. The South—particularly the 'old' and traditional part—is not a happy place today."

Andrew Gay and his family would not agree; the St. Louis House and the St. Louis Plantation stand firm today because they do not agree that the old Southern style is finished.

THE PREACHER

REX HUMBARD

The man of God stood in the center of the spotlight and gazed beyond its beam, beyond the faces of the five thousand people who filled the stadium, straight into the eye of the television camera. He flung out his arms in a gesture of supplication, even crucifixion. "How many of you expect me to ask for money?" There was a pause. Hands began to show among the audience, many hands. "I . . . will . . . not . . . disappoint . . . you," he intoned slowly. He smiled at the laughter that rippled through the crowd. And as his small army of servitors, in red blazers, appeared—as though by magic—with the white plastic buckets in the aisles, he moved into the next stage of his sales pitch.

Rex Humbard, traveling evangelist, man of God, son of a preacher, was doing—once again—what he does most naturally and best of all; gathering souls for God—and money for his cause.

"I'll tell you what I'd like to do." He managed a confidential manner in front of his huge audience. "I want to make this a one-hundred-percent occasion. I want EVERYBODY here to help me make it a one-hundred-percent occasion. You may think it will cost you to say you will help—but it won't cost you in quite the way you think. You see, I want everybody here to say to me: *Rex, when you take up that collection I'll give the BEST GIFT I CAN.* Now what is the best gift? Some of you might be able to write a sizable check, some of you might be able to give a ten- or twenty-dollar bill, some of you might only give a dollar, some may only give a coin.

"And there may be somebody here tonight who has not one penny. Well, I want to say to that person: You are so welcome in this meeting and we are praying that God will provide for you. But you can give too. You can give prayer. If that's your best gift, prayer will do.

The organ behind him had been playing softly during the message and now it swelled to crescendo reinforced by the prepared music tapes, amplified by the multitrack mixer. Rex paused and smiled, his hands clasped in front of him as the music boomed out and the ball-point pens scratched and the checkbooks and the wallets of his audience rustled quietly. The attendants collected their white buckets and, as the music faded, Rex started again: "Now you know I've told you that if you haven't money prayer will do and what I want from you is the best gift you can give. And isn't that a wonderful thought? Isn't that the most wonderful idea in the world? Now what I'd like you to do is to stand up if you've been able to give your best gift, just stand up if what you are doing is giving your best gift." Slowly they began to stand. Eventually all of them, some on crutches, stood. The invitation was irresistible. The response from Rex was fulsome. "That's so wonderful, dear Lord, dear God that's so wonderful. Now all of you remain standing because we are going to talk to God, now."

America was first settled and then opened up by men and women who came to escape religious persecution, to find the freedom to worship as they chose. And America is still, on the whole, a God-fearing country. More than half the population of the United States belongs to, and attends, a church. There is, of course, no established church in America, no formal link between church and state, so that in the United States today there are more forms, more sects, of one religion, more subdivisions of Christianity, than anywhere else in the world. And far and away, the most colorful part of this growth always was, and always has been, the traveling evangelist, the "circuit-riding preacher."

In the early days, the tented meetings, the singing, the hand-clapping, the fire-and-brimstone sermons brought a kind of entertainment into what was for the most part a lonely frontier life. In a way, there wasn't all that much of a difference between the rainmaker, or the patent-medicine man, or the preacher. For the men and women wresting a living from the land, each of them represented escape from boredom and routine. And the circuit riders had one thing in common, they were all hustlers of a kind. They made a buck, or broke a heart, or won a soul—and then moved on.

Nowadays the preachers and traveling evangelists—the circuit riders of the twentieth century—use all the weapons and devices of this electronic age. In the Cathedral of Tomorrow beneath the black-domed ceiling and the giant cross, illuminated by over 6,000 bulbs and 60 permutations of color—a setting more like Radio City Music Hall than a church—Christianity is brought to the masses—and projected beyond to the unconverted. But this is where Rex Humbard preaches, every Sunday, to a congregation of five thousand and a television audience of twenty million viewers around the world. Rex Humbard is among the most modern of a small

The circuit rider played an important role in American history.

army of traveling evangelists who have discovered the electronic age. But in one fundamental respect he differs not one jot from his nineteenth-century predecessors. And he will cheerfully admit it. He needs your soul for God—and your money for his cause.

He *is* a religious man, there is no doubt about it. Many authors, and critics, have descended on Akron and driven to the Cathedral of Tomorrow with their preconceptions at the ready. From outside the complex looks more like an athletic training center than a place of worship and the two-hundred-foot-high half-finished "Prayer Tower" is known to local airline pilots as "Rex's Erection." The writers may have come in order to investigate, to scoff, to expose. Their personal cynicism about religion and evangelism may remain unaffected by Rex Humbard's genuine sincerity and his plausibility. But any attempt to expose Rex's purpose as irreligious has always failed. Most American Christians take their religion in small doses in small communities, in what they think of as a closer relationship with their pastor—and perhaps with God. But it is also true that, these days, more and more Americans are prepared to endorse the flamboyant preaching style that reflects the age we live in—and Rex Humbard.

Rex Humbard was born on August 13, 1919, in Little Rock, Arkansas. His parents, Alpha and Martha Humbard, were both evangelical ministers who had, by the time Rex was born, founded several churches in Arkansas and traveled frequently on evangelistic crusades. Rex was the eldest of six children, all of whom, as soon as they were old enough, worked in the crusades, providing the music either by playing or singing. Rex Humbard was ordained in 1943 when he was twenty-four years old, by the Gospel Tabernacle, Hot Springs, Arkansas. Now he has an Honorary Doctorate of Divinity degree, from Trinity College, and is a Doctor of Humane Letters, from the Oral Roberts University.

But his childhood was far from academic, it was in fact a traveling, impoverished and hectic time not unlike the childhood of any youngster living with a traveling circus; coming into strange towns, putting up tents, putting on a show for one night, and moving on. The significant difference always was that the Humbard family were poor and worked hard to become rich, not for themselves, but for God and God's cause. In his autobiography Rex says: "Father was a poor hard-working boy who had little education and no religion. His own family never attended church, but one Sunday he slipped off to Sunday School with some neighborhood youngsters and the Sunday School teacher gave him a bible. Dad read the Word of God every chance he got. He went to several churches from time to time and it puzzled him to find that each church told him that the others were wrong. But he continued to pray alone and read his bible. And when he read 'Take up thy cross and follow Me,' he vowed to save *all* people, not just those of one sect. We always had a family altar at home and, from babyhood on, we literally lived by faith. We were poor by many standards but we were rich in the presence of God.

"I was the eldest of six children; my sister Ruth was born a year and a half later and was followed by Clement, Leona, Mary and Juanita. During the twenty-five years that my mother and father spent rearing us they were constantly in gospel work. They traveled all over the United States and Canada, and Dad pioneered and built many churches. He was a simple old-fashioned down-to-earth preacher. He believed the inspired Word of God and preached it with power. Mother had real faith, too. If one of us kids needed a new pair of shoes, or if there was no food on the table (and there were lots of times like these during the Depression), Mom would go down the hall, close the door and start praying. Whenever we had a need we always told her and, if she went to that bedroom to pray, we knew something would happen."

Millions of Rex's followers have read his autobiography and heard him tell such stories from it during his services. He has come a long way since then.

Even by the age of thirteen, Rex believed that his father's style of preaching was not having the impact it ought to have, in an increasingly technological world. The young Rex was already a veteran radio broadcaster, an accomplished guitarist, and a leading light in the Humbard singers. But he was, also, very much a product of the twentieth century and he gazed at its achievements and technical advantages, not with puzzlement and awe, but with the enthusiastic idea of putting them all to good use—in God's cause. He told me: "As you know, we were very poor and because my Dad was a great preacher but not any kind of businessman he didn't know the advantage of advertising or getting through to people by electronics. From the age of thirteen I had to assume the management of all of the family evangelistic crusades. I organized the churches, I rented the auditoriums, I placed newspaper ads, and then I would become master of ceremonies and announce the services as well as leading the singing and, finally, I would take up the offering after my dad had preached.

"But what I used to do, as well, was to give the invitation to the congregation to pray with me. After a while, no one in my whole family would give an invitation to pray, as long as I was on the platform. My mother, my dad, my brother, my brother-in-law, all of them were preachers. But after they had spoken they would go and sit down and then I would get up, they would want me to, and I would be the one who asked people to pray. I have always felt close to people, and their burdens, always felt connected to their needs and, in some way, I have been able to relate to them and lead them to prayer.

"So there I was at the age of thirteen, the business manager of the Humbard crusades. But I have seen meetings, for instance during the days of the Depression, and even into the early forties, when we would have ten thousand people attend a meeting and we would still have to sell the spare tire out of the truck or mortgage a truck or something like that just in order to get out of town. We weren't making enough money to cover our expenses and we certainly weren't making enough money to really help God's cause. We never seemed to have enough for what we were trying to do—and poverty was part of our life the whole time. We had to do something about it.

"Our first big break came when I persuaded the manager of a Hot Springs radio station, KTHS, to let us appear on a number of two-hour Saturday evening country-and-Western music programs, which were called *The Saturday Night Jamboree.* Soon our gospel music became a regular feature on the Saturday night program and we became better known—the Humbard Family Singers. Later, as well as the Saturday night performances, all of us Humbard teenage youngsters started a Saturday morning gospel music program on the same station."

Rex Humbard had been manager of the family crusade, lead performer as well as organizer of the family singing group for five years, and was a self-reliant—perhaps even overconfident—man of the world when at eighteen, he met Maude Aimee Jones, then aged fifteen. She was also a singer, also in the evangelical business, and, what's more, named after one of the most famous women evangelists of all—Aimee Semple McPherson. Rex started courting. It must have been one of the most rigorously supervised courtships of the day. Wherever Rex and Maude Aimee went Maude Aimee's mother went too. When they were married in 1942 after four years of keeping company, they bought a trailer to live in and continued to travel with the Humbard crusade, with Maude Aimee's mother living in the trailer as well. When Rex Junior was born Mother became the babysitter while Rex and Maude Aimee sang or preached at meetings. By then, their work in radio was increasing, their fame among listeners was spreading, and Rex was restless. It seemed to him a logical step from radio to the new medium of television, but he couldn't find a way to move the Humbard Family Singers over to an electronic audience that could see as well as hear them. For twelve years, he and Maude Aimee and Maude Aimee's mother, as well as the Humbard children, traveled from town to town in their house trailer. Finally, when Rex had decided that a traveling crusade wasn't enough, wasn't sufficient achievement, they reached Akron, Ohio—and Rex decided to stay.

"We were using a tent in Akron that seated six thousand people and

Aimee Semple McPherson—Maude Aimee was named for her.
Maude Aimee.

some nights there would be eighteen thousand cramming in and many, many more outside. We were very successful and it was obvious that the people of Akron liked us and needed us. But one day a man said to me: 'There are more people alive today than have ever lived on earth, since the time of Adam and Eve until now.' And when I worked this out it disturbed me very much and I said to Maude Aimee, 'We're not reaching those people, the population of the world is multiplying so fast that however many years we spend traveling around on our crusade, however many thousands of people we reach each night, however many spill outside the tent, they are still only the tiniest fraction, of a fraction, of a fraction, compared with the four billion people on earth. And we're not reaching those people; we can't even teach them to read and write as fast as new people are being born. Now,' I said, 'there's this new thing called television, people are fascinated with it, they are even standing looking through the plate-glass windows of the shops that have the TV sets, they're glued to it. Now that's powerful, that's the way. I think that God gave us television. God gave us television to reach the world.'

"So I told my whole family that I was going to stay in Akron and build a large church and go on television and get into every state of the Union, via television. I was going to tell people about Jesus through electronics. My family were shocked and didn't want me to do it. My dad didn't want me to stay in Akron, my brother didn't want me to stay. There wasn't a row or a fight, but they didn't like it on the day they pulled out of town and I stayed. I felt funny too on that day. I had just sixty-five dollars, a wife and two boys, no church, and no members.

"We went to the local TV station and it was pretty hard to get them to take God seriously and they particularly didn't want it from us. They had many big-time speakers on television already. So I went from one TV station manager to another. All in all it took me fifteen years to build up the worldwide network of TV stations that we now have. Just think, these days our services are seen each week on more that five hundred television stations and we are televising to all six continents of the world. In some continents where there is no television we broadcast on shortwave radio like those in Manila and Portugal. But I believe that television, in particular, was given to us by God at exactly this time in the world's history so that we can use it to bring about the greatest, worldwide moral and spiritual awakening in the history of mankind."

The Television Temple that Rex Humbard planned was originally to cost only $2.1 million. No bank would lend him the money. "We'll give you all the money you want for a shopping center, or an industrial park, but not a church. If we had to foreclose the mortgage what would we do with a church?" The Humbards decided to raise the money by selling church bonds. By this means they brought in $12.5 million toward their new Cathedral of Tomorrow. Then, they also borroweed $5.5 million from Jimmy Hoffa's Teamsters Union and that brought bad publicity. It didn't seem to matter to the Humbard family. They had the money and soon they'd have the means to spread the message—by television.

The Cathedral of Tomorrow was opened in May, 1958. It has 5,400 seats; two television studios; one recording studio; more than $8 million worth of sophisticated television equipment; a warren of small chapels, and more than 150 classrooms, off the corridors circling the central auditorium, used for Sunday schools and other purposes. It also has a 200-bed nursery and a crèche, a large public buffet and five dining rooms, to cater to the less spiritual needs of visitors to the Cathedral. There is a hydraulic device to raise and lower the center of the 170-foot cathedral stage. The curtains, lighting, and audio equipment on stage use more power and are more complicated than those used in the largest Broadway theaters. Behind the stage is a total-immersion baptismal font complete with changing rooms. There is an office block with computers, addressographs, stamping machines, printing devices, a complicated telephone switchboard system manned twenty-four hours a day so that the pious who feel in need may telephone to consult the "dial-a-prayer" service. There is, as well, the two-hundred-foot-high "Prayer Tower," needing further funds before it can be completed, intended to bring the dial-a-prayer service nearer to God. In the main cathedral are makeup rooms, offices, cloakrooms, choir-robing rooms, and fully equipped cuing positions for the stage managers. In the middle of the 5,400 seats are two fixed television cameras; two more are fixed to the roof of the auditorium and the side aisles. The domed roof of the auditorium is supported by forty-eight pillars, which Rex and Maude Aimee intended to represent the forty-eight states of the Union in 1956. The color scheme of the auditorium is startling, almost overwhelmingly so. Black (for the sins of the world), red (for the blood of Christ), white (for purity). In the center of the roof of the auditorium is the largest indoor cross in the world. It has over 6,000 light bulbs and is capable of switching through 60 different color combinations, to match the mood of the service. In fact, the place and the statistics are, together, almost too much.

Behind the architect, driving the builders, supervising each brick, and every drop of paint, was Maude Aimee, designer in chief, supervisor supreme. "I love the black and I love the red in the Cathedral and I think that many people come here because it's an unusual place and then stay to worship," she told me. "Actually, I didn't want it to look like a church. It was to be called the Cathedral of Tomorrow and we settled on the name

The Cathedral of Tomorrow cross.

Checking the tape in the TV control room.

before we even saw the design. I was tired of seeing pink churches, blue churches, beige churches, green churches, I wanted something very, very different. I wanted the Cathedral of Tomorrow to look as if it was of tomorrow. For instance, you won't find a piece of brown wood in any part of the building, not in any part of the complex, except occasionally in some of the desktops. (Sometimes some of the younger business managers in the operation will bring in desktops when I am out of town on a crusade and they have brown tops, then I raise Cain.) I don't like brown. I like black. So when the roof of the auditorium was finished the foreman of the builders was very proud of it, it was all in wood, good-quality highly polished wood. Brown wood. He thought it looked nice. I said to him, 'Paint it black.' He was astonished. He couldn't believe what I'd said. 'You can't mean it?' he said to me. 'I do mean it,' I said to him. 'Do it.' He just couldn't bring himself to do it. 'I can't, I can't,' he said. So I got a bucket of black paint and climbed up the scaffolding and the ladders and I threw it at the roof and it made a great big ugly black splash on that wood that he loved. 'Now you'll have to do the rest of it, won't you?' I told him.

"Then there's the cross. Rex used to say to me, 'When they leave the building I want them to have something in their minds that they distinctly remember about the church, something that will help them to remember the message.' That's when he designed this large cross. They'll never forget that. I hope they'll never forget the whole place. We always admired the large stage at Radio City Music Hall, in New York City, so we modeled our stage the same way. I just love those curtains that lift up and down in great festoons."

Rex had little trouble in raising the money for the Cathedral. He is a persuasive and magnetic speaker, sincere in his purpose, convincing in his ambition. The faithful responded by putting their hands into their pockets and shelling out. The church bonds sold completely. But nearly twenty years later the Federal Securities and Exchange Commission charged the Cathedral of Tomorrow with the illegal issue of bonds to raise the construction funds. Rex explained: "They told us it was against the regulations to have sold bonds and notes, without issuing to each investor a formal statement of debts, liabilities and assets. When I first learned about the filing of that suit against us for illegal action, a suit which threatened to black out the whole television network we had built up by then, I felt that all my hopes and dreams for the future, all my work as an evangelist, had been ruined. We couldn't understand why we had been singled out, from all the churches in the United States, to be charged and charged publicly for a so-called violation. Maybe it was because we were the only independent church with a television congregation larger than that of all the combined memberships of all the other churches. And maybe it was because we weren't associated with a nationally organized association, like the Baptists, the Methodists, or the Lutherans, to whom we could turn for support and protection.

"But it proved to be a blessing in disguise; at first we thought that we had been ruined, finished, and that the forces of jealousy and evil had been brought to bear upon us. But a few months later we realized that it was God's way of getting rid of our troubles and strengthening our ministry. When that financial crisis forced us to stop deficit spending I realized that God was telling me that, in our eagerness to expand our television ministry, we had gotten ourselves too involved in commercial business enterprises. From then on we must limit our work to the service of God. Instead of trying to supplement our church offerings and donations from outside business ventures, we should trust in God to provide for his work. I prayed, and I prayed, and I prayed, and I said to the Lord: 'God, you've got a problem. I'm in sales, not in management. I'm letting you take care of making ends meet, from here on.'"

By then the Cathedral of Tomorrow had become deeply involved with "management," with the business life of the community. They owned businesses and property which included a girdle-making factory. They were worth $45 million. The roots of their earthly existence may have been designed to support their heavenly project but they were so clearly connected with the materialistic life of the people they were preaching to that it may have been this that aroused the Federal Securities and Exchange Commission. Rex said: "I asked them what they wanted me to do and they said, 'You've got to pay it back.' Now, at that particular time we had twelve and a half million dollars worth of financing out through church bonds and the thought of paying it all back looked like disaster. All my colleagues and helpers thought we were wiped out."

At about this time the Cathedral of Tomorrow's deficit spending was running at $5.4 million a year. In order to pay back their debtors they had to cut back heavily on their expenditures. They sacked 200 staff members. They sold the Real Form Girdle company in Brooklyn, their small printing and advertising agency, their two airplanes, their wire company, their downtown office block on Cascade Plaza in Akron, Ohio, and their Mackanac University. They closed Cathedral Tele-Productions, which was on the verge of becoming a million-dollar-a-year business, making TV commercials. They changed and simplified plans for the two-hundred-foot Prayer Tower—and it still isn't finished. And they set about raising the money to pay off those bondholders who wanted their money back. They estimated that this might work out at about 30 percent, but in fact, more than 60 percent wanted paying back. And they managed to raise, by donation, the necessary $8.3 million in less than two years. As a business operation, taking up an offering on a gigantic scale, it was impressive. As a businessman Rex Humbard is extraordinary. He may say "I'm in sales, not in management," but nevertheless, at the management of God's business he is quite as sharp as he is at the selling of God's message. I asked him if it didn't seem inconsistent that his church had roots so firmly in the world of Mammon. Rex had clearly heard the challenge before. "It isn't money, but the love of money that is the root of all evil," he says.

Rex Humbard is Chairman of the Board of Trustees of the Cathedral of Tomorrow and all the subsidiary enterprises that market the Word of God. He also runs the executive committee that looks after the day-to-day business of this complex and hugely costly missionary business. They spend more than $1 million a month just on buying the television air time for the programs. They close their books every month and audit twice a year. Their computer chief used to be a top man in the secular business world. They pay good salaries and employ hundreds in the letter-opening and mailing departments. They use the best television technicians and directors. They pay them competitive salaries but don't allow swearing, drinking, or morally bad behavior. This means, I observed, that they have the most polite, softly spoken, early-to-bed-and-early-to-rise hard-working television team I have ever met. The Humbard family earn personal salaries for their work, but Rex Humbard will tell you that he considers himself the most underpaid man in the world in terms of the number of hours and the number of programs he makes. He used to be paid a little over $25,000 a year.

Rex and Maude Aimee live in one of the quieter parts of the smartest suburb of Akron, Ohio. Their $200,000 house is guarded by high brick walls and "Keep Out" notices. It is a nice house, obviously the home of a successful man, with its four-car garage and a double avenue of military-smart privet trees leading up to the front door. But the privet trees will always be well manicured. They are plastic. Inside there are white carpets trodden only by stocking feet—Maude Aimee insists that all visitors, whoever they may be, remove their shoes. Rex drives an executive car with white leather upholstery and, on the whole, lives the affluent life of any successful managing director. He enjoys his life-style and will point out the houses of other successful businessmen, most in the motor tire business.

But Rex is still defensive about his personal wealth, about the house, about the car, about his smart clothes, about Maude Aimee's jewelry—she has much gold and some impressive diamonds—and he will explain quickly: "The house belongs to the church and the car belongs to the church. You see, I happened to know the attorney who was handling the sale of this house and he gave the church a very good deal on it. We use the house for entertaining friends of the church, many good friends who work for God, like Johnny Cash and Oral Roberts, and Billy Graham and Pat Boone. The car was given to the church by an automobile dealer in Columbus, Ohio." As for the jewelry, "They talk about my diamond and gold ring. But I don't have a diamond and gold ring. My son, Rex Junior, has a diamond and gold ring and the newspapers confuse it with that. But I don't pay too much attention to it, I watch the people that I am serving. They are my customers and I am in business to please them and as long as the auditorium is packed that's what I am concerned with—not the critics."

I asked Rex if he was worried about retirement when it seemed quite possible, according to his own account, that he would be without a roof over his head or a car to drive. "I *was* worried about that," he said. "But about three years ago we were going through some difficult times and I began to think, Look, you're getting a little older, we better do something about it. So in our organization we set up a proper retirement program with very good insurance for all our executives when they come to retirement age. Now all of us, including all of our ministers, pay into the retirement program and the church matches the amount they pay in so that our own retirement policy will now compete with any business organization in the world. There are also tax advantages both at the time when you are paid and when you come to retire. So I'm not so worried now."

It is very easy when talking to Rex Humbard about his sophisticated and global operation to lose sight of the original financial basis of all evangelical missions. At the end of the day somebody passes a bucket and money is dropped into it. Is the Cathedral of Tomorrow still financed that way?

Rex answers: "Yes, it's still basically what we do. Through television we may be reaching every country in the world and millions of people but our entire worldwide program is still supported almost entirely by individual contributions. And the vast majority of those contributions are still just five or ten dollars a month. We do have many wealthy people and they do sometimes make huge, generous donations to our cause, but most of our money comes from little sums of money, from little people who want us to continue in our work. And, at the meetings, I admit I am pretty good at twisting arms, making sure that they give the best that they can for the cause. I have become skilled over the years at getting money into those buckets. But I really would rather the people give in the way that they should. The Bible says, 'The Lord loves a cheerful giver,' and for me to just go up there and say, 'Hey folks, if you don't give enough money today my television program won't be on the air next week,' wouldn't be the right approach at all. That's why I never mind telling them jokes." At meetings, while the organ music plays on and Rex prays, in a side room off the stage Rex Humbard's staff always quickly and roughly assess the amount of money collected. At one meeting they whispered to him that the collection was very low. It is said that Rex stopped his praying and told the congregation that he was locking all the doors and then he asked them to contribute again. The money was forthcoming. Rex—and the congregation—prayed with relief.

Rex Humbard's business is first and foremost a family business, all the family, every single member. And when the giant theatrical curtain lifts slowly at the beginning of every one of his Sunday morning "performances" to reveal the massed choir behind, it is only after all the Humbard family have made their carefully timed and rehearsed entrances, right down to the grandchildren. And a congregation who may have come to worship is certainly entertained. The cast for that entertainment is controlled by Rex Junior, at thirty-three the administrative officer of the organization and responsible for the general running of the ministry and for the television production of the Sunday shows. He is married with three children, fights a waistline problem, and enjoys the pressures and demands of the production of a highly complicated television operation. Next is Don Humbard, twenty-nine, the assistant administrative officer, also married with three children. Both brothers, both their wives, and all six children sing on stage as part of the show. Then there is Aimee Elizabeth, "Lizzy," seventeen, with long blonde hair and her face already on many record albums. She sings solos in the show and undoubtedly causes many a male teenage heart to flutter in the congregation and the television audience. She clearly enjoys her "Top-of-the-Pops" world. Her younger brother, Charles, aged fourteen, is still at school but also sings in the group.

On the day of the show, if it's in Little Rock, Arkansas, or Dallas, Texas, or Manila in the Philippines, or Tokyo, or Israel, or even back home in the Cathedral of Tomorrow, all the family report, as for any television production, in time for makeup and costume. Maude Aimee supervises the vast and complicated wardrobes. The women all wear the same dresses and the men wear matching suits. (When on tour, they travel in style in a private airplane equipped with telephones, offices, beds—even special rooms where the younger members of the family can practice their singing and guitar-playing. Normally another plane will fly behind, carrying additional members of the television production as well as equipment. In addition, a convoy of heavily loaded trucks will drive overland with scenery and the heaviest of the television equipment.)

On the first day I called at the Cathedral of Tomorrow I found Maude Aimee on her knees scrubbing the vast floor in the front entrance hall. It hadn't been finished to her satisfaction. Her sense of tidiness and her concern with finish and cleanliness is almost obsessive—and well known among all the Cathedral staff. That accounts for the fact that she can carpet her home with white piled rugs, and her personal bedroom in the private plane in the same way and, years later, not have a spot on any of them. I have seldom spent so much time in my socks as on this assignment. But the Cathedral staff and the Humbard relatives are well used to it. During the first television program that I watched, Maude Aimee rushed at a television cameraman who, with a heavy hand-held electronic camera, had climbed on to a piano stool in order to achieve a better close-up angle. She beat with her fists on his back until he hopped off—fast. "That piano bench goes with the concert grand and I bought that in the memory of my mother when she passed away. And even if I hadn't bought it in the memory of my mother I still wouldn't have anyone put his feet on the furniture. I wasn't brought up that way and I won't be around with people who behave like that," she told me.

Maude Aimee is a force to be reckoned with, a formidable, impressive, and driving lady. She told me, "All our married life we have never had an argument about anything, Rex and I. I have the last word about the children. Now some people say that isn't scripture and shouldn't be so and that the man is the head of the house. But I say to them that may be so, but I am the neck that turns the head. We made a pact when we got married. He makes all the major decisions and I make all the minor decisions. So far we've never had a major decision."

In Little Rock, Arkansas, while on tour with the crusade, Maude Aimee descended on her favorite dress shop in order to stock up on the full-length chiffons and the powder blue two-pieces for all the ladies of the show. The shop had heard that she was coming, and they were ready for her and nearly as eager to sell as she and her daughter and her daughters-

Rex's daughter Liz—now she's top of the pops.

in-law were to buy. The Humbard women went through the racks like locusts descending on corn. Backless, sleeveless, crossover, tailored, full-flowing, fur-trimmed: within an hour they had a whole range of dresses to be worn as the accoutrements for a Bible lesson. Maude Aimee remained sharply the arbiter of taste and adjudicator of price throughout the whole frenzied operation. She told me: "We may wear the dresses only at the Cathedral or we may wear them only on television. But we have to remember that what we wear for a television audience we are also wearing for a church service. And then we must also bear in mind that we are an entertainment, the program has to attract and hold viewers, so we can't have something so formal-looking that it would look out of place on a Sunday morning." Maude Aimee broke off in order to supervise, some might say censor, Liz. Liz, with some glee, was trying on a clinging black number that I thought very attractive. Maude Aimee obviously did not agree, and told Liz to take it off at once. I asked Maude Aimee why the dress was unsuitable. "I think that it's unbecoming because it's too sexy. You mustn't dress for the opposite sex, you must dress for yourself and I don't want to dress to overpower people. I don't want Liz to come out in a dress that causes people to look at her and think thoughts that take their minds off the words that she is singing. Anyway, that dress is not becoming to a fourteen-year-old girl." There was a pause while Maude Aimee remembered that Liz was seventeen. "It's not becoming to a seventeen-year-old girl either."

She went on: "I have very clear ideas about what shouldn't be worn by the girls in the show. I don't think that there should be plunge necklines, and I always think that the arms should be covered up. Also, you must remember that nothing we buy is too expensive. It all has to come out of the money contributed to the Cathedral so we have to be careful about it. And I'm a good marketing lady and I always make sure that we get a discount. Sometimes it is as much as forty percent or fifty percent off and in any case I try to keep the dresses we wear in the fifty to sixty dollar range. Just once in a while we spend a little more on something that one of the girls is very fond of but for the most part we keep the price down."

Maude Aimee has another theory to support her economic policy. She believes that if women television viewers thought that the dresses worn by the Humbard family women were obviously expensive or exclusively designed, they would likely become so jealous of the clothing that they would be diverted from the religious message. "Some women do have a little jealousy so when you have something like that you have to be careful to look well but not show off. We have to look our best for the work we

Rex and Aimee, warm in the snow.

are doing but not so well that people become bothered about how we are dressed. For that reason I am very careful about how much jewelry I wear on television. I have been given so many beautiful things, rings and bracelets and pieces of jewelry by admirers and friends, that it would be a great temptation to me to wear them and show them off. They are beautiful and they are mine and I am not ashamed that people want to present gifts to Rex or me. And it would be offensive if we turned down those gifts. But it would be equally offensive to wear any of those gifts in front of the people we are broadcasting to. After all, we are asking them to give all they possibly can to God's cause and it wouldn't look good if I was wearing diamonds and gold and costume jewelry.

"Now I do have a mink and I know that the press has talked about that as though it was something wicked for me to wear. It is a beautiful white mink coat and it was given to me by a friend, a true believer. I have heard tell that the press has said that I have fifteen minks and anybody who said that to me I would turn to them and say, 'Oh you're just a liar, just a real liar. I don't have fifteen minks, I have one mink.' "

If he had not been a preacher most people who have met Rex Humbard believe he could well have been a successful businessman and, to an extent, he would agree: "I love mathematics, I love bookkeeping and that kind of thing. I like organizing and organizations, so I suppose I could have been a businessman. But you have to remember that when I was a small boy of thirteen I was truly called to God. One night, listening to a visiting evangelistic preacher, I knew God was speaking to me. Suddenly it was all different. When the preacher gave the altar call and the music started, I felt a small voice calling me to go forward to claim Jesus Christ as my Savior and Lord. I had been brought up in church; I went to services just about every night and my folks were what most people would label 'religious.' But right then I knew I had to make my own decision; neither church nor my parents could determine my standing with God. I hesitated, but evidently the Lord knew I needed a little push, because a Christian woman stepped across the aisle to ask me quietly, 'Are you saved?' I walked down that aisle and knelt at the altar and opened my heart to Jesus Christ. Light flooded into my soul and I became a new person. I really wanted to live for the Lord. In that moment God took my shyness away and made me an extrovert. I started talking about Him and I haven't been able to stop since.

"From that night on I was often the first one in our meetings to jump up and testify for the Lord, something that had always embarrassed me before. The Lord changed my heart and made me over. It wasn't until several years later that I studied courses in the Bible and religion, and was formally ordained as a minister with a license authorized by the International Ministerial Federation, an association of independent and inter-

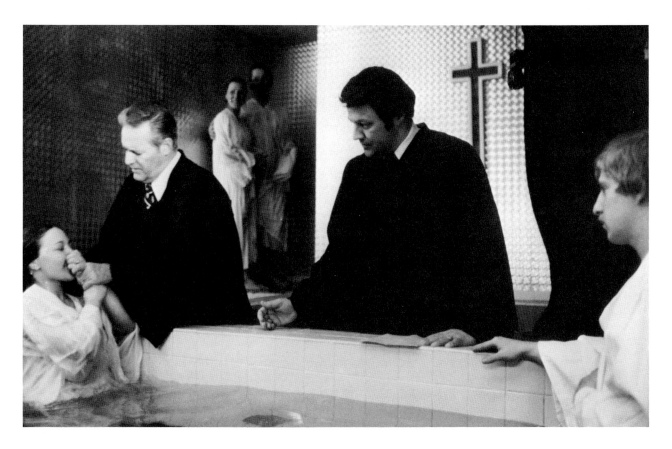

Rex baptizes a young believer.

denominational ministers. But when folks ask me today when I became a minister, I say with a smile, 'At the age of thirteen,' because I really feel that I started to work in God's Ministry on that great day when I was converted and the Holy Spirit changed my heart.''

Rex Humbard is a charismatic and magnetic person. Does he believe that there is a danger that his congregation will find themselves sold on the man rather than the cause? "They'll never buy God unless they buy the man. I think that people are vulnerable to persuasion and our congregation is no different but they won't listen to God's story unless it is told in a way that's attractive to them so first they buy the man, and then they hear the message, and then they buy the message.''

Rex Humbard also believes that the Second Coming of Christ is likely to happen within his lifetime. He states it simply, as a matter of fact, and isn't prepared to argue about it. He just knows that it is going to be so. "I believe we are approaching the end of what I call the Holy Ghost Dispensation and nearing the return of Christ but I can't set an exact date, I wouldn't want to do that. I do have my own ideas but I don't expound them on international television because people wouldn't understand; in Africa, for instance, they wouldn't understand, and in many of the other countries that we broadcast to. But let me tell you how I work it out. It's to do with numbers and mathematics. You see, there were two thousand years between Adam and Eve and the Flood; and then another two thousand years until the coming of Christ; and now we are approaching another two-thousand-year period. And seven is God's perfect number in the millennium and at the end of this two-thousand-year period the time of Christ will return. No man will know the exact date and the hour. But the 1967 war had something to do with the prophecy in Israel; it said that Jerusalem shall be trodden down by the Gentiles until the end of the Holy Ghost Dispensation and then God will return to speak to his people. Nineteen sixty-seven was an important date, because it also says in Matthew that 'Generations shall not part until all be fulfilled.' So 1967 plus thirty-three years, which is a generation, goes on to another two thousand. But Matthew twenty-four said that God cut the time short because the wickedness of man was so great that they would destroy themselves when Jesus returned. So, looking at all that, we seem to be approaching the end of this dispensation. Now how short God will cut the time I don't know. So, no man knows the exact date, or the hour. But in fact I hope to be living when Christ returns. However, I am hoping to live for a hundred years, so it could almost be at any time. Anyway, I propose to go on living as if I'm going to live for a hundred years or as if I'm going to go tomorrow so that whatever happens I'll be ready. If I'm still here on earth I'll be ready and I'll be ready if He takes me up sooner.

"People ask me, what do I think that He will make of me and my work? Well, I think that God has told evangelists like me to go out into the world and to use television. I feel that God gave us radio and television to supplement His Word and I hope He'll believe that I was carrying out His work in that way."

Rex Humbard believes in the Commandments. He believes in Hell and Damnation but he is sensible and intelligent enough to preach in twentieth-century terms. Fire-and-brimstone are "out"; lost-souls-in-misery are "in." But personally he has little doubt about the unequivocal demands of God and the unenviable fate of those who fail to follow perfect ways. Rex Humbard talks about the Commandments a great deal, insists that his own life is lived, daily, by their measurement. He will happily and easily grant one concession, one particular similarity to his circuit-riding predecessors. He admits to being a "hot gospeler." "Oh yes, I am a hot gospeler because the gospel is hot and I'm there to spread it. There's nothing wrong in being that kind of evangelist. It's the kind my dad was. It's the kind I am. It's the kind I hope my sons are. It's the kind God needs —and man needs. I believe in the Word and the laying on of hands, I

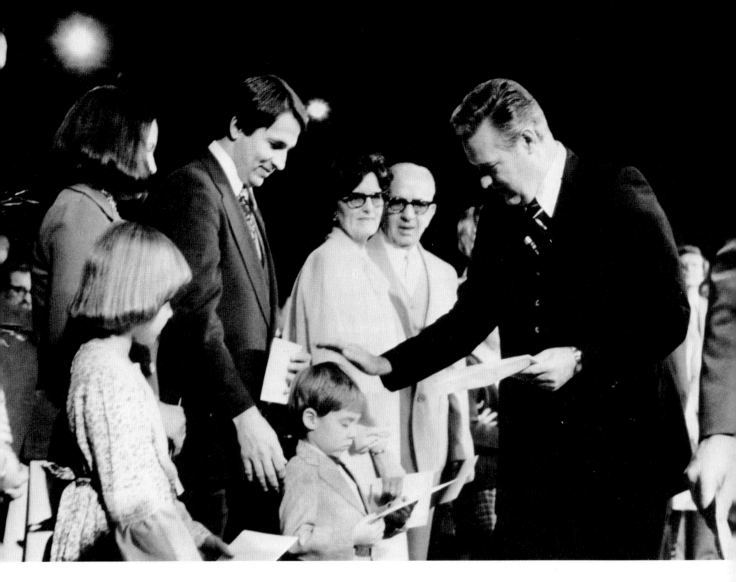

Coming forward to be blessed.

believe in coming forward to testify, I believe in the healing spirit. I am one of the old-fashioned preachers who invites the newly converted to come forward. I believe in God and I believe in the Devil. They are there all right. They're all around us."

Rex may follow the old-fashioned preaching ways of his father but he disagreed strongly and fundamentally with his father's inability to come to terms with modern business methods. "My father was strongly against debt of any kind. He couldn't understand that you could actually borrow in order to build, in order to earn, in order to pay back—in order to spread the Word of God. I wanted Dad to stop traveling with the tent and to find a base and expand the mission that way. This is where we disagreed. He preferred an old-fashioned tent full of people wanting to be converted. He wouldn't see the real value of the public media, or radio or television. My dad never announced a radio program in his life. We traveled all over

America, as a family, but in the largest auditoriums and the biggest tents he still would not have found, in a lifetime of traveling, as many people to listen to the Word of God as I can reach in one hour on a Sunday morning.

"You know, years after I had built the Cathedral of Tomorrow and separated from my dad I brought my dad back and he stood in the Cathedral and preached on television one Sunday. Then we went home after the service to eat dinner and I couldn't find him when the time came to serve dinner. I discovered him in the bedroom crying. And I said: 'Dad, what's the matter?' and he said, 'Go ahead and eat, I'm not going to eat.' And I said, 'What are you crying about?' and he said, 'Rex, I stood there today, after preaching for fifty years all over America but today I have preached to more people in one hour than I have preached to in my whole lifetime, and I'm worried about you and your responsibility. It is so great that I am worried about you.' There he was weeping because he felt my responsibility. But I tried to convince him that it was just that responsibility I wanted, and that I was ready for it, and that it was a good thing. Because, however many millions we reach out to, our style of worshiping God is still simple, natural, and down-to-earth."

It may be a simple message but it is carefully planned, scripted, and rehearsed. It is always written on teleprompters placed strategically in Rex's eyeline so that, in a voice choked with emotion, he can tell the congregation at one of his rallies (and the millions on television) some simple story about his Maw and Paw and their simple beliefs. It will always have a homespun readiness about it, which belies the fact that every word, even every intonation and every folksy inflection, is written down. I asked him whether all this wasn't "preaching down" to his congregation. He said: "I'm folksy to start with so I can't be 'preaching down,' I'm just being me. It may be that I go back to my beginnings and think about my beginnings when I write these sermons and then the language becomes language that people will understand. But, as I told you before, I'm in sales —not in management. If that's the way I have to sell the message then that's the way I'll do it. Remember that Christ talked to farmers and fishermen and he didn't preach as if he was talking to intellectuals or university professors.

"Now, I know people have criticized our use of music. They think it is sentimental, sloppy, and too persuasive. But that music is only what we call a bridge, it's for when we change mood. We may have been talking about the letters that have been sent to us so that we can pray over them; or about the people that have phoned in during the week for help; or we may have been talking about our need for money to spread God's word to other countries. It's then that we need a bridge to change the subject and the mood."

The order of a Rex Humbard service is complicated. They are recorded for television at greater length, then later editing will take out, for instance, the urgings during the collection or the occasional "fluffs" by the family. Although the television production team always makes sure that the cue cards and teleprompters are within eyesight, Maude Aimee is farsighted and Rex is nearsighted. And that constitutes a major problem. Standing side by side, as they invariably do, it may be possible to share God's work but it certainly isn't possible for them both to read from the same teleprompter. Rex has found a unique way of solving the problem: "I use one contact lens in one eye; that means I can use one eye for seeing the audience and doing my normal work as a preacher and the other eye for reading the same teleprompter as Maude Aimee," he said.

He may be a Man of God but Rex Humbard is also a "television" preacher. At 26,000 feet in the family prop-jet, flying between Akron and Little Rock, Arkansas, at the beginning of one of his sweeping rallies (sometimes as many as six services in a week) he was using the private telephone to speak to the manager of the local television station two miles beneath the aircraft. With whoops of glee and shouts of victory, he announced to the family that the Humbard show had beaten the highest rating ever recorded by that station for any program.

Rex also specializes in spectacular conversions; like Bill Coad, his computer chief. Bill told me: "I had a background of considerable success in the secular world but I served the Devil with great vigor. Now if I can serve Jesus Christ half as well as I served the Devil then I'm going to be a tremendous success here in the Cathedral of Tomorrow. I made a tremendous amount of money and had big houses and cars, and I belonged to country clubs and I used to drink alcohol and indulge in gambling. Then one morning, at home, my wife turned on the television set and she said to me, 'Come and see, there's this preacher from Ohio.' And it was Rex and I don't remember now what it was that he said but he said something that made me want to come back the next Sunday and the same for about five Sundays. And then, on November fifteenth, nineteen seventy, at home, I got down on my knees in front of the television and, with my wife, I started bawling like a baby, all two hundred fifty pounds of me, total exhaustion, ready to accept Christ with no reservations. After that I came to the Cathedral of Tomorrow and started talking to the pastors and I met Rex and when I heard there was a job here I came to join the mission and I have never regretted it."

The organization is sharp and professional in following up the acquisition of a name and address. The supplicant receives the monthly and bi-monthly magazines and is, sometimes, persuaded to buy special versions of the New Testament or Rex Humbard's autobiography. In every publication there is always the name, address, and telephone number of

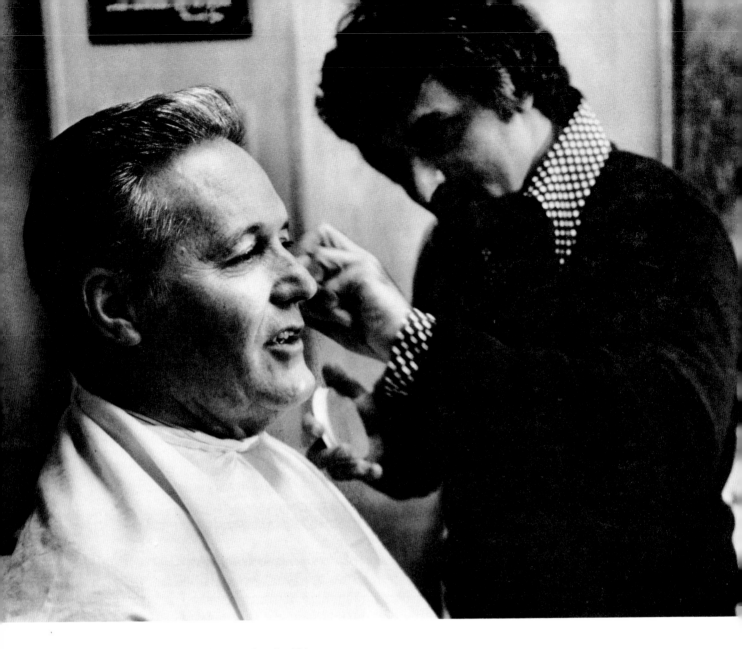

Finishing touches for TV.

the Cathedral of Tomorrow. And at the Cathedral of Tomorrow there is somebody waiting to receive a call or a letter. I met a couple from Pennsylvania who, when coal was discovered on their dairy farm, poured the money into Rex's mission—$50,000 in all. At one small rally of hand-picked followers, Rex raised—for his work in Brazil—$300,000 in less than two hours of passionate soliciting.

The Humbard family don't register in hotels as the Humbard family. Although they can hardly be mistaken for anybody else they still use other names to prevent the persistent and bothersome phone calls from hecklers—or converts—that would otherwise get to them through the switchboard. They always travel with tutors for the young children, usually the wives of associate pastors. Before they arrive in town, the local TV station plays carefully placed commercials advertising the crusade in the local auditorium and the broadcast on Sunday morning. It's a well-organized, professional, experienced traveling circus. It operates efficiently and tirelessly. And it does it in the name of God. It also does it abroad. The Humbard family will think nothing of piling into the family planes and flying 12,000 miles in order to make their TV show and bring their message to prisoners under sentence of death in Manila; or the enthusiastic, but barely comprehending, Japanese; to the Christians in Israel; and the new converts in Brazil. The television crew, always conscious of the need to behave themselves as Christians as well as good technicians—and equally conscious of Maude Aimee's eye upon them if they don't—frequently work forty-eight hours without sleep or a break in order to erect the sets then dismantle them for the next production. They're paid standard union rates and do well on overtime. But their enthusiasm and spirit is clearly also an affection for and identification with the program they make and the family for whom they work.

The circuit-riding Humbards press ahead. But who will take over from Rex? "This is a great concern of mine—who will take over when I'm gone. Of course I trust that the future is in the good Lord's hands, but I am trying, however, more and more, to involve my three sons in what we are doing; to make them spokesmen; to make them feel the congregation the way I do. I've been making changes these past few years. In the past I used to rely upon musicians from outside the family and singers other than the family. But today I've confined it all to the family—I want it all to be the Humbard Family. I'm hoping that one day my own son, Rex Junior, might become the minister. Gradually Rex is coming out from behind the machinery, from behind the administration, and taking a role in front of the camera, in front of the congregation.

"Remember also, that we are a church with trustees and we have taken out a huge insurance policy on my life. It is true to say that I am most probably the most valuable man dead in the ministry because our organization carries over ten million dollars worth of life insurance on Rex Humbard. But that is to cover them so that if things do happen, like my death, then what we have built need not collapse and they can meet their obligations and regroup their forces.

"It's then that I hope my son Rex Junior will be able to play a part. And I feel sure that God will allow the Humbard name to continue.

"After all, if God approves of evangelists, then the Humbards might be allowed to stay around."

THE INDIAN CHIEF

JOE DE LA CRUZ

The chief sat quietly and calmly, his face immobile, only his eyes revealing alertness.

In the land where the white men said that they would finally be left in peace, the elders, the leaders, the wise men, and the lawmakers of the tribe were gathered for a pow-wow. On the edge of the booming Pacific, in the state of Washington with the cedar forests stretching behind them, the Quinault Indian Nation were meeting in formal session, to decide their day-to-day affairs—and debate their whole future. These days the pow-wow is actually called the monthly meeting of the tribal council, but it is, nevertheless, where the decisions are made.

The chief, Joe de la Cruz, is a young man. If he were mayor of any small city or community in the Pacific Northwest he would still be considered young. As chief of his own tribe—elected as tribal chairman—he seems even younger when considered against a tradition of wise leadership by tribal "fathers," which may stretch back as far as 25,000 years. But Joe de la Cruz will be a name to remember. In 1977 he became paramount chief of all the tribes of all the Indian nations in America. And the Quinault tribe, his own people, have known for some time that they and their chief are mentioned with respect in Congress and the White House. Joe de la Cruz is leading his people in a battle to regain their independence, their wealth, and their dignity. His own name may well go down alongside those famous chiefs of history such as Sitting Bull, Red Cloud, Crazy Horse, Geronimo, and Cochise. Instead of warriors, he uses words. Instead of bows and arrows, he uses law books. Instead of spears, he has honed and forged land-preservation and wilderness regulations. His weapons are those of the white man and with them he has already become the victor in several major battles against the white man's rule. He has, undoubtedly, altered the future of his tribe and shown a new way to all other Indian tribes.

The only true native American *is* the Indian. For 30,000 years, or more, he fished the rivers and the shores, hunted the forests and the plains, worshiped in the mountains and buried his dead in the open, migrated with his tribal nations across the vast and fertile lands of North America. But then the white man came. In just four hundred years he slaughtered and fought, and finally drove the people he called "redskins" into reservations where they were shamefully neglected. The history of the American Indian is littered with hundreds of broken promises and dishonored treaties. And the chart of the white man's relationship with the natives of the land he came to settle is spattered with betrayal and blood. It is not a new pattern nor, when compared with other violent colonizations, is its style particularly more brutal and insensitive. On other continents, in recent history, the Conquistadors, the French, the Belgians, the Germans, and the British were responsible for excesses of brutality beyond any perpetrated by the new settlers of the United States and their troops. But in a nation with a history so short, it is a pattern that stands out.

There are still nearly one million Indians living in the United States today, but only half of them left on reservations. The Quinault reservation is three hundred square miles, about the size of a small county anywhere in the United States. Once it was a beautiful land, part of what is arguably the most beautiful corner of the whole of the United States, the Pacific Northwest. The white men drew up a treaty protecting it for the Indians in 1855. And then, over the years, they persuaded and led and herded the various Indian tribes from the entire region into the reservation. In fact, there always had been an Indian settlement at the mouth of the Quinault River. There always had been long houses and giant cedarwood canoes drawn up in front of them. And it always was a mystic, sacred, bountiful place with a calm and recognizably Indian spirit, that atmosphere which seems to be about peace and closeness to the land.

The atmosphere is still there even though nowadays less than 1,600 Indians live in a reservation that was originally intended as a kind of human dumping ground and has, despite all the painful history of the last 125 years, retained a special Indian quality. The main village was called Taholah, after the first chief, and it is an easygoing place of small purpose-built houses, attractive children, and friendly dogs. It could be any early American settlement—except that it's "late Indian." Unlike those on many reservations, the Indians here have never actually starved. There has always been salmon in the rivers, game in the forest—and these days an income of $8 million a year from government and other outside sources. That may seem a great deal of money, a comfortable form of existence, subsidized by hard-working tax-paying Americans but, in fact, it is only just enough to help them exist, never enough for them to grow and prosper. The Quinault Nation always needed more than money, they needed the spirit to grow strong again. And now they have found it.

The Indians in the reservation are, of course, Americans, but they are also *all* Indian. They point out that almost anybody can become an American and almost every kind of person has. The immigrant arrives, settles, applies for citizenship. His children are born and they are then Americans. But nobody can become an Indian—he must be born one. By taking pride in that fact, by using it as the slogan of "winning-team politics," the Quinault Indians are restoring their own ancient native dignity—and severely denting the pomp of the white man. Joe de la Cruz puts it this way: "We all understood quite well that when our people signed the treaties and gave up vast areas of land in the Pacific Northwest that we were agreeing to go to live in a smaller area, a reservation. But we always thought we would be able to keep the rights that were written into those treaties; rights to do with fishing, with the resources of the land, with the timber, with the game, and with the shorelines. The treaty also guaranteed that we would be left in peace, that we would have control of our own destiny and the way we handled our life on the reservation.

"And what we are saying now, to the American nation, to the whole world, if you like, is: 'We lost a lot and now you've taken away even more. But what we have left is ours and, even if it is not in very good shape, we still want to be left alone, not interfered with anymore. As to help, what we really want is some help to rebuild what we have been left with. That will help us to rebuild ourselves as a people, it will help us find our way to prosperity, it will stop our being totally dependent on America. But, much more important, it will help us find our dignity again.' "

Even when he was a child growing up on the reservation, Joe de la Cruz was aware of that Indian spirit, the dignity that he now wants America to recognize in the Quinault Nation. I asked him if, when he was a youngster and during his years at school outside the reservation, he ever thought of himself first as an American, and then an Indian. He said: "No, I think there was always the feeling in me that I was first and foremost an Indian —and secondly an American. Even as a young child it really was a very deep feeling. I always had it ingrained in me to be proud of my background, proud of my culture, and even though I was educated in a school system where every day we pledged our allegiance to the American flag, where every day we said Christian prayers for the American nation, where every day we had to memorize three or four verses from the Bible; I still had this feeling deep in my heart that I was an Indian first, a native of this country, the only proper native of this country. Those prayers and those pledges of allegiance were just something that happened in my life because there was a place called America. It was the name, for my land, that had been chosen by the settlers and the white men. They were Americans. I, too, was American, but first I was Indian—something they could never be."

Joe de la Cruz was trained and prepared to be chief of the Quinault. His predecessor, a big, dark, impressive man named James Jackson, appointed him business manager of the tribe when Joe returned from a spell of working for the United States Government in Portland, Oregon, as a hydraulic engineer. As business manager, Joe was closest in the tribe to "Big Jim," went everywhere with him, studied his methods, learned his style and his strategy. Chief Jackson suffered a heart attack and was told by doctors to take it easy. It was almost inevitable that Joe would be elected to take his place.

"I owe everything I've learned to Jim Jackson," Joe told me. "He would always tell me not to hurry at things, not to feel violence or aggression, because that would spoil our chances of winning. Jim Jackson knew the right way was to use the laws that were there for everybody to use—not just Indians, but everybody. The financial grants that we have are in fact grants which are available to any white community, if they'd take the trouble to make the application and work out how to do it properly. It was Jim Jackson who suggested to me that we weren't using laws and lawyers enough. Now we are and now we're beginning to win. But he set the groundwork and started it all off. In his day things were really very much worse. When he was a young man Indians were treated without any consideration and were completely neglected by the local community. Now, at last, things are beginning to change a little."

As a boy Joe grew up in the village of Taholah. "I went to school here, up to the sixth grade. In those days children spent a lot of time with their grandparents and I was no exception. I lived both with my grandparents and my parents and I traveled back and forth between both families and that meant that I spent a lot of time with my grandfather, who was a very wise and wonderful old man. My grandfather was one of the last Indians who still fished for salmon fifteen, twenty miles up the River Quinault. I wouldn't say that the community was poor when I was a boy, although many people outside must have regarded it as poor. But it always seemed to me that there was an abundance of fish and most of the people could sustain themselves on fish and what game they found in the forest. Now, these may be the memories of childhood coloring the truth, but I don't think that there was actual poverty in terms of not having enough food.

"But in those days things were a lot slower, a lot easier, and we weren't forced to try and measure up to the outside world as we are today. I didn't even feel the presence of prejudice so much in those days, when I was young. I suppose it must have been present but it's possible that, because

the pace of life was less fierce, it wasn't expressed so much, people were more polite to each other—even to Indians. We were always raised by my grandparents and my parents to believe that we were all equal and that we were just as good as anyone else and that the same applied anywhere in the world. At school I wouldn't say that I was a particularly bright kid although I did what was necessary to get by. I suppose it would be true to say that I was a popular kid, I was elected a class officer. But I don't want to place false emphasis on that because it was mainly because of sports. I was very active in all kinds of sports at school, running and, particularly, fighting. I was a good boxer and I was well taught by a marvelous old man in the tribe, called Charlie, who had in his time been a professional boxer. He passed on everything he knew to me. What was particularly important to me was his teaching me not to lose my temper. He used to tell me, 'Lose your temper and you lose your fight.' I have never forgotten that. It served me well in school and has done ever since."

High school for the young Joe de la Cruz, for any family living on the reservation, meant traveling outside the reservation—to the small town just on its borders, Moclips. There was no high school on the Indian reservation, there still isn't one, and these days, one of Joe's priorities is to persuade the authorities to subsidize the building of a Quinault Indian Reservation High School. So far, he hasn't won that battle. In Moclips, Joe and the other Indian children mixed with local non-Indian children, fought with them, made friends with them, and also discovered from them the prejudices of their parents and the rest of the world outside. They learned, too, that even though Moclips is a small and struggling community living largely off tourism, logging, and local fishing, life for the white people there was still very much more affluent, more comfortable, and more secure than life on the reservation. So perhaps it is hardly surprising that when Joe finished with school and college and married an Indian bride, he decided to try to live away from the reservation—in Portland, Oregon.

There, he worked as a hydraulic engineer on government-sponsored conservation schemes and lived in the suburbs with Dorothy, a full-blooded member of the Colville tribe, and the family they started to raise. But after only a few years of suburban America he began to feel restless and unsatisfied, began to experience a deep longing to return to the reservation—and his own people.

He discovered, on a trip back, that the job of business manager for the tribe was to become vacant. He ran for office, was elected, and started to work alongside the chief, Jim Jackson. He had education, personality, youth, energy, and—much to the point—had acquired a detailed, working knowledge of how non-Indian business and government departments operated. With his mentor, Jim Jackson, he made a combination that was to prove deadly effective. Joe de la Cruz was being molded as a future chief, a man to lead his people in battle, a man to restore both their fortunes and their faith in themselves, a modern Indian chief.

The stereotype of the Indian is probably developed from the over-colored descriptions of the Sioux and other tribes, at the time of the Indian wars. But the Quinault were different. They are a fishing tribe and their traditional dress, a magnificent woven cloak and a Polynesian-style basket hat, is a long way from the feathered dress and war paint that we have come to expect. The Quinault spirit, though, has in the past been no less fierce and warlike than that of other tribes and certainly presages the fighting spirit they have found today. They may be winning battles, but there are no "scalps"—even token ones. Joe was quick to remind me that taking scalps was not an Indian invention. This savage aspect of the conflict between the original Americans and those who came to settle the country was first used as a method of bounty-hunting by white men. Joe de le Cruz described the way he sees Indian nature:

"Whatever most people think is probably false. They get their ideas from the movies, the television screens, and from the prejudiced stories of other white people. They think in terms of firewater, tomahawks and war parties. But in my own experience I would say that the Indian is among the calmest of all people that you are ever likely to find. It is pretty hard to get an Indian excited about anything. I'd say—in the majority at least—that they are a very passive people. You know, no matter what kind of conditions they are living in they are still capable of being contented. Accepting fate has become a way of life for the Indian people, because they have had to learn to go without, and be content with so very little, for so very long, that now they have become used to it and are passive about it—it can even seem that they are content, or satisfied, with it. It doesn't mean that they are dull or beaten, just that they have developed the strength, the stoic capacity, to cope with whatever life hands out.

"It's something all Indians have. I'll give you an example. When I was working on the reservation as a young man (after I had returned from Portland), I was acting as a guide and taking fishing parties up and down the river. I would take pride in the fact that I could stand the cold much more than any of the hunters or tourists or fishermen could. All Indians are like that. You learn to tell your body not to feel what is happening to it. You learn to tell your stomach not to feel empty. You learn to tell your brain not to be tired. This is part of the Indian closeness to nature and the spirit of the land, you draw your strength from that. I don't mean all this in a pagan or irreligious sense, although even those of us who have been brought up in the Christian faith—I try to be a good Catholic—are still very close to those old faiths and beliefs and the spirits of the forest, the influence of the ocean and the rivers. When you inherit all that it isn't

hard to see how one can come to accept what is done to you as being part of the pattern of nature. If you can accept the cold, the frost and snow, the wind, then you can accept the hunger and the conditions in which you live.

"As a young man I did what all the young Indians have done throughout the ages, what they still do today. It has always been part of our religion, our capacity to survive as Indians, to be able to go away into the forest or up the river for days on end on our own—with nothing other than a few hunting things—and live quietly in the forest and move about silently and meditate and think about nature. And we still try and keep that up. It is now a deliberate part of our school program, here in Taholah, to take the children into the forest on trips. We point out the different kinds of trees, the different creatures, and we deliberately try to start in them the beginnings of those spiritual urges that have motivated and protected Indian people throughout the ages. We hope that in elementary school they will begin to feel the pull of the Great Spirit of the Forest so that when they become men and women they will want to go into the forest—like we did when we were young—to discover for themselves the strength that comes from meditating with nature. Now, while that is nothing new for us, it's just become very fashionable with the non-Indian people of America to discover the strengthening and healing effect of living close to nature. Perhaps it's a pity they didn't think about it when they herded us all into reservations."

There are twenty-six miles of beaches bordering the Quinault reservation, deserted, log-strewn, beautiful beaches, in stark contrast to the dirty, littered, and tourist-filled miles of beaches outside the reservation. In the small town of Moclips it is almost impossible to see the beach, or the sea, for the campers, the tents, the shacks, the pickups, and the groups of weekend clam diggers and fishermen—the American nation in search of the great outdoors. At one time, the same sprawl spread into the reservation. City people built shacks along the shoreline, retirement bungalows in the woods behind. The richer commuters from Seattle and other towns bought, through developers, plots (land bought in the first place from individual Indians, usually at bargain prices) designed to be the building sites of more costly homes on the clifftops overlooking some of the loveliest views in America.

The indiscriminate "development" of the Quinault reservation began to look like an ugly boom. It was under Chief Jim Jackson and, later, Joe de la Cruz, that the tribe began to wake up to the fact that their reservation was becoming little more than an extension of the already spoiled and

The Indian beach.

Digging for the razor-shell clams.

overcrowded holiday areas of the Olympic Peninsula. The tribe, led by
Joe, sent for help. They brought in lawyers, specialists in civil rights and
minority rights legislation, they armed themselves with experts who understood the controls that might be able to halt the accelerating destruction of their reservation. They looked, also, for ways to qualify for grants
from the government to improve their lot. They discovered methods of
obtaining federal aid which were actually open to all American communities but not much known and used. They went to work with a will—a will
to win. It was hardly Red Power, it wasn't a second battle of Wounded
Knee, with guns and violence. But it was as determined and as remorseless
as the movement of a glacier, slow and irresistible. The Quinault Indians
were on the move and determined not to be stopped. They did nothing
illegal, but what they did caused more pain and outrage than if they had
run out of the reservation armed to the teeth and shouting war cries.

They closed the beach.

At first they put up notices announcing that the beach was tribal property and was for the use of the tribe, and only the tribe, and nobody who

was not a member of the tribe was permitted on the beach. They discovered that they were entitled to do this under wilderness-protection legislation and they carefully framed their ordinance within its terms. The weekend campers, the beach bums, the surfers, the tourists, were given their marching orders—politely but firmly. The tribe appointed a beach warden and he usually carried a shotgun which was described as "necessary for self-defense." He patrolled, with shotgun, to see that strangers carried out the tribe's new "get out of town" policy. It caused an uproar. The beaches of the Olympic Peninsula—including the Quinault tribal beach—are the only beaches, outside Alaska, where the razor-shell clams may be found —and dug.

This clam is a prize delicacy, expensively served in local restaurants and hotels. And searching it out on local beaches is also a form of sport. The clams are dug for and captured only at certain times of the tide—it always seems to be five or six o'clock in the morning—in the freezing waters at the ocean's edge. They burrow to escape and must be dug quickly with a specially shaped spade. After shelling and washing, the succulent clam meat will retail as high as five dollars a pound. Digging the razor shell may

Another major source of income comes from the clams.

be sport for the tourists, the weekenders, the campers, the American outdoorsmen—but it is income for the Quinault Indians.

With the beach closed to outsiders, the tribal council appointed a fishing committee charged with the supervision of the clam harvest, for the benefit of the tribe. Today on the Quinault reservation the clams are dug only at the best and most profitable times and only when the digging will not interfere with their reproduction rate. It is a policy of conservation which has produced an awesome increase in the clam crop for the Quinault Indians. Indian traders buy the clams from members of the tribe— on the days that the beach is declared open for digging—and then sell the clams to the hotels and restaurants outside the reservation. But closing the beaches, explosive though the reaction was, was still only a small skirmish in the battle of the Quinault.

After the beach, they moved against the weekend homeowners and the land developers.

The tribe issued stop orders on half-completed buildings and demolition orders on homes that didn't conform to regulations designed to protect both the appearance and the future of the shoreline. Soon summer homes and bungalows were up for sale, others were abandoned or pulled down and taken away, and some that had been started were never completed. It was obvious the tribe meant business and the reservation was no longer a breeding ground for summer homes and a gold mine for get-rich-quick developers. Nothing was done illegally. Each time the regulations were tested in the courts they were upheld.

Next came the fishing.

Salmon—on the Quinault reservation there are four kinds, king, coho, chum and sockeye—has been the center of the Quinault life for as long as they can remember. They catch the salmon by dropping fine mesh trap nets, from stakes, across the width of the Quinault River on its twenty-seven-mile run from Lake Quinault to the Pacific Ocean. Under the 125-year-old treaty, the Indians living on the Quinault reservation, and all those in the area, were allowed to retain their rights to fish: "in all their usual accustomed grounds and stations, in common with all the citizens of the territory." But, like all treaty promises, that provision was ignored and broken until the Indians of the area, with the Quinault, decided to test it in court. In 1970 a fundamentally important decision, called the Boldt decision after the judge who handed it down, ruled that the Indians were not only entitled to all the fish in the lakes and rivers of their reservation but also they were entitled to half of all the fish in all the rivers, and all the coastal areas, of *all* the land they had surrendered more than a century ago, when they signed the treaty. It may seem, in legal and moral terms, only just and fair. To the Indians it was no more than the restoration of

Drying fish in Pacific Northwest at the turn of the century.

the rights that they had been guaranteed. But the decision caused an uproar.

Salmon fishing in the Pacific Northwest, both by sportsmen and commercial interests, is very big business indeed. The court ruling, which would in theory allow the Indians fifty percent of all the fish in all the area, threatened the livelihood, as well as the sport, in a region heavily dependent on both. And when the white man feels that his living is threatened by the Indian he behaves as he has always done—violently. There were incidents in bars, fistfights, shotguns fired in the middle of the night, and —more by good fortune than good sense—no serious injuries. But there was a return to all the old prejudices and hatreds.

Did Joe de la Cruz think that this time he had overdone it and brought on a potentially counterproductive backlash? Was he in danger of separating the identity of the tribe from their overall American identity and risking loss of support from fair-minded non-Indians, among their neighbors in the Pacific Northwest? He told me: "I don't believe that we are in danger of cutting our people off from the American identity because I believe that everybody realizes that we are no threat to the overall American people. We are a tiny part of America, only asking to have our legal rights recognized. What bothers us is that other ethnic groups have actually come into America and have insisted on being allowed to practice their ethnic culture within this polyglot society of ours. Indeed, they have been encouraged to do so. They managed to keep their language, their culture, their social differences in such a way that the American people not only recognize their right to behave like this but take pride in it. Nobody interferes with them. The Spanish, the French, the Italians, the Poles, the Swedish, the Germans, the Russians, the Greeks, and many, many others who have arrived in this country to become Americans continue to practice their particular way of life. It's only with the truly native Americans, the Indians, that this desire to teach our children the ways of their great-great-grandparents, to keep alive the songs, the culture, the beliefs of our race, is resented."

Is Joe in danger of starting the Indian wars all over again? "In a sense, this may be happening," he told me. "But if that is what people feel as the result of these court cases then that is what I am afraid they must go on thinking. We don't believe that we are creating Indian wars. We just believe that the Indians are saying to the American people: *These are our rights, please recognize them and let us have them.* Eventually people may see that we are benefiting the whole of America. After all, it is the Indian people who have taken the only worthwhile steps for the conservation of the razor-shell clams. We are, as well, showing the way to the rest of the world in our conservation plans for the salmon. We have a salmon hatchery and breeding station which enables us to study and regulate the movement of salmon so that they shall not be overfished and threatened with extinction. Then, our logging practices are better than those that have been used in our reservations by the non-Indian logging firms. We're showing the way in terms of restoring and conserving the resources of our reservation and the whole area. By winning these court battles—these Indian wars, if you want to call them that—we will show the way to the rest of America. It is difficult for stiff-necked, prejudiced people (with more pride than sense) to accept that the way we are going and the example we are setting is the best way.

"For generations now white people have regarded Indian reservations as more or less open territory, free to be exploited. White people never felt that they had to offer the Indian a fair price for his land, sometimes they didn't even bother to buy it from him at all before they built on it. What hurts the white people is the fact that we are now behaving exactly like Americans—and they would like us to behave exactly like Indians. They see Indians as a beaten people, as losers, without rights, able to be exploited as

The Quinault salmon factory.

second-class citizens. That just isn't true—legally, historically, socially. And we are the people helping *all* the Indian tribes to prove it.

"It may be uncomfortable for them to accept it. But they are going to have to live with it—whether they like it or not."

And it is true. Nowadays the Quinault reservation is moving toward self-sufficiency. The Quinault salmon fishery exports frozen salmon all over the world, to Europe, Japan, South America, and the rest of the United States. The clam-digging brings tribal members an excellent income.

But the forest remains a problem. For fifty years or more, outside logging interests were encouraged by the government Bureau of Indian Affairs to log the giant cedarwood trees from the Quinault reservation. It takes five hundred years for a cedarwood forest to grow (and, in these northern latitudes, it is rare to find a cedarwood rain forest like the Quinault reservation's), but it takes only a generation or two to lay it to waste. There was nothing illegal or technically improper when ITT Rayonnier and Alohoha Mayr, the two main logging companies concerned, purchased the rights to log in the reservation. Under the original Indian Acts the reservation was divided into parcels of land among the tribal families, amounting to about eighty acres a family. The Bureau of Indian Affairs, as guardian and caretaker of Indian interests, was entitled to put together

these eighty-acre parcels and sell off huge tracts of logging land. But cedar trees are cut at a high point from the ground. After these giants of the northern forests—many of them fully grown before Columbus set sail across the Atlantic—are dragged out what is left behind becomes an almost impenetrable mess called "the Slash." Little grows in the Slash. The streams, which are the breeding ground for the salmon, become choked with debris, soured and foul. Secondary tree growth may spring up but is commercially useless, thin and spindly. The land becomes locked in a rigor mortis caused by man and not curable by nature. These days the logging companies admit that in the past there was little or no replanting, hardly any clearing out. Now, the area looks like the ruin left behind by war.

The Quinault are doing what they can. Because cedarwood does not rot, the debris can be dragged out and turned into "shakes" (shingle tiles), much prized in the building industry for their durability and attractive appearance. The tribe has set up a Quinault shake mill, where members of the tribe work at the dangerous jobs of splitting and sawing. But it is a slow process. The Quinault have discovered that they can clear just about 1,000 acres of Slash a year—and there are 90,000 acres left to go. At the present rate it will be nearly a century before the Quinault Indians complete the restoration of their devastated forest.

The Quinault tribe has its own police force, its own laws, its own court, its own judges—and its own prison. As you drive into the reservation a large metal notice identifies the area, tells you that you are on Quinault tribal property, and warns you that you must obey tribal laws. The notice was resented by some whites outside. They pulled it down. The Quinault put up another. It was pulled down again—and the Quinault replaced it again. Then it was burnt. The Quinault left it as it was. It is still quite legible and somehow the scorch marks add fierceness to the notice. It was an effective move on the part of a tribe who are becoming increasingly more surefooted in dealing with prejudice.

I visited the small police force and seven-cell prison. The only tenant at the time was a middle-aged white logger who had been drinking and fell asleep at the wheel of his truck beside one of the few main roads that run through the reservation. The police had picked him up and brought him in. The chief of police, himself a Blackfoot Indian, explained why the man had not been released on bail and was still in jail, awaiting trial: "Normally when we pick up somebody who is intoxicated and is a member of the tribe we know exactly where we can reach him so we wait eight to ten hours until they are physically able to drive their car or walk home and

Joe walks in "the slash."

163

if they then don't appear in court, when they should, we can go and pick them up. But because of the feelings that were aroused in the State of Washington, when it was ruled that our court has jurisdiction over non-Indians as well as Indians, we're forced to hold a non-Indian in jail until he either posts quite a substantial bail or until the trial happens."

The prisoner himself was mildly hung over and not unhappy. He cheerfully admitted that it was not his first spell in jail and, compared with some he knew, the food and care were good. Later that morning a passive, and impressive, judge listened to his plea of guilty and fined him seventy-five dollars plus costs. When I left the logger was cheerfully negotiating for time to pay.

The tribe is run from the tribal office, an octagonal cedarwood building alongside the mouth of the Quinault River, where a staff of eighteen, including the group of very busy lawyers, work at administering the tribal enterprises, collecting the tribal income, enforcing the tribal regulations, and planning the future of the Quinault community. They use the latest typewriters, computer programs, modern dictating machines, teleprinters, and all the other weapons of business competition. The electronics of the twentieth century have replaced bows and arrows, lawyers have taken over as warriors, and accountants have become battle leaders.

The tribe also runs, with the help of grants and aid from outside, a free medical and dental clinic, where a dedicated non-Indian staff provides excellent service. Alcohol has always been a problem in Indian tribes and although the stereotype image of Indians fighting drunk on "firewater" owes more to movie scriptwriters than fact, it has become the basis of a deep, and largely false, prejudice. These days there is little more alcoholism inside the Quinault tribe than outside it. There are no bars, no liquor on sale.

The resentment toward the Quinault achievements by the white people outside the reservation is explosive. I met with a group who had bought properties or plots on the reservation just before the Quinault took action to control the developments. One man told me: "Really, we became the victims of a change in the way the Indians were handled by the federal government. My wife and I came up in here one Sunday afternoon in about 1967. There was a real estate development going on at the time and we saw this really beautiful spot and decided that it was just the place for a retirement home. Within a few days we had purchased the property and had fallen in love with the area. But of course we were not aware, at the time, that there was any real trouble brewing with the Indians."

A neighbor of his told me: "I was the first person the Indians took action against. I received a summons instructing me to stop work on my house when it was almost finished. Even though they had observed me since the time I started building it, they didn't inform me that I was not supposed to until it was almost finished. Then they hauled me into court and issued an order that I should tear the house down within thirty days or they would do it themselves and charge me for it. They also said they would evict me from the reservation using as little force as necessary. I was advised that they were legally in their rights to do all this. It didn't make me feel any better. They said I was violating the wilderness order that was passed which did not permit the building of homes between the highway and the ocean."

Business in the tribal office.

Grandma Black, a revered old lady of the tribe.
A beach picnic—salmon Indian style.

There were a dozen similar stories. These were ordinary Americans believing that they were behaving only as Americans in America but discovering, to their chagrin and anger, that they were in fact behaving as Americans in an Indian reservation. They may have been ill-advised, they may have been uncareful and overenthusiastic. But they can be forgiven, perhaps, for not expecting trouble when for nearly 120 years there never had been any trouble and white men had always behaved as freely within the reservation as outside. Joe de la Cruz led the tactics that brought a virtual end to white property development within the reservation but he has some sympathy for the householders who found themselves caught in a squeeze play. "We felt in the tribe that they were the victims of very unfortunate circumstances. We had every sympathy with them because they had been caught, rather unfairly, in this situation. But we were determined to restore our rights to our tribal land and to do it legally. They had been deceived, if you like, into thinking that they had more rights than they did. And our reply to them is that they should sue the development corporation that sold them the land in the first place."

Dewey Whittacker, for many years, saw himself as the leading developer in the Quinault area. He is a proud old man with harsh opinions. His forebears came to the area with ox-drawn wagons. He believes the Indians have too much power and are getting out of hand. He says: "For the benefit of the Indian people, as well as the people on the outside, they should not be given any more power and what power they have should be taken from them. What we need to do now is to dissolve the reservations and rescind the treaties. We need one nation and we need it united and we should have it. These reservations should be made part of the American nation. Never mind what it says in the treaties. Whoever heard of treaties made more than a hundred years ago being effective? They ought to be torn up and the Indians forced to join the mainstream of the American people."

Opinions like those didn't ease the situation between the Quinault tribal leaders and the property developers. One night during the height of the struggle, Dewey Whittacker's office within the reservation and one just outside were both blown up simultaneously. Dynamite is easy to get in any area where there is logging, but the suspicions of the local population (and quite a few Indians) were aimed at the Quinault tribe—and Joe de la Cruz. Eventually a non-Indian was caught, tried, and convicted. But the effect of it all was still to hasten the end of housing development in the Quinault reservation. "For sale" notices went up overnight on nearly every beach cottage or retirement home on the Quinault shoreline.

The criticism most often voiced is: "We pay taxes to support their schools, build their houses, provide their welfare, buy their food, clothing, and practically everything that they have. It's our money, so surely we have the right to come and live on their land." Joe de la Cruz replies: "This tribe alone pays more into the United States Treasury, by way of tax on our resources, and individual tax on our tribal members, than what it costs, in fact, in grants for all the tribes in the western part of Washington State. Ten years ago we didn't know this, but once we got lawyers and accountants on it we were able to discover exactly what we were worth, exactly what we were contributing. So, we're not freeloaders. We're taxpayers. Anyway, the grants that we do get are available to any community in order to develop." He sighed for a moment, a flicker of what could have been humor crossed his passive Indian face. "But then, I suppose we Indians always have been cast as the bad guys. The cowboys never seem to lose, do they?"

The man who took over from Joe de la Cruz as business manager of the tribe is Guy McMinds, a big, affable, rocklike Indian, contrasting strongly with the quiet, thoughtful image his chief projects. He lives with his wife and daughter in a magnificent house overlooking the Pacific. He managed to buy the house from a non-Indian, when a bomb blew up a neighbor's house. The implications seem obvious, but Guy McMinds just laughs. "Not guilty," he says, "but I'm happy to be living here all the same." He, as much as anybody in the tribe, watched over and masterminded the fishing dispute during the years it took to go through the courts.

Guy McMinds points out: "You know, people say that because the treaties are more than a hundred years old, they have no validity or constitutional value. But the Constitution of the whole country is more than two hundred years old and people have just finished celebrating that fact. We're not saying that we're superior citizens, we're as much American citizens as anybody, but we've discovered that the white man doesn't want to face the Indian, he wants him to disappear. He wants to get rid of him."

Historically speaking, Guy McMinds echoes the past. When the treaty with the Quinault was signed in 1855 it was only two years after Washington became a territory of the United States. Isaac Stevens, the new Governor and Superintendent of Indian Affairs, was eager to open up the territory as soon as possible. He set out to solve "the Indian problem" and within a year of Washington becoming a territory he had succeeded in pressuring most of the Indian tribes into signing treaties which extinguished their title to a vast sixty-four million acres, in exchange for the reservations. Subsequently national policy for Indians in reservations was directed toward the termination of the reservations and moving the Indian into the mainstream of American culture. A Zane Grey novel, written in 1925, was called *The Vanishing American* and, at that time, that was still what national policy intended the Indian to become. The Indian, it was said, must either accept the white man's ways (a car, private property, learn

Joe's children on the stairs.

English, become educated) or become extinct. Either way, as a problem, he would "vanish." Only in the last twenty years has American national policy reversed its thinking about breaking up the reservations.

These days, hundreds of tribes are following the example of the Quinault, using the law and the courts to win the latest "Indian war." Joe de la Cruz says: "There's a long way to go, we have much to do. We are creating a great deal of bad blood by winning these battles. We must win the battles. But then we must restore our good relations, wipe out the bad blood, and bring back the good feeling." His wife Dorothy, small, attractive, the mother of five children, knows that she will see even less of her husband as he flies frequently from Washington State to Washington, D.C. Just before he left on one of these trips, there was a funeral in the tribe for one of the leaders, an old, wise man. The whole tribe turned out. After the funeral Joe said to me:

"The tribe was paying respect to the hereditary descendant of the blood chief of the Quinault tribe. It was his grandfather who negotiated and signed the original treaty. Henry Mason approved of the progress we were making. He thought we were right to do it. But he warned me to be careful not to forget the things we really should struggle to protect. He warned me against the danger of becoming greedy and ambitious to gain victories in an American way rather than an Indian way. He said we don't need to be gigantic business successes, we don't need to be gigantic property developers. We should protect the basic things of our life, the fishing, the forest, the beach, the game, and the rivers." I asked Joe where it might all end: "I believe that America will one day look to us, as the first Americans, to take our place among them with pride and not lose our culture in the melting pot.

"As for me? Well, one day there will be another chief of this tribe. It's as it should be. Somebody will take over from me, there are young men almost ready to do it now. I shan't be unhappy about that. I won't be dead. I expect I will do a bit of fishing, a bit of hunting. I'm a good fisherman and I can dig clams and I can hunt in the forest. It's the way an Indian ought to live—even in America today."

THE PRIVATE EYE

JOHN O'GRADY

Safely in his office, he unzipped the plastic briefcase, took out the heavy chrome-plated Colt .45 automatic, slid open the middle drawer of the desk, and laid the gun on top of the papers. He shut the drawer.

From the pocket of his Hawaiian sports shirt, he flipped a pack of Luckies and a book of matches onto the desk in front of him. He unwrapped a stick of gum as he reached for the telephone to make the first call of the morning.

Outside, Sunset Boulevard was hardly awake, but Hollywood's Number One Private Eye, John O'Grady, was already about his business.

John O'Grady—like the opening words of this chapter—has become a parody of the fictional private detective. But that *is* how he starts his day. He does have real clients, real cases, and is, often, in real danger. It is just that the adventures of Philip Marlowe, Sam Spade, Travis Magee, Lew Archer, Frank Cannon, and a score of others have so fixed the public image of the private detective that John O'Grady's clients wouldn't recognize, or believe in him, unless he behaved "in character." And it is because of Hollywood, more than anything else, that the Private Eye has become one of the best known of the American archetypes—alongside the Cowboy, the Indian, and the Sheriff. The fiction of the private eye as a hard-bitten "loner," in a world of guns and gangsters, booze and fast dames, has filled our movie houses and television screens for so long that, by now, the sometimes heroic but mostly rather seedy adventures of those "gumshoes" have become an essential myth of our time.

But the "fact" behind the "fiction" is that there are more private eyes in Los Angeles than in any other place in the United States—any other place in the world. A few, in fact, operate as "loners," from small offices tucked into the corners of this stucco town, with its Disneyland architecture and neon-lit people. You can look them up in the Yellow Pages. It is there that you will find the Sunset Boulevard address of the ex–Los Angeles Police Department inspector who, without modesty, lists himself, quite simply, as "Hollywood's Number One Private Eye—John O'Grady."

He looks something like Robert Mitchum and he doesn't mind the comparison; indeed, I suspect he goes to some trouble to maintain the similarity. He's tall, heavily built, and may be fit enough to take on the kind of trouble that could still come his way. He has hard, heavy-lidded eyes and stooped shoulders. He wears smart sports shirts, tucked into expensive slacks, white buckskin shoes, a diamond ring on each hand, a gold wristwatch, the inevitable necklace, tortoiseshell sunglasses. He drives a Cadillac convertible which has seen better days.

He'll tell you it's all part of a deliberate image he's trying to create. It reflects the world of his clients. Unlike his fictional counterparts, he seldom wants to right injustice, clear the innocent or the wrongly accused. His world and his work are dominated by money. Nearly all his cases are connected with money, or property, and nearly all his clients are motivated by suspicion, or greed.

He operates from a small office in a two-story block on Sunset Boulevard. The other occupants of the building include lawyers, dentists, and accountants. The raised letters on his door are chipped and the apostrophe between the *O* and the *G* in his name is missing. He says somebody stole it. He uses a part-time secretary and an answering service. Despite a comfortable couch, the furniture in the office is cheap and in bad taste and the impression given to clients is that of a private detective who has invested as little as he could get away with. John O'Grady denies it. He believes the clothes he wears and his office furniture are smart, even sophisticated. "My shirt cost a hundred fifty dollars alone—that is three times the price of my whole uniform when I was a cop." He argues that an address on Sunset Boulevard is a must. "Where would you have me? In some lousy walk-up on Fifth Street in downtown Los Angeles?" he asked me.

He takes on most kinds of assignments: tracing missing persons; running investigations into the backgrounds of employees-to-be, husbands-to-be, and brides-to-be; checks on errant spouses; divorces; rows about alimony. For defense attorneys he will build a case for their clients, often a case against the police. He charges high fees. He has bodyguarded Linda Lovelace and been retained by Elvis Presley. He liked working for Presley, disliked Linda Lovelace. He boasts of a score of other Hollywood celebrities as his clients. He's been shot at, knifed, beaten up, and on the wrong side of barroom brawls more times that he cares to remember. But for

"An office on Sunset Strip is essential."

John O'Grady there is somebody who waits, who would mourn if, one day, he didn't come back in one piece. He has a wife, Ginny, and two sons. He's proud of them all and tries to keep them separate from his working life —as if he fears that the seaminess of it might rub off on them and damage them.

John O'Grady is the son of a cop who himself served the Los Angeles Police Department for twenty years, twelve of them in charge of the Narcotics Squad. He became one of the best known—and one of the most hated—of Hollywood's real-life cops. John O'Grady busted all kinds and took particular pride in putting the famous behind bars. It was his evidence that sent Robert Mitchum to jail for marijuana smoking, his methods that embarrassed the well-connected and the influential, caught out in the name of the law. In the end, his punch-ups, his shootouts, and his publicity paste-ups became too much for his police bosses. They transferred him to the San Fernando Valley and assigned him to quieter duties; even then he managed to wind up investigating murders, even then his tough methods continued to bring complaints. Times were changing, so were police methods. More and more ordinary citizens knew their rights —and more policemen had to learn how to respect them. So John O'Grady took his pension, and his flamboyant reputation, and set up shop as a private eye.

I went with him on one case. This time he was not alone, he brought along an electronics expert, with a suitcase full of specialized equipment.

O'Grady explained: "The case involves an industrialist with a successful international product but he keeps being underbid in competition for contracts. In all probability there's a leak somewhere in his office; maybe one of his staff, or even one of his partners, is selling him out. But he's very reluctant to admit that this might be the case. You know, nearly all employers are reluctant to recognize disloyalty and treachery in their own organization—they think it reflects on them personally. So he's called me in to see if I can trace the leak and stop it. The first thing I'm going to do is look for an electronic bug; it is a possibility that there could be a transmitter in his office—once we've checked that out then we'll know what to do next."

O'Grady and his assistant had already been given the keys to the executive board room and office suite. They went to the office late at night, after the staff had left, in order to avoid tipping off any defector in the firm. They searched the paneling, the carpets, the furniture, the telephones, the typewriters, the light fittings—even the executive lavatory—for bugs. It took three hours and at the end O'Grady was able to pronounce the place clean. What then?

"Well, he's been underbid at least six times, and it has upset him and it has cost him a lot of money. So what I have to do now is prepare a false bid and run it through the company with only two or three people knowing about it so I can isolate where the leak is. Then if another company comes up with a bid fractionally below our false bid we'll know what's happened." But before adopting that plan, John O'Grady drove out to one of the plushier sections of Beverly Hills to report to his client. He was charging $2,500 a week plus expenses, and for that kind of money the private eye always visits the client at home. The industrialist, a worried, intense man surrounded by expensive furniture and many paintings, reluctantly gave the go-ahead for the false bid. Two weeks later O'Grady went back to the industrialist, reported that one of his long-time employees had been selling secrets. The employee was quietly fired, the rich industrialist became a little more cynical than he already was—and his secrets were safe once again.

That particular case came to O'Grady because he already knew the industrialist—he was the tenant in one of his buildings, and had run security checks for him before. But most of O'Grady's work comes from attorneys. He prefers it that way, believes that the possibility of not being paid is reduced when a lawyer acts as a middleman. Although you can find him in the Yellow Pages he is violently disinclined—unlike his fictional counterparts—to take clients who come in off the street, or telephone him for help. Why not? "I made a decision when I went into this business that I'd only work where there's a legitimate right to investigate. Now if some person has to scan through the Yellow Pages to find a detective it may be something shady, something I don't want to do, it may not be a sufficiently confidential relationship (as it would be with an attorney) and perhaps they don't have any money and they're just shopping around." I suggested there could be another reason: it could be someone genuinely in need of help, sincerely reaching for the aid of a private detective. But too much of Hollywood and its values has rubbed off on O'Grady. He countered: "Well, there's more than a hundred fifty private detectives in the Yellow Pages—and I'd just as soon they go to the other hundred forty-nine."

O'Grady is in the job to make money, but if he has made a great deal it doesn't show. He lives modestly in Glendale, a respectable suburb of Los Angeles, in a small bungalow with a small swimming pool; his two boys are grown up and at college; his wife, largely because of her husband's erratic hours, has learned to develop her own interests, lead her own life. But he likes his job. He told me: "It's not a routine job, I'm not punching a clock, I've no supervisor or management man over me. If I don't like a case I can withdraw from it instantly without too much going wrong. And I don't have to feel that I'm doing good, either. I'm not a cavalier or St. George trying to put the troubles of the world right. I'm just an ex-cop making a living as a private eye."

It wasn't always like that. In his days with the L.A.P.D., Inspector O'Grady was a gangbuster to be reckoned with, a man for all headlines. His superiors frequently chastised him but his methods didn't change. He liked to cut corners. "Why bother with a warrant to get into a place when, by shouting 'Fire' outside, the door will open and you get all the access you need," he told me. "I knew what my job was when I was in charge of the Narcotics Squad. The law was quite unequivocal in those days. Any kind of drugs meant a bust. These days, you wouldn't do a day in jail for the kind of marijuana offense that cost Robert Mitchum a year behind bars. I didn't like the way society was changing, I thought it was too goddam easy for people to get off. Police work was becoming too pussyfooted. I wasn't sorry when the time came for me to decide to quit. Some of the best times of my life have been on the police force, but the kind of justice and kind of system we have these days makes me sick. Every street punk has so many rights that the average policeman winds up in the hospital from a broken skull before he's finished reading them out to him. It wasn't for me."

Most of O'Grady's work in his heyday as a policeman centered around Sunset Boulevard. He came to know it well. He still does: "The Strip is a rip-off now. You park your car here and go in for a pack of cigarettes or a cola or something and you come back and they've taken your spare tire. If they have time they'll jack up the car and take all four wheels. I've had luggage taken when I've only parked for a few moments. But I know the Strip well, I know every joint, every massage parlor, every bar, every restaurant along here. I've watched it change over the years but I wouldn't operate anywhere else, it's always been my beat. I don't mind it being tatty, I don't mind the nude shows, I don't mind the girl parlors. But some of the heavy things in the days when I was a cop I was determined to break up—and I did. I didn't like the drug scene, the blackmail, the extortion, and the violence. And I stopped all that. I didn't care who was involved, I didn't care who they knew, I didn't care what big names would be mentioned, if I wanted to raid a place, then I raided it. And I raided them all. I raided private homes up in Beverly Hills, I raided the homes of the top stars, and I raided plenty of parties right here on the Strip.

"I remember one unusual incident when we raided a lesbian party. We were bundling all the girls into paddy wagons and two of them refused to put clothes on. I think they were under the influence of marijuana at the time and I found it quite an unusual problem, one I'd never had before. So I had to call the night chief of police and get him off his dead little ass—he was asleep someplace—and get his permission to bring the ladies in naked. He said yes, I could. So when I reached out to pick one of these girls up she damn near bit my finger off. After I'd arrested her and booked her I turned around and sued her. The city paid for everything, all my legal costs, and I collected two-hundred-eighty-dollars for punitive damages. It turned out to be the first police case in the United States where a police officer got punitive damages for a physical assault. I was proud of that."

O'Grady, at the wheel of his Eldorado convertible, drives up and down the Strip reminiscing, showing off. "Now that's a place where hoodlums used to eat," he told me. "The number-one table was right at the back by the stairway, and I was sitting there one night chatting with a very attractive blonde when some idiot walked up to me with a beer bottle in his hand. It was a crazy scene, almost straight out of a Western. It seemed I had sent his sister to the penitentiary and he was going to kill me. Now I didn't know the man from Adam, and I didn't want to create any further scene in a place where there were hoodlums because things might have gotten out of hand. But at the time I couldn't remember if I was wearing my gun on my left side or my right side so I kept the conversation going while I sorted it out and I finally recalled it was on my left side and while we were still talking I stood up very quickly with my gun in my hand and I put it right underneath his throat and I said the usual thing that I always say with all of them: 'If you want to get your ass blown right off, hang on to that bottle.' "

O'Grady is frequently seen around the night spots of Sunset Boulevard with an attractive girl on each arm. He even boasts about it, claims that it is all part of his front, necessary to his image as a private eye. At first I didn't believe it, but after talking to some of his escorts it became clear that it is just a front. Even private eyes, it seems, sometimes suffer from

These days it's bugging, anti-bugging, and surveillance.

a machismo problem. And O'Grady is more concerned with machismo than most. His own anecdotes are always at their most scathing and destructive when he's talking about "fags" and "closet queens." He remembers, apparently with greater pleasure and clarity than most police incidents in his career, all the arrests, all the fights, even the shootings that have been connected with raiding homosexual establishments.

Back home, Mrs. O'Grady remains unimpressed—and unworried—by her husband's chest-beating behavior. She continues to love him, admire him, and, certainly, understand him. She told me: "It's true that there is a tremendous phoniness about the world he lives in. It's not my world. I don't participate at all in his business life and I try to keep our home life separate from it, that way our home life remains real. I think home is a necessary and vital reality for him, it's where I exist and it's where he returns to. In his business life he constantly associates with insincerity, treachery, and false values. He lives and moves among liars and traitors. He doesn't know from one moment to the next whether a person is telling him the truth or not. Now it's his job to sort out the phonies from each other. But I have nothing to do with that, I don't want to know about it, and I think I keep myself stronger for John by being separate from it. He knows he can always come back to me and what I have here is the true part of his life.

"Oh, I know he goes out with other women, I know it's necessary for him to do it for business. I don't feel threatened or insecure or jealous about it. If I did, then we wouldn't have a proper marriage. I know that behaving like that is part of the phoniness in his life. But he has to do it.

"Now I *do* know that some of that phoniness rubs off on him. He is the John O'Grady I know, an honest, true, responsible person. But he is a tough, hard man, living in a tough, hard, dirty world—and it does rub off on you. But I say to myself, so what? Everybody is a little phony in one way or another. At least I'm able to know which part of him is phony and which part of him is true. And underneath it all he is a very gentle, very sentimental man. Perhaps one of the reasons I don't worry about other women, when he goes out with them, is that I know how attached he is to me and to our home life. I know that he needs the calm, ordinary domestic stability that we provide for him but I also know that he needs that other life, that phony, flashy, gaudy life of his. I understand his need for it, although I don't want to share it with him.

"I know about his clothes, for instance. He's always liked classy clothes, he always dresses up. He was the first man in the Los Angeles Police Department to wear Bermuda shorts, or a pink shirt, and that created quite a scandal at the time. Can you imagine?—a big tough policeman wearing a pink shirt, let alone Bermuda shorts. But it means a great deal to him to be thought stylish. That's why he wears the jewelry, the shoes. But you must remember, too, that John actually is a very glamorous person. He is a Hollywood policeman and Hollywood is a glamorous place. He does have all the ingredients of the television private eyes. He does have glamorous clients who are immensely rich and immensely famous and who like him and trust him because he solves their problems for them. The attorneys that use him come back to him again and again because they like him and because they know that he gets results." As she talked her eyes were bright with wifely affection and loyalty, the kind of loyalty that sees beyond the sports shirts and white buckskin shoes. John O'Grady may be a good detective, and he's certainly a lucky husband.

He was brought up strictly, in a large Catholic family. "Until the day he died, whenever my father saw me smoking he would lean over and take the cigarette out of my mouth, because he disapproved of it so much. When we were youngsters he would beat us if he thought we were doing wrong, but I approved of the way he brought us up. He would never allow bad behavior from any of us in front of our mother, he taught us to respect each other, our parents, and the law. When I see some of the married people I know today and the way they speak to each other or the way they let their children speak to them, then I know how good my father was for me. As a young boy I remember playing on the block and seeing two men draw up in a car and hide a small box in a tree. They behaved very furtively and very oddly and they didn't look as if they were about any kind of honest business. I noted the position of the tree but did nothing about it while the men were around. Then I went down to the police station and told the police officers about it. They were very excited because it turned out that the men—I gave them a description—were part of gang they had been watching for some time. So they staked out the tree and when somebody came along to collect the box they were able to make a bust. I was about eight at the time and after that I knew I had to be a policeman like my dad. And that's what I became."

On another case, I went with O'Grady to Brentwood. There are very few poor people in Brentwood. As O'Grady puts it, "You've got to be loaded to live here." He had been sent for by the recently divorced wife of a man with considerable property. A woman we will call Linda Manning believed that her husband had concealed assets at the time of the divorce and she wanted them traced, wanted her share of them. She was lonely—and left behind. It's a bitter combination for women like Linda, too frequently found in places like Brentwood. O'Grady is used to listening to stories like this. He promised to do what he could to trace the assets. In his car afterward he told me, "I'll use another investigator, who specializes in this work, to dig through city records and corporate records to discover what he can. Maybe I'll be lucky, but it's very difficult. If a man wants to conceal money in a situation like this he will go through so many cover-ups that it would take me years to find it—by which time all the assets that I could discover for Mrs. Manning would be spent on my fees.

"It's true to say that most of the clients I get are acting out of paranoia or some personal greed. After a while you get used to living with the fact that everybody is suspicious of someone else, believes that they have been double-crossed, fears that they are going to be cheated. Does it make me feel the same? Well, I don't know. I'd like to say it doesn't rub off on me. But I think it probably does." In the case of Linda Manning, O'Grady has so far failed, with his fellow investigators, to dig up the evidence she needs to go to court. But he's promised to go on digging and she's agreed to go on paying.

O'Grady is very conscious of money, talks about it all the time, assesses everybody he meets in terms of income and power. He equates money with sex, with attraction, and with survival. In his world he is very probably

A "citizen's" arrest by a private eye.

right. When I watched him at work questioning Linda Manning I knew I was watching a scene that Raymond Chandler and a score of imitators would have approved, the classic gumshoe setup; the sunlit terrace, the film-set background, the *genuine* call for help in a town that is always shrill with *artificial* noise.

John O'Grady practices his craft in the footsteps of historical predecessors stretching back through American history as far as 1844. The prototype was called Pinkerton, a Chicago cop who turned private eye and bequeathed the world a tradition which has since made fortunes for the storytellers. On the screen most people think of Humphrey Bogart in *The Maltese Falcon,* playing perhaps the most famous private eye of all, Sam Spade. But there have been scores of others on the bookstands and our bedside tables; hundreds of late-night adventures with heroes invented by masters of the gumshoe style. Now there are the television private eyes: Jim Rockford, a man who is cheerfully a coward and doesn't carry a gun; Harry O, who is unofficial and travels by bus; Frank Cannon, who is fat and flawed and credible.

And in a town where fortunes are made out of private-eye stories, John O'Grady wrote his own—the true story: *O'Grady, the Life and Times of Hollywood's Number One Private Eye.* O'Grady admits that deftness with language is not his strongest asset, so he shared his author credit with Nolan Davies, a former correspondent for *Newsweek* and now a writer for a television network. The book sold only modestly but then came the Hollywood twist. A syndicate, headed by Ida Lupino, is considering making a television detective series out of O'Grady's book. The programs would be set on Sunset Strip and would capitalize and enlarge on the O'Grady stories. It doesn't seem odd or confusing to O'Grady, that now there may be a fictional O'Grady, based on a factual O'Grady, who modeled himself on his fictional predecessors.

O'Grady also advises other private eyes. He drove one morning to the boat basin in Marina del Rey, the largest in the world. The boats that bob up and down at their moorings represent a floating investment that would impress any banker—and at least one belongs to a private eye. Mike McCowan is a private eye who specializes in tough insurance claims. The problem he put in front of O'Grady sounded tough enough to qualify for any television drama. He told me: "I am supposed to bring back four hundred thousand dollars worth of diamonds that were taken out of the country by a person who got hold of them for appraisal and then skipped out and used them to get a loan. What he's done is unethical but not altogether illegal. Nevertheless, those jewels are now in Switzerland and the insurance company who risked that four hundred thousand dollars wants them back. The man concerned has vanished but there are quite a few risks involved because now there are several other people—the wrong kind of people—who know about the diamonds and might like to get their hands on them. It's my job to get them back into the country and safely into the hands of the insurers."

O'Grady advised him to use the services of American Express, to set up decoy travel arrangements while genuine, bonded couriers brought the diamonds in. Mike McCowan didn't like the idea, commented that it sounded too predictable. So, they discussed disguises. They also dis-

THE LATE ALLAN PINKERTON.

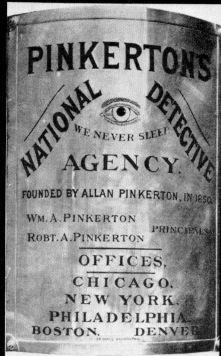

cussed the fact that, recently, on a similar assignment, a New York private eye who was supposed to take jewels from Chicago to Los Angeles was found dead in an alley. McCowan justified the use of disguises. "I often do it," he told me. "I'll masquerade as a lawyer, a doctor—once even as a priest." O'Grady (remember he has firm personal opinions about gay men) capped McCowan's story: "I've even dressed as a fag on some occasions and infiltrated gay bars as an old closet queen in order to get information." For him it was, clearly, the most courageous act of all. In the end McCowan did use a disguise. He traveled to and from Switzerland posing as a man with a broken neck. Everybody was very kind and helpful —and nobody noticed that the diamonds were concealed in his surgical collar and neck brace. The whole operation took less than a week—and the fee was $25,000.

One of O'Grady's recent lawyer-referred cases came from Burton Marks, a well-known criminal attorney who sent for him to investigate an alibi for a client who had been accused of rape. The case seemed pretty thin and the police already appeared to have quite enough evidence to convict. In situations like that there is, according to O'Grady, only one way. It's called "pounding the bricks." It means footwork, miles and miles of it, ringing doorbells and asking questions, listening to answers, waiting to find one witness who may be able to break the police evidence. It didn't work out, in this case. The young man was convicted.

O'Grady doesn't inquire too closely into the innocence or guilt of his clients. He told me: "I like to think that everybody I work for is innocent; if I was told that a man was guilty of a terrible crime before I was asked to take the case I suppose I'd have to say no. But no lawyer is ever foolish enough to do that. Mind you, if you do dig into their lives, even though they are your client, you may find out facts about them that make you sick, you wouldn't even sit in the same automobile as some of them. There have been times when I've worked successfully for a client, got them off charges, and I've hated what I've done.

"There was one particular case, a sex case which involved a girl under age and a very elderly married man. He had been arrested and charged. I dug around, I searched for a defense for that man. I dug up a great deal about the private life of the mother of the girl, so much so that in court the attorney was able to blacken her reputation and get his client off. But I didn't like doing that one bit, that was a case I was really rather ashamed of. Some years later the attorney rang to say that the man was in trouble again for the same thing and I told him where he could put his client and his case. The attorney didn't resent me taking that attitude. But then, even when I was a policeman, I had to do things that I didn't really like. It's only in detective thrillers, and on the television screen, that the private eye is able to have a noble cause and compassionate heart.

"In this country today we have five thousand murders a year, we have street crime, robbery, violence, lying, fraud—all on the increase. I believe it's probably true to say that there are more crimes committed here today than in any other country in the world. And I think that one of the causes is that people have just too many rights. We have a society too full of social engineers and it's time the pendulum swung the other way, time we took away some of the rights that are hampering the policing of our society. But until that time, I am afraid there will always be work for the likes of me. I am, if you like, a gun for hire—in the Old West tradition. But the vigilantes of the frontier days did serve a useful purpose. And, believe me, California is just as wild today as any Western town was a hundred years ago."

O'Grady has a specialty. He's an expert with the polygraph, or lie detector. He has a portable suitcase model which he can put in the trunk of his car and a larger, more impressive version in his outer office. His skills at lie detecting are used by attorneys investigating molestation cases, rape charges, and paternity suits. Frequently they demand in court that their client be allowed to take a lie-detector test in the hope that the results will convince a jury of his innocence. O'Grady charges several hundred dollars a session for his skills in that kind of case, but—for seventy-five dollars a throw—he most frequently does security vetting on potential employees. He has a list of prepared questions designed to test the honesty and loyalty of any employee. Many of the questions seem almost impertinent and personal. Do the employees ever object, I asked him? "Oh yes, they have the absolute right to object," he explained to me. "But then the employer has the absolute right not to hire them. If they want to be hired then they take the goddamned polygraph test. Actually the worst question for them is a trap question in which I say, 'I am now going to ask you a personally very embarrassing question,' and I watch the point of the needle very carefully. If they react in a certain way then I know that the person is innocent. A truly deceitful employee, planning some disloyalty or treachery, would react in a different way, might be more prepared to lie."

When putting a batch of girl stenographers through the polygraph test for a large corporation in Beverly Hills I noticed that John O'Grady wore a white cotton jacket, rather like a dentist or a pharmacist. "I do that because it gives a kind of reassurance to women. Men don't need it but it works very well with women. They think of me as a sort of technician and then they relax and lower their guard—if they're planning anything deceitful it's easier for me to get a reading on it. Mind you, because of all these years as a policeman and private eye I don't need a lie detector to tell when someone is lying."

O'Grady's job as private eye has taken him around the world several

The lie detector test.

times; in one case he travels, always, with frustration. For nearly seven years now he has been pursuing a cashier from the Robert Stigwood organization, who took off one night with all the funds from a very fat company account. So far the errant cashier has stayed one step ahead of O'Grady, although on occasions they've been in the same town. Once in Estoril, Portugal, he was close enough to touch him—and then O'Grady was arrested on a passport technicality. O'Grady admits that the cashier is good—smart: "I tell you if I do catch him then probably I'll be scared," he told me. "You see I'm convinced that he's brighter than me and that frightens me. Chasing him, catching him has become the biggest challenge of my life, but when I do catch him it will not make me brighter than him, probably only luckier. That might prove to be a bad day for my ego, when I catch up with that cashier.

"And, anyway, by that time the statute of limitations may well apply, and it might be impossible to arrest, or charge, the man and we'll probably just have a drink together. God damn him."

All O'Grady's macho fears apart, the case of the cashier is nevertheless clearly one of the more glamorous in his working life. Another was the time he was asked to bodyguard Linda Lovelace, the star of *Deep Throat*, because of threats to kidnap her. He switched hotels for her, registered her at a little-known place under another name, spent three days camped in the outer room of her suite. But he didn't like that bodyguard duty: "Oh she's all right, I suppose, but I don't really think that she's a lady. One time we went shopping in a big store and even though it's all right for women not to wear bras these days, it was obvious from the see-through and clingy nature of her dress that she didn't even wear pants. The manager of the store came up to me and said, 'Sir, will you get that woman out of here, we only like to serve ladies.' And you know, I agreed with him. I didn't like that one bit, it didn't excite me at all. Later in her suite she offered me a sip of her drink and I couldn't drink from the same glass. I could see it embarrassed her—I didn't mean it to."

O'Grady has become an experienced hand at private bodyguard assignments; he was retained for many years by Elvis Presley to organize his bodyguards. He once offered his services to Robert Kennedy and was turned down. Two nights later Kennedy was assassinated in Los Angeles. O'Grady believes that if he had been on the job it might not have happened. I suggested that this was vain and unpleasantly boastful. He responded: "I am saying it because I believe that a bodyguard is only effective if the person he is protecting will do exactly what the bodyguard tells him. Bobby Kennedy died because he would not completely accept the advice of the Secret Servicemen in his bodyguard. If I take an assignment of this sort then the individual has to do exactly what I say. I would not have let Robert Kennedy move among the people in the way he did

and certainly I would not have let him behave in the way that he did on the night of his murder. If you're going to be a bodyguard you've got to be a successful bodyguard. If you're going to be a successful bodyguard then the requirements have got to be that your 'body' agrees to be guarded."

O'Grady augments his income—which he estimates at about $75,000 a year—with a great deal of telephone detection. Hired to discover facts about an individual, O'Grady first phones government offices, insurance managers, personnel offices, accountants, even the honorary secretary of a Rotarian organization. He carefully times the calls for the lunch period when the supervisor of the department is likely to be out and when his understudy is more likely to be persuaded, or bullied, into parting with confidential facts about finance or marital status.

While I was with him O'Grady pretended to speak for a Rotary group considering awarding one of their members a "Businessman of the Year" certificate. He called the man's home and spoke to his wife. The wife revealed that the man had left home three months earlier. O'Grady expressed confusion and regret at causing bother. But he had discovered what he wanted to know (he had been asked by a potential employer if the man had a stable background). He calls this telephone detection "stiff calling." I suggested it was "conning." He agreed: "But a lot of detection is conning," he told me. "I don't see why an investigator should be deprived of the capacity to con when the crooks know all the angles—and have all the protections and are allowed to con as much as they want. A lot of my clients have been ripped off in divorce cases by husbands who concealed their assets; or there are employers who are being deceived by people who want to get on the payroll. There's no law against what I'm doing. You can take it from me that I'm pretty versed on the laws of this kind of operation. It's subterfuge—and subterfuge in itself is not illegal. I always use my own name, always say I'm John O'Grady. But I also add the name of a company that doesn't employ me. That is not illegal—just subterfuge." O'Grady's rationale for his telephone method may be worth debating among lawyers, but it's doubtful if anyone could ever put a stop to it. And, certainly, he's right when he says every detective does it.

O'Grady's relationship with the Los Angeles Police Department is cautious and, in this area, only occasionally does he resemble his fictional counterparts who have continuing wars with various police lieutenants and sheriffs. O'Grady knows only too well that to get in the way of real police work, to incur the wrath of real detectives would be to restrict his abilities as a private detective. As an honorably retired policeman he is entitled, for the rest of his life, to carry a gun—and he does so. Yet he wouldn't dream of trading too heavily on his background as a cop. "My clients don't like it," he told me. "When I walk into their homes or offices

Detection by phone—"stiff calling."

to be briefed on a job, they like to see me in casual sports clothes, packing a .45 Colt, wearing good jewelry, decently barbered, shaved, and groomed. If I went there in a suit with a shirt and tie then my image would scream 'Cop'—and most people who send for a private detective do so because they can't send for a policeman. It's not that they want to do something illegal—just that they want to operate a little closer to the edge of the law than any policeman could. Most of my clients don't like police-men, but they want the experience that having been a policeman gives me. They like to know that I was a tough one, even a rogue one."

O'Grady reads detective books, and likes them. He watches detective thrillers on the television screen, and enjoys them. He's at home in Holly-wood and he claims that he feels comfortable and at ease anywhere in the world.

One day he hopes to retire, perhaps to Hawaii. At least, he talks about it, although the possibility of it really happening is remote. But what is clearly true is that he's beginning to feel bad about his work. "Sometimes, just sometimes, you get sick of all the clients and their dumb stupid problems. And you think of all the greediness, all the jealousy, of all the sickness—all the violence. And you think that they—the clients—are just using you to produce more of that—and then you get sick of your own job too.

"But I suppose that's the way any private eye is bound to feel—in real life, anyway."

THE GENERAL

THOMAS TACKABERRY

He sat in the open door of the military helicopter, his feet dangling above the scrubland, three thousand feet below. The heavy thumping of the giant rotor blades made talking impossible. The "static line" from his parachute whipped and tugged in the slipstream; the wind was 15 knots, a little too much. Earlier, while waiting for takeoff, he had told me: "I am always nervous before I jump—I always was. You wonder if there's going to be a chute failure, then you wonder if you can pull the rip cord on your chute in time, then you wonder if the reserve will work. But you have to jump, you must do it." He was fifty-four years old, the oldest man in the Division and the most senior—the General.

Major General Thomas Howard Tackaberry, hovering above the pines and sandy hills of the dropping zone at Fort Bragg, North Carolina, was waiting, along with the newest group of volunteers for the 82nd Airborne Division—America's Guard of Honor—for the jump sergeant's signal. Seconds later a scream of "Go" and a slap on his helmet pitched him, face forward, out of the open door of the helicopter. The parachute opened.

The American Army has a long history of arriving just in time to save the day, a history which goes back as far as the days of the early settlers in the West when the cavalry would gallop to the rescue, with trumpets blowing and colors flying. These days the American soldier makes his entrance no less dramatically—but usually from above. One factor has remained constant since those days—the American soldier has always been a closely integrated part of the American way of life. Even the latest twentieth-century fighting man is still the boy next door. And the leaders of the army, the generals, have always ranked high among American hero figures; ten generals have been elected President.

But despite all that, the army general in America today has to be more than a hero figure. He must defend his shrinking service from Congressional budget cuts, he must put the shine back on a military image tarnished in Vietnam, and he must train peacetime soldiers to think of war. The general officer who commands the elite 82nd Airborne Division must be part businessman, part diplomat—and all soldier. He has to be fighting-fit, instantly ready, motivated to obey—and to win. Major General Thomas H. Tackaberry is commanding officer, ultimate authority, almost godlike in his power, to 15,000 men—and it takes everything he's got to stay on top of that situation.

Earlier that windy spring day in Fort Bragg, before driving out to the parked helicopters to make the first of a number of training jumps with a batch of three hundred new recruits to the Division, he had addressed them in one of the mission assembly rooms on the camp. He is a small, wiry, taut-faced, good-looking man, appearing neat in his combat fatigues, laced-up jump boots, and the khaki canvas belt and holster carrying an inextravagant pistol. He wears his red parachute beret over closely cut hair with a little sign of gray in it. His authority and his command are obvious and three hundred enlisted men of all shapes, sizes, and colors sat nervously waiting on hard wooden chairs with several things in common: their heads were newly shaved, their first parachute jump with the 82nd Airborne was about to happen, and "the Man" himself was coming to talk to them. They had already learned, from their NCOs, the ritual greeting of the 82nd Airborne, the military version of "Good morning, how are you?" As the General swept through the door they leaped up and came swiftly to attention. The General saluted casually and used the first half of the ritual: "Airborne," he said. A bellow roared back from three hundred throats in unison: "ALL THE WAY, SIR."

"Be seated." He took his place naturally on the rostrum and spoke clearly but softly. They strained to listen. "You know that the nickname of this division is 'America's Guard of Honor' and I'm here today to tell you something about it. First we guard America's honor, that's just what we do. Think about that. This division has the mission to be prepared to go anywhere in the world, if the President desires to have ground forces present; at any time; at no notice at all. We are the ones. We are the ones ready to go. So we have to be ready today, tomorrow, or next week to get on these aircraft that are always parked right outside here, that are ready to fly off at no more than two minutes' notice. It may be the Middle East, it may be Africa, it may be the Far East. It doesn't make any difference where it is—we have to be ready to go.

"You've joined this division and now you are part of that duty. You will be trained to peak condition and kept at that peak all the time. We have

He commands 15,000 men.

The men of the 82nd Airborne
are triple volunteers.

to have good people, people we can depend on. I want you to understand that every man we have in this division—and we have fifteen thousand—every man has an important job. I don't care what your job may be, whether you are an artillery man, whether you are a medic, whether you are a military policeman, whether you are working in supply, whether you are driving a truck, whether you are firing a rifle—every man is important."

They had arrived at Fort Bragg, ten miles north of Fayetteville, North Carolina, from other units all over the United States, during the previous two weeks. They are volunteers from other parts of the American Army for this elite division. The 82nd Airborne is only one of the units contained within the vast boundaries of Fort Bragg. But the minute you join the 82nd Airborne you are made to feel that there is no other fighting force worth reckoning. The camp is thirty miles across, vast acres of sandhills and pine trees and row after row of hutlike buildings and houses. As military camps go it is considered a good posting, plenty of activity, plenty of sport, plenty of things to do.

General Tackaberry went on: "I want to tell you men that if you want to be a soldier, a good soldier, then this is the place to be. You have come to the best division in the United States Army and the best division in the world. It is a division with a great history. We are the only division in the United States Army that is parachute-qualified. We are the only division to have the mission to go anywhere in the world. As a result we get top priority, we have the best equipment—we get the best men.

"Most of you men are triple volunteers. You volunteered for the army, then you volunteered for parachute training, then you volunteered for this division. We couldn't ask for any better men than we get. Just like you men sitting right here today.

"Right now we have one-hundred-four-percent strength in our division. That may sound ridiculous to some of you, to be above one-hundred percent strength, but it is deliberate. At one-hundred-four percent strength it means that even if there are a few guys ill in hospital with broken legs or with sickness or injury, and even some guys on leave who couldn't get back in time, it still means that whenever we have to go at an hour's notice we go at one-hundred percent strength. The United States depends on us to be the quick-reaction force so we have the best men, the best equipment, and physically and psychologically we are always ready.

"Now I want you men to always wear your uniforms properly, to look sharp, to salute sharp. And I want to talk to you about saluting. Saluting is not the servile respect that you pay to officers. Saluting is a gesture that says, 'I'm glad to be here, I am glad to be in this outfit, I am glad to be Airborne,' because that's what it means. It's a military gesture and, here in this division, you will find the officers saluting you before you get a

The start of another day's training.

chance to salute them. We salute better than anyone else in the world, we wear our uniforms better than anyone else in the world, we do everything better than anyone else in the world. We run faster, we look better, and we're better soldiers. And when one of us says 'Airborne,' the other will always reply 'All the way' and it doesn't matter who says what. If you say 'Airborne' to me then I'll say 'All the way' to you or the other way around. That is the greeting between fighting men. That is the way we greet each other in the eighty-second Airborne.

"Now in a few minutes we are going to leave here and you are going to be privileged to jump from helicopters at a height of three thousand feet. This is a higher-than-usual jump and is, therefore, longer and more exciting for you. Also, if anything goes wrong with your chute it enables you to use your reserve chute. We do that so that you can stay alive to enjoy life in the eighty-second Airborne! It's an impressive experience. In other, weaker, places some people would call it a frightening experience. But for us in the eighty-second Airborne it is an expensive privilege that we give to newcomers and that we enjoy ourselves. I shall be jumping with

you. I shall jump several times today. I will enjoy it. I know you will too."
And suddenly, as if he had been turned off, General Tackaberry stopped
speaking. The silence hung in the room. He stepped back a pace from the
rostrum, snapped himself upright, looked at the men in front of him,
picking out faces, remembering one here, another there, starting the
process of getting to know the men who must serve under him, fight for
him—and may die at his command. "All the way, men," he said, sharply.
"Airborne, sir," they roared back at him.

Already the process of boosting morale, maintaining esprit de corps,
was under way. General Tackaberry, in private, may concede that the
Marines and other regiments also have esprit de corps. But the job of
military commanders is to make their men feel that they, and the officers
they serve under, belong to the best. The General told me: "This makes
my job more demanding since these men have volunteered, because they
are immensely active. There must always be plenty for them to do, otherwise they will get bored and be less than ready if we have to move. Also
they'll get into trouble. This is the toughest part of my job. It means
exercise training, athletics, competitions, parachute jumps, anything at all
to keep the men interested and at top mental and physical strength."

The army has suffered inevitable cutbacks during the period since the
withdrawal from Vietnam. So far the 82nd Airborne Division has been
unaffected by the cuts. Every man, every NCO, and every officer in the
Division, knows that this can only be true if the Pentagon also knows that
the 82nd Airborne Division is able to defend—or more to the point,
invade—at a moment's notice. In the meantime battle exercises occupy
most of the time and effort of the men of the Division; parachute-dropping
men and equipment at simulated battle zones; using live ammunition,
hurting—and sometimes killing—each other as part of this training for
instant readiness. Civilian critics and political opponents have described
the activities of the 82nd within Fort Bragg as "playing at war." The 82nd
hardly "play" at anything. And their war games are deadly serious, carried
out with admirable efficiency and leadership. The 82nd Airborne Division
is more than impressive, it is amazing.

Every day starts with a run, for every man, for every officer, for every
cook, every orderly and clerk in the Division; particularly, for the General.
The minimum run is four miles, though sometimes it will be six or seven
miles. By 7:30 A.M. the run is over, the officers and men showered, fed,
and about their military day. The General is at his desk determined to
finish administrative duties and mounds of paperwork in the first two
hours of the day, in order to allow the rest of the time for what he calls

---

The chute opened.

The oldest man in the division jumps several times a day.

"proper military activity." This means that before most American businessmen in any equivalent position of authority are at their desks, General Tackaberry has run four to seven miles, showered, eaten breakfast—usually from a paper bag at his desk—and dealt with two hours of paperwork. And this is only the start of a normal twelve-hour day. He is probably the fittest man of his age that I have ever met.

General Tackaberry earns a comparatively modest salary of a little more than $30,000 a year and he knows better than anybody in his division how uphill the work is ahead of him and his men. Restoring the image of the military, after Vietnam, is not easy in a nation where the people have turned away from war and soldiers, sometimes in disgust, often in protest. In the back of his staff car on the way to visit the divisional commander in another part of Fort Bragg he talked about this. (He served two tours in Vietnam himself, and he was decorated for valor there.) "We in the military felt that we had done what we were supposed to do, what our government had dictated we should do. If our government felt that we should come out, then we were ready to come out. If our government felt that we should continue then we would have continued. It was a very limited war and therefore we were confined to limited objectives. But there was a big controversy about what was meant by 'winning' the war. If we were to 'win' the war it meant going into the whole country and taking it over completely. And we could have done that. We could have taken over North Vietnam—our country has that capacity—but we weren't about to do that because our political leaders had told us not to.

"So that I think, for the military profession, there is every reason to feel satisfied with the job we did in Vietnam, it was the job our country wanted us to do. The fact that men were dying and we were appearing to 'lose' as far as the public was concerned was because most of the population in this country didn't understand the limited military objectives that we had been given. They weren't told. Those were tough times for us and our men. But I think history will show that the American armed forces did an exceptional job in very bad conditions in Vietnam. It was a tough war, a really tough war—and I've seen three of them."

General Tackaberry has more decorations than any general, more than most people in the army. He plays them down, shrugs off his ribbons as "luck." "Let's face it, it only happens if a man's in a place at the right time." Pressed to describe the incident which won him a medal for bravery in Korea, he told me: "Well, we had two patrols ahead of the enemy lines, each of them in charge of a lieutenant—about seven or eight men and a lieutenant in each patrol. They got into a fight with the Chinese and both of the lieutenants were wounded fairly seriously, one shot through both legs and the other shot through the eye, with a broken arm and leg. Therefore, although the men weren't leaderless and were in themselves quite resourceful they were without the really tough leadership that they needed at that moment. Daylight was coming and the men had to traverse about a thousand yards of open country with the enemy gazing straight at them, down the barrels of their guns. I could see that the men were disorganized a little and there didn't seem to be anybody there to help, so I just ran out down the slope of the hill toward them where I could get them together, organize them, and bring them back. At that time we were getting shelled pretty heavily and we needed several people to get the wounded back. Before we reached our own lines the enemy started coming over the hill toward us—which was a little disturbing. I called back to our own lines to get some stretchers out and we got the wounded in. And while that was happening I stayed there, with one corporal, and we sort of held off the enemy. And a lot of the guys managed to get away back into our lines before the corporal and I took off like greased lightning at the last moment. It was, I suppose, pretty hairy in a way." He paused for a moment. "You know, I never did find that corporal again. I wonder where he is today?

"Anyway that was the situation and if you're there, then you've got to do something because, if you're the only one that can do it, that's why you're there." It was a masterpiece of understatement which would have made any parody of the British look clumsy. I wondered if, at key moments like this, the soldier ever feels real fear, second thoughts, and regret at having plunged into the situation in the first place. The General replied: "Probably he does if he has time to think. The important thing is not to have time to think, to let the pace of events dominate you so that your training, psychological and physical, takes over. It is different, sometimes more frightening, with parachuting. During a parachute jump you *do* have time to think; while you're waiting on the ground to load into your aircraft while it flies to the dropping zone, and while you sit or stand there with the door open waiting to fling yourself out. You may think that the wind is pretty strong, that the ground is pretty bumpy, that the trees can smash you up. And you do reflect, What am I doing here? But you jump anyway. That's willpower, discipline, determination—and training."

Nowadays, outside the base the men from the 82nd Airborne Division wear their uniform with pride. It wasn't always so. Just after Vietnam most regular soldiers knew that in order to avoid fights and ugly scenes, off the base civilian clothes were safest. The army today is a volunteer army and, says Tackaberry, "It's working beautifully. We're getting the numbers of people we want and we're getting the quality. In this division, right now, eighty-eight percent of the men have a high school education, virtually

Office work is done just before dawn.

every officer has a college degree, and we are at one-hundred-four percent strength. We're sitting on top of the world."

Before commanding the 82nd Airborne General Tackaberry served as senior liaison officer in Washington. There he fought quite explicitly for the army in its battle to persuade Congress to keep up defense appropriations. His only weapons were persuasion and argument. How does a general sell the idea of a strong peacetime army—an expensive peacetime army? "All a man has to do—and I've told this to our politicians—is to watch television and observe that we have fighting going on right now in the Middle East, in several places in Africa, problems in Southeast Asia. You can just tick off the dozens of countries where they have military problems. Now, we know that if a country is weak somebody is going to move in there and take over; if you look at the statistics of history you know what is going to happen. I think it was Will Durant who said that out of the last three thousand years we've only had about two hundred sixty years when we didn't have a war going on in the world. So that's a pretty good reason for supporting and maintaining a strong army.

"Then I would tell them to look at the situation in the U.S.S.R. There, they have four-million-one-hundred-thousand men under arms. Ask yourself why they keep that number of men armed when they have no war going on. And the answer is bound to tell you that you need the American Army. If we don't have strong military forces we are bound to lose the things we have now, the things that we hold dear. We can't take that chance. So it comes back to the fact that the army is a big insurance policy. It's worth the money because we're only spending a sixth of the gross national product on our military right now. We can afford that—we're not a poor country."

The leathery, weather-beaten, and war-toughened men gathered for a lunchtime beer in the senior non-commissioned officers' mess would not only agree with their general, they would argue that he ought to take a tougher, more unequivocal line. They themselves are known as "The Hard Core," the toughest of the tough fighting men with the best qualifications—they have lived through it all. One told me: "I don't believe that Russia can beat us, that China can beat us, that anybody can beat us. Nobody actually beat us in Vietnam. We had the war won, it was just a matter of the politicians saying 'Do it'. I have the confidence that we can go in and win anywhere. The only thing that is going to stop us is the people back home here."

Another added: "Vietnam was a bad time for us, it was a tough war, perhaps the toughest. And to have your fellow countrymen hating you for fighting in it was what made it worse. I remember once coming back through a California air base, I had been wounded and I was returning Stateside for a few weeks to recover. I was brought off the plane on a stretcher and I was glad to be home. Then a little old lady, in glasses, came up to me when I was being carried through the airport on a stretcher and threw a glass of lemonade straight in my face and told me that I was a warmonger and that I should be dead rather than be home. It's that kind of thing that gives you a bad outlook, that makes you feel apart from civilians. I knew that we shouldn't be running in any popularity contest. But we did feel at the time that nobody understood what we soldiers were going through."

A master sergeant alongside him said: "The American public didn't believe in what we were fighting for and the way we were fighting. They didn't believe a word of anything we were doing. They couldn't make up their minds, why the war was costing two to three million dollars a day. At one time in Vietnam we had six hundred thousand troops and that's more than enough to wipe out the whole country in just three days—but the civilians and the politicians wouldn't let us fight that war. If it had been left to the generals and the fighting men like us we could have won it in six months."

Thomas Howard Tackaberry didn't set out to be a general. He was born in Los Angeles, California, in September, 1923, the son of a barber. At school he did well in academic subjects but excelled at sports. He wanted to be a physical education teacher; he had no thought of a military career, no belief in himself as a man to lead in battle. The soft sunshine of California is an unusual background for successful military commanders. In the past they have tended to come from Eastern, Midwestern, and Southern backgrounds tending to reflect either puritan, or more disciplined, or more dedicated beginnings. In March, 1943, Thomas Tackaberry was called into active service in the army. He served as a private soldier in various infantry and parachute units and was posted to Europe. He was commissioned second lieutenant before the end of the war and served with the Army of Occupation in Germany from November, 1945, to June, 1948. In 1948 he joined the 82nd Airborne Division at Fort Bragg in North Carolina as a lieutenant. He received his regular army commission a year later—until that time he had been on short-term commission. In June 1952 he joined the 2nd Infantry Division in Korea and served there as a company commander. He studied Italian at Monterey, California, attended the Italian war college at Civitavecchia in Italy, served on a staff of the allied forces of Southern Europe in Naples, and in various senior posts in the Pentagon. He joined the American division in Vietnam in 1969, where he commanded the 196th Infantry Brigade. After his return from Vietnam he served again in the Pentagon as chief of legislative liaison in the office of the Secretary of the Army. In October, 1974, he returned once more to the 82nd Airborne Division at Fort Bragg—to take over as the commander general. He knew, all too well, that the job he had been posted to was usually seen as a step to higher things. The men who have commanded the 82nd Airborne Division have nearly all gone on to become three-star generals. And for Thomas Tackaberry that third star is important.

A two-star general, a major general, serving a normal military career, usually retires when he reaches his mid-fifties. A three-star general is allowed to serve another five or six years. And *that* is Thomas Tackaberry's ambition. "I love the army, I know almost nothing else. This is the best life I can ever experience and I want to go on in it for as long as I can.

"I think the initial reason for my becoming a soldier was because I like the kind of life, I like working with people, and I like working out of doors and not always in an office. I particularly like the challenges. The fact is that I always felt—even when I was a young lieutenant and applied to stay on in the regular army—that we needed an army to protect our nation and to protect the free world. I wanted to be a part of all that. I don't know how else to explain it, except that it's an important job, it ought to be done, I hope I'm good at it—and I'd like somebody to allow me to go on doing it. I've been in the army thirty-three years now, and I'd like to stay in as long as they'll have me. I know many soldiers become cynical about the way the country regards them. But we are here to look after the fools as well as the wise men and we shouldn't worry about that.

"Does it make me feel more American to be a soldier serving America? I suppose it does really. I am in the army to maintain an American kind of freedom, to protect that freedom. It's the kind of freedom that allows the civilians to say and do the things that they do about the military, to hate us if they wish to. That's a very American thing and I'm proud to be part of it. So I'm proud to be American."

These days, one conflict of loyalties for any soldier, any commanding officer, comes when he has to bear arms against fellow Americans. The 82nd Airborne Division trains also for military duties that they, and the rest of America, may well hope will never happen—but it does happen sometimes. What they dislike most is when they are called to reinforce the police or the National Guard during civil riots and disturbances. The 82nd was called into Washington, D.C., in October, 1967, and again in April, 1968, to deal with the riots that followed in the wake of the assassination of Martin Luther King. And in Detroit, in the long hot summer of 1967, the men of the 82nd Airborne faced their worst civil disturbance. In that riot 40 people died, 500 were injured, 2,500 arrests were made, 5,000 people were made homeless. Tackaberry dislikes that kind of duty intensely: "If we had a choice we wouldn't want to be involved in any kind of law enforcement or anything like that. These are our own citizens, our own friends, our own brothers. We don't like this kind of mission. But we are ready for it, we'll do it if we're called upon to do it, we've been trained and prepared for exactly this kind of mission and we know how to do it well. Those who go in know exactly what they've got to do and our tactics are defensive rather than aggressive. We have special teams trained to take out snipers, for instance. My men have been taught to use only minimum force, to behave only defensively."

The 82nd Airborne Division was founded in 1917 at Camp Gordon, Georgia. Since then they fought persistently in two world wars, many minor skirmishes, in Vietnam—and in civilian crises at home in the United States. The divisional shoulder-patch has the letters "AA" under the Airborne insignia, standing for "All Americans." Previous commanders were Major General Omar M. Bradley, Major General Matthew B. Ridgeway, and many other aspiring general officers whose names were to become famous in American military history. The Division has distinguished itself in most major battles, and an impressive number of troopers have been decorated for valor—including General Tackaberry.

Historically speaking, army personnel have always been closely involved with American government. From Washington on, ten American Presidents rose to the rank of general in the army. The most famous, apart from Washington, were probably Jackson, Grant, and Eisenhower. But the army produced, as well, a collection of internationally known folk heroes. General Custer, standing alone at Little Big Horn, was probably the most written-about army general in American history. Then there were General Patton and General MacArthur who, like Custer, were controversial and to a large extent unattractive figures, but still achieved hero status in the nation. While it is interesting that America has consistently made heroes of its generals, England, since 1789, has only had one military man as Prime Minister, the Duke of Wellington, known to friend and foe as "the iron Duke." But few military leaders can match the American commanders for eccentric and colorful reputations. Andrew Jackson, veteran of the 1812 war, was nicknamed "Old Hickory" by his soldiers, as the toughest thing they could think of. General Grant was tobacco-stained, sometimes drunk, and wore a private's tunic. Theodore Roosevelt took twelve pairs of spectacles with him to the Spanish-American War because he was so shortsighted. Old Zack Taylor rode through the Mexican War swearing, as he wore and occasionally chewed on an old battered straw hat.

Today's American soldier is better educated, expects a better wage and better conditions, even fairer treatment, than in the past. He won't even necessarily obey an order just because it is an order. As General Tackaberry himself points out: "Our soldiers these days want to know more about what they're doing. We try to tell why they are doing something.

They train, in peace, for war.

The role of the leader in the army has changed. We have developed a form of leadership in which instant obedience, in battle conditions, is expected from the men, but in other conditions the men have learned that their commanders and NCOs will explain to them the reason for an order—and will even allow discussion about it. This may seem like heresy to some of the leatherneck, hardcore, NCOs with twenty or thirty years' experience, but the fact is the oldest and the toughest have proved to be among the best at adapting to this new form of leadership. It stems from education. Once you get a better-educated soldier you get a better-thinking soldier. Once you get a thinking soldier, then you get a soldier who questions what's going on around him. If you want that kind of mind to work well for you in the army then you have to allow it to work at all times."

While General Tackaberry has to train his hardened old-timers in new and heretical ways of command he also has to provide his troops with a great deal more than the simple bed, board, and training of the old days. Fort Bragg at times seems more like a giant holiday resort than an army base. In his opening address to the new volunteers the General was at pains to point out: "Now, there are lots of things to do on this post. You don't even have to go off the army post to have fun. We have three bowling alleys, three big gymnasiums, two with indoor swimming pools, there are basketball courts, weight rooms, sauna baths, tennis courts. During the summer months we have four or five outdoor swimming pools, there's a riding stable, there are auto workshops for your use, a scuba-diving club, a sky-diving club, and many other facilities. In addition we have twenty-one chaplains, twelve lawyers, divisional finance officers, doctors, dentists, and all the professional expertise that you could want. If you get into trouble outside the base, there's a lawyer here to help you; if you become ill, or have toothache, we have a doctor or dentist to heal you. If you need advice, and you can't go to your officer or your NCO, we have chaplains who are experienced in every area of trouble. If you don't want to go and see a chaplain, if you think that's soft or sissy, then go and see the Inspector General or go and see one of our lawyers. Whatever happens you don't have to feel that you've got a problem on this base that we can't help you with. You don't have to run away from Fort Bragg, you don't have to run away from the eighty-second Airborne."

Tackaberry is proud of the fact that fewer men go AWOL in the 82nd Airborne than in any other military division, although he feels that even one man absent is deplorable. "If they go AWOL too often, we'll fire them. We don't want a man who doesn't want to stay, he's rotten and that spreads among the others. But if he's likely to go AWOL because he has a problem then we want him to know that we're here to help him, counsel him if he's got trouble at home, or if he's in money trouble, or if he's being sued by outside people. We're here to look after him."

The General is, as well as commanding general, chief judge and arbitrator in his division. One of his daily tasks is to decide what action should be taken when one of his soldiers may have broken military or civilian laws. His biggest problem is drugs, an offense he detests and cracks down hard on. While I was there he had to handle one case where a man was accused of pushing four hundred tablets of LSD. He told me: "Most of our problems have been with drugs and if we didn't have any drug problem we would have almost no courts-martial here in the Division. I think the main reason the drug problem grew up is that we have become a target for the pushers and the big gangs. Every payday there is ten, fifteen million dollars paid out to the men on this base and you'll always get people trying to take that money away from them—and some will be doing it by pushing drugs. But I am still sure that we have less of a drug problem here than in any American city of a comparable size. But even if we only had one drug case, it would be one too many."

Some of the "hardcore" NCOs manage to endorse the General's new leadership approach to the educated soldier and still maintain a level of discipline in the old harsh traditions of the army. Deadpan, they explain that the men want it that way. Sergeant Major O'Neal, one of the younger NCOs but battle-experienced and tough, told me: "I'm what you would call 'a mean ass' and I don't mind being known as that. I think society has produced attitudes and ways of life in young men these days that sometimes come into the ranks of the enlisted men when they arrive as volunteers. I don't think that helps them with the rigors of army life and I think it's my job to point out that defect in their background and make sure they enjoy the real prospect—the rigors of army life—that I hold out to them. Just give me six months with any soldier, and I don't care what he's like, how educated he is, how clever he is, I'll make a soldier out of him. I haven't any time for the man who says 'Why?' when I say 'Pick up that cigarette butt.' I believe in the old standards of discipline and I believe that respect and obedience make for a proper army. I'll go along with the educated man but I won't go along with them using education to duck responsibility and to avoid discipline and I'll bet that the General will back me to the hilt in this. The worst thing for the peacetime soldier is boredom. It's NCOs like us that make sure that they don't get bored. We keep them too busy to become bored."

Another NCO said: "In the old days when men came in they were told how hard it was going to be. Nowadays they're told how easy it's going to be. I've discovered that they preferred it the hard way. Many of them have said to me that they wished that the army would go back to the regular strenuous type of training."

Thomas Tackaberry's career as a soldier marched inexorably toward the rank of general. He served with distinction at every stage of his career, but as promotion went on when did he see the rank of general ahead of him? "I don't think I ever thought about it in that way," he told me. "I never really thought, Well now, after so many years I'll become general, or, I'm going to make general or die. I don't think I started thinking about becoming a general until sometime after the Vietnam war, when I was a colonel and then some of my contemporaries were making general, some of the people around my own age. Then I thought, Well, here's this man a year older than I am and he's made general, perhaps I'm going to be considered."

Perhaps the most difficult part of any army officer's career is the strain it places on domestic life, especially for a man with a wife and family who must frequently be left to their own resources for long periods. Thomas Tackaberry has had five children, loves his family deeply, and has always found separation from them hard. "I was gone for a full year in combat during Korea and my wife was home with three sons and then later I was two years in Vietnam. It is times like that that are really rough, particularly on the wives. It is also rough on the officer but he's occupied doing his job. Nevertheless he wants to be home to help educate his sons. He wants to be there to play baseball with them and look after them and be a strength when there's illness or disaster in the family. That's the sort of thing he misses. It's particularly bad for the wife. She has to make all the decisions. She has to take care of the house, take all the children to school, she has to see to all the bills. For her it's like being a widow."

General Tackaberry's children are his pride and they are equally proud of him. One of his greatest wishes was that one or more of his sons would follow him into the army. But he insists that he never pushed any of them in that direction. Now the two eldest, twins Burt and Kief, are both captains in the U.S. Army. His third son, Tom, turned down the chance to take the examination for West Point. His father was proud of him for making his own decision. To his children Tackaberry is an old-style hero-figure and father-figure. His third son is at college and wears his hair much longer than army length. Tom cheerfully puts up with the nagging about it he gets from his father. "He's always been my hero. I've always said that if in my lifetime I can be half as successful as he has been then I'll be a success indeed." Tragically, General Tackaberry's daughter Lilian was killed in a car crash a little while ago. She was much loved and is deeply mourned by the whole family. I met her when they were all together at a family barbecue at Fort Bragg. Then she spoke of her father: "He's a very, very special man for me, he's so intelligent and humorous and he always makes me feel so good. I know this may sound soft and girlish, but

He goes to work by helicopter—seen off by his wife Lilian.

he's like a knight in shining armor to me, he's so good-looking, so calm, so sure. He's all that anybody would want a father to be."

There is no greater fan, friendly critic, or cynic about army life, than the General's wife, Lilian. Her nickname for him was "Two-star Tommy." She sends him up and loves him deeply, travels with him whenever she can, and when she can't she looks after her family and the house. She's a large, attractive, smiling blonde woman with a passion for bridge playing —which her husband doesn't share—and an understanding of the army which he respects and admires. She is a general's daughter. But Tackaberry insists: "I didn't mean to marry a general's daughter. I thought it was a distinct disadvantage, and in terms of my career, at the beginning, I'm sure I'm right. In terms of my marriage I couldn't have done better."

They met at an officers' swimming pool when he was a young lieutenant on a military base and an hour later the forceful Lilian was telling her mother, the commanding general's wife, "I've met the man I'm going to marry." At that point in time, the man concerned didn't know himself. Nor did Lilian care whether the man she'd chosen became a general or not —or even stayed in the army: "I never gave that any thought. He was just wonderful and a great person to be with. I also knew he was a very serious person and that I wanted to spend the rest of my life with him and go wherever he went. I am terribly proud of him. I'm proud of what he's done, I'm proud of what he's achieved, I'm proud of what he is." She laughed: "I've tried for thirty years to get him out of my system. But there's no way I'm ever going to. I'd rather be with him than do anything else in the world."

At home the General's life is quiet. He fights off bridge playing, watches television, does some reading, hosts dinner parties, mostly for other officers and their wives. On weekends they play golf and go for bicycle rides. Lilian has even taken to parachuting in order to be closer to her husband's work. She trained with the Fort Bragg sky-diving club and then parachuted from a helicopter, at three thousand feet, with her husband. They jumped from the helicopter hand in hand. On landing she broke her ankle. She hasn't jumped since but their sunporch is now covered with plaques from The Broken Bone Club and The Order of the Crutch.

On full training days for the 82nd Airborne the General is collected— as a VIP military commuter—from the front door of his house by helicopter. On training days the Division is more than impressive—it's spectacular. They use live ammunition, drop tons of equipment including tanks and field guns, maneuver jointly with helicopters, planes, and ground vehicles. The Division trains all the time. On one exercise when I was with him, the General parachuted twice, went without sleep for two days, and was back at his office desk at 7:00 A.M. on the third morning—after his four-mile run.

The problem ahead of General Tackaberry was the problem of promotion. Would he make three-star general? If he did, he could stay in the army, which he loves and serves fiercely, for some years longer. But promotion to three-star general is a matter of selection and, although Tackaberry denies it, the jump from two-star to three-star is also a matter of military politics. To make that jump, the candidate needs the endorsement of other generals and of the top men in the Pentagon. Although few commanders of the 82nd Airborne have failed to go on to three-star general, Tackaberry remained modest: "I'd like to be a three-star general. I think I can do the job and I'd like to go on serving longer."

A year after I first met him, Thomas Tackaberry was promoted to three-star general. He was transferred to Europe, where he is now serving as the United States representative to the permanent military deputies group in CENTO, the Central Treaty Organization. He is happy. He can continue to serve the army he loves.

THE IMMIGRANT
LEON STEIN

H
e had never visited the place, although for more than forty years he has talked about what happened there, as if he himself had been present and experienced it. Now, aged sixty-six, an American citizen, an American Jew, he stood in the middle of the decayed and crumbling Great Hall, listening, in his mind, to the noises and the voices, long since gone—echoes from three quarters of a century ago.

Leon Stein, all-American family man, trade union leader, newspaper editor, and author, a New Yorker born and bred, had come to Ellis Island on a personal pilgrimage, a return to his origins.

"I think there isn't a single day, hardly a waking hour that I do not feel aware of my immigrant origins." He spoke, softly, in the damp silence of that Great Hall; a short, plump man with a fine head of silver hair and large, liquid brown eyes, an incongruous woolen scarf knotted under his chin. "I never shed that feeling, that connection with my immigrant beginnings. Wherever I walk in this city, this big, big city, I see signs of other newcomers. I am surrounded by immigrants, and in everything that I think and do, all the judgments that I make, I am affected by their presence.

"The influences that come from within me are immigrant and arrived in this country only a generation ago with my parents. My parents came through this place, at the turn of the century. How can I stand here and not be moved?—I feel it is haunted. I think if you become really quiet you can actually hear all the crying, all the feeling, all the impatience, all the misunderstanding that went on in this hall. Being born again is not an easy thing and the people who came through here were being born again. This was their gateway to hope, to a new life. Right across the bay those tall skyscrapers must have looked fantastic and, for the immigrants, those were the towers of paradise. They didn't understand it, at the time, but what they were looking at was the East Side ghetto. That's where they were headed.

"It must have been a terrible experience; I'm proud of my parents for going through this, I'm proud of anybody who came through here. Why do you think that, even though I was born in America, I feel so close to this place? I think the people who came through here were the best, America got the best of Europe. It took such courage to make that leap. People may jump with parachutes and do other brave things these days but nothing matches tearing up your roots, working your way across Europe, getting on to a ship and heading for the unknown. I know that my father told me that when they were twelve days out of Liverpool all the people in his immigrant ship were convinced that there really was no such place as America. They thought they had all been hijacked, or that the ship was going to sink and they had no choice, they were trapped. Can you imagine what happened when they finally saw this land? My God, it must have been wonderful. Abe Cahan, the Jewish leader and immigrant author, stood at the prow of the ship, when it was near the coastline, looking for Indians. He'd read *The Last of the Mohicans* and he thought that they were still running around this part of America.

"My father often talked to me about his journey here and his arrival on this island. His adventures on the ship were really all summed up by one love affair. He fell in love with a herring. All his life he'd only ever had the tail of a herring to chew on. He'd been part of a big family and that was all that was usually left for him. But on the last day, before they reached New York, there was a party in the ship's hold given by the ship's captain and my father found himself confronting an entire herring—a symbol of wealth to him. He remembered that moment for the rest of his life. It was, for him, the symbol of America—enough to eat.

"But then there was Ellis Island to be faced. There must have been so much confusion, so much doubt, so much fear. People were turned back, you know, families were split; daughters were allowed in, parents were kept out. There were such agonizing decisions to make that few families today could even begin to cope. A million heartaches went on in this hall."

For millions of immigrants to America their first real sight of the New World was the Statue of Liberty. It represented freedom and welcome, although most of them would never discover the words inscribed on the base of the statue (itself a gift from France to the United States).

> *. . . give me your tired, your poor,*
> *Your huddled masses yearning to breathe free,*
> *The wretched refuse of your teeming shore,*
> *Send these, the homeless, tempest-tossed, to me,*
> *I lift my lamp beside the golden door.*

Dining room for detained immigrants at Ellis Island around 1900.

The Great Hall, Ellis Island—"You ca

The full poem ("The New Colossus") was written in 1883 by Emma Lazarus, a scholarly member of a wealthy New York Jewish family. The words were an accurate picture of American society and its front door until well into the twentieth century. And in the great halls and corridors of the Victorian buildings, erected on the 27 acres of Ellis Island (the island was itself constructed of three smaller islands and landfill), every day was a babel of noise and confusion, a bedlam of people. At the beginning of the century, when the pogroms in Europe caused terror and exodus among the Jews, the staff of Ellis Island were forced to handle as many as 15,000 immigrants a day.

Inspectors questioned them to see if they were criminals, or feeble-minded. Doctors and health inspectors examined them for disease. Their hopes for a new life could be shattered by the stroke of a pen or a chalked letter on their clothing. H for heart disease, E for eye disease, like trachoma. Chalk marks could divide families, split married couples, separate children. But most of them made it. In the first twenty years of the twentieth century, fourteen and a half million immigrants passed through Ellis Island. Few of them spoke English, nearly all of them were from Europe, and by far the most desperate of those millions were the Jews—escaping persecution and vilification in their own land. The Jews brought with them their own special skills and talents, and most of them stayed in New York, swallowed by the East Side ghetto. They became part of the garment industry—the rag trade. That is what happened, nearly seventy years ago, to the parents of Leon Stein.

In search of a population to work its wealth and fulfill its promise, the United States threw open its doors. Although the restrictions sometimes seemed cruel they were kept to a necessary minimum, the least inhibition which would remain a protection for the country. And the words inscribed on the base of the Statue of Liberty were true. ". . . give me your tired, your poor . . ." But President John F. Kennedy, in his book *A Nation of Immigrants* (published in 1964), commented: "Until 1921 it was an accurate picture of our society. But under the present law it would be appropriate to add—'As long as they come from Northern Europe, are not too tired, or too poor or slightly ill, never stole a loaf of bread, never joined any questionable organization and can document their activities for the past few years.'"

Ellis Island was built in 1892 as the successor to Castle Garden on the southern tip of Manhattan Island in Battery Park, and was designed originally to handle only five thousand people per day. The need for an island as an immigration control center was decided on because of the number of "escapes" from Castle Garden while immigrants were waiting to be processed. Once clear of Battery Park, in Manhattan, the crowded ghetto quickly swallowed any escapee. Nowadays, Castle Garden is gone and

Battery Park is where you line up for the Staten Island ferry. Ellis Island, abandoned and rotting, is guarded by a lonely park ranger living on its edge in a trailer, complete with a portable chemical lavatory, and supplied once a week by tugboat.

Leon Stein has nearly reached what he calls his "threescore and ten." His children have grown up, married, and left home; his wife has gone back to college, to take a degree in social work. All his struggles, and probably most of his achievements, are behind him. His mother, when she first became too old to live alone, moved into Leon and his wife Miriam's small home in Brooklyn. But she missed the company of people during the day and missed even more the sound of voices, preferably speaking Yiddish. They found her an old people's home in the Bronx.

It's a Workers' Circle home founded with International Ladies Garment Workers Union funds, for the senior citizens of the garment industry, men and women retired from the rag trade. Here they are able to live out the end of their lives in the country which most of them first came to as immigrants, surrounded by the language and the manners that they all brought with them. Many of them—indeed, most of them—suffered in the pogroms of Russia and Poland and Lithuania at the turn of the century. Among them they speak nearly every language of Europe, plus Hebrew and Yiddish—and, of course, American.

Leon's mother told him she knew the place was right for her on her first visit, when all around her she heard Yiddish spoken. Now a sprightly eighty-six, she helps look after the older folk (she doesn't confess to being old herself). She speaks on the telephone every day to her son and looks forward to his weekly visits. It is very much an American pattern, but with strong European and Jewish overtones. Leon's mother still remembers, as though it were yesterday, the day in 1908 when she left Lithuania as an immigrant, destined for America.

She was brought up in a small village. Her parents were too old to drag up their roots and try again in the New World. She was going, with cousins and friends, to join relatives already in America. She was leaving behind her parents, most of her neighbors and friends—and all of her life for the past seventeen years. With a handful of clothes, she was traveling to the nearest town by horse and cart and, from there, by train and boat to America. "I remember it clearly," she said. "The whole village turned out to wave us good-bye and we were all sitting in the cart with our little bundles on our laps and our shawls round our shoulders. I was excited a little bit, but mostly rather miserable and frightened. As the cart got to the end of the village street I could see the group of villagers who were waving us good-bye was getting smaller and smaller, but I kept my eyes fixed on my mother in the front of that little group. I didn't take my eyes off her, I hardly blinked. Then, just before the cart turned the corner and

The gateway was Ellis Island.

I lost sight of them, I saw my mother faint and fall to the ground crying and weeping, and I saw the rest of the group bend over her to pick her up, and I tried to get out of the cart and run back to her and stay with her. But the others with me in the cart stopped me and held onto me. And the cart turned the corner. And I was weeping and struggling and they were holding me. And I never saw my mother again.

"After that it was all journeying, traveling, madness and nightmares. On the boat there was a big storm in the middle of the sea and we all thought we were going to die and the captain came down into the hold and said, 'Those of you who know prayers had better say them.' So that when the storm died down the captain came and said, 'Thank you for your prayers.' Then, we landed at Ellis Island and it was frightening and noisy and I felt lost and I thought I was going to die and I didn't know what was going to happen to me, and I spent the night in Ellis Island while we were all being sorted out. But the next morning the relatives I was to stay with came to the island to collect me and they took me by ferry to Brooklyn, to stay with my cousin." She paused, and her still beautiful face lit up with what was clearly a deeply moving memory. She grinned at me. "I remember," she said, "they gave me breakfast in Brooklyn. We had kippers for breakfast. My first meal in America was kippers. It was truly, truly wonderful."

Later in the crowded Brooklyn streets she learned to speak English, began to feel American—and met, and married, Leon's father, who had come through Ellis Island from Poland a year after her. They went to live in Williamsburg, even these days one of the humblest of New York City neighborhoods and still very much a Jewish quarter; somehow European, romantic—and definitely foreign. Then it was all of those things and overcrowded too. They had a fifth-floor apartment and both of them took jobs in the garment industry—in sweatshops. (She was still working in the rag trade at seventy-seven when her children demanded that she retire.) Shortly after the birth of her two children, Leon and his sister, she and her husband split up and divorced. Her husband, who remarried later, is dead now, and so is her daughter. Only Leon remains of her family. In her late eighties she is becoming religious, visits the synagogue in the old people's home nearly every day. She told me: "I have always felt Jewish first and American second. Being Jewish is the most important thing in my life. It is because we were Jewish that we had to come as refugees from Europe. We were oppressed for being Jewish and now it is a good and happy thing to be. Also, when you grow older, the temple, the Jewish holidays, become more important to you—and more comforting for you."

Leon Stein may feel and think like an immigrant but he is completely American. If you met him anywhere in the world and asked him what he was he would reply, naturally: "I'm an American." But what makes him different from other Americans is that he is also a Jew. That fact totally affects his work, his thinking, his family life, his daily existence. He is not religious, but that doesn't matter. For Leon Stein, and six million other Jews in America like him, it is as if he belongs to two countries. The one he has been born in, the United States, and the one that his father, and all his ancestors, are part of.

Leon is cautious of the question: "Are you first a Jew and second an American?" "I am simultaneously both," he says. "I walk on one leg that says 'Jewish' and on another that says 'American.' And if I limp a little, once in a while, it's because there are times when one leg is stronger, or weaker, than the other. But I don't see any contradiction, any rivalry between the two elements of my background. I have this very strong feeling that the better I am as a Jew, then the better I become as an American. I'm not sure if that works on a vice-versa basis but I hope it does. In any case the immigrant experience is one that we have shared with the Irish, the Italians, the Swedish, the Spanish, the Chinese, and many others. When I meet a group of newcomers, whoever they are, I try to point out to them that they're not the first, that their experiences have been shared by others who went ahead.

"They must all go through this excruciating experience of accommodation, of arrival, of learning a new world, of finding a place. Others have done it and haven't been damaged by it—they became Americans. The country is just a conglomerate of all these newcomers. We are all immigrants here, descendants of immigrants, or immigrants directly. So it's part of the American character.

"The *Jewish Daily Forward* is the Yiddish-language newspaper which became the daily necessity, the bulletin, the bugle—almost the Bible—of Yiddish-speaking immigrants in this country. You know you could go to Strauss Square in those days and its name would be up in lights. It always used to impress me as a boy because the word *forward* was so positive and this was the first country in which Jews could proclaim, as loudly as they wanted, their desire to go forward. The personal advertisement columns of the *Jewish Daily Forward* were full of fascination, every entry a story in itself. It was in these columns that immigrants who had lost touch with their relatives—or even their closest family—would advertise for contact, or news: mothers hoping for information about sons; daughters trying to make contact with fathers; cousins, engaged to marry, who had somehow missed each other. It was in the columns of this newspaper that the mistakes, the partings, and the miseries that were so often part of Ellis Island would sometimes be put right. You could read the little Jewish heart-cries, written in Yiddish, as people tried to find each other—so that they could settle down in this new land of theirs."

I walked with Leon through the streets of Williamsburg to the apartment block in which he had lived as a child. Compared with many, it was almost middle class, neat, shabby rather than rough. But the street was run-down, most of the street lamps out of order. It still had very much the flavor of the ghetto. I asked him if he would have described his childhood as an "all-American" childhood. With considerable indignation, he told me: "You bet it was. It was a good childhood, too. This was my village, my town, the streets were my playground. We had a sizable gang of kids around here and we played all games that children play; dodging streetcars, kicking cans, playing with balls. I had fun growing up here. I'm sure that my parents were going through agony at the time, both of them working in the sweatshop trying to stretch every penny and dime. But on this block, as children, we were able to find any kind of adventure, any kind of color that we wanted.

The *Daily Forward*—a story in every personal ad.

He lived as a child in Williamsburg.

"We had a mountain on this block. It arrived every lunchtime, when little Willy Bratlov's father came home to have lunch and take a little snooze. He would park his horse-drawn wagon, stacked high with beer barrels, right here in front of the apartment block. We kids would gather around and, if Willy was in a good mood, he would let us climb to the top of that mountain, over all the barrels. Once we had an avalanche when one of the barrels slipped and came thundering down. Nobody was hurt, not by the barrels at any rate, but Willy Bratlov's father would have liked to hurt us—if he could have caught us. We even had a whole scout troop here. My cousin Joey, who was working for his Eagle Scout badge, came home one weekend and said he was going to organize all the kids to take a hike. Now where the heck can you take a hike when you live in a concrete jungle like Williamsburg? But Joey had it all worked out. We had about fifteen kids in the apartment block and ten across the street so one way or another he had about two dozen kids and he organized them to meet on Saturday morning. And we all stood out here in front of the apartment block with our haversacks and our bedrolls and our tents and our equipment and he blew the whistle and said: 'Ready men, follow me.' And we marched off. We followed Joey down the block with all our mommas and poppas hanging out of the windows and waving to us. And we marched all the way down the avenue and we came to Bridge Plaza and we marched all the way around Bridge Plaza and back up the other avenue into the block. It took about two to three hours. We were sweating, tired, grimy. We were carrying our knapsacks and little brown paper bags.

"But instead of dismissing us and letting us go back into our apartments he marched us right through the tunnel and down the side passage alongside the apartment block into the back yard. You've seen that back yard. It's about forty feet long and twelve feet wide and nothing but solid concrete. Never mind, we pitched camp right there, right on the concrete. It was a bit of a problem, how to keep tents down, but we found stones to do it. We sat around in the tents that night and we made a meal and we told each other stories about Africa, stories about lions and tigers. And we discovered one small spindly tree there, so that was our forest and we studied the tree. And we saw wild animals when Joey picked up a slab of concrete and we saw all the grubs underneath. During the night it rained a little and the sound of the rain on the canvas was very exciting. Some kids cried and one kid was just a little too nervous and we had to hand him out of the tent through the rear window to my Aunt Anna, who was the janitoress of the block. She took him to the lavatory and he did what he had to do and then she handed him back out of the window and we took him back into the tent and he felt able to face the African jungle all over again. And we heard the wind whistling all night and in the morning we played Reveille on the bugle and we got up, rolled up our bedrolls, and folded our tents.

"And I looked up from that back yard at the high slab sides of apartment buildings all around us and I saw a sight that I don't think I'm ever going to see the likes of again. There, on two rows of fire escapes at every window level, were all the poppas in their undershirts. They had slept out on the fire escapes all night long—like protective guards hovering over our camp. What a night that was. Anyway, we broke camp and we marched out front again and we reversed the entire circle. We marched down the block and around Bridge Plaza and back again and when we got back to the apartment block, all the mommas and poppas were waiting to welcome us as though we'd been away on a safari. And we *had* been away on a safari. We were American kids behaving like Americans—using our imagination. But since then, I have realized that for all our mommas and poppas, who entered into the spirit of the thing so well that most of them were moist-eyed about it, it was something else, something very special. Here they were, immigrants (most of whom had fled from persecution to this country) watching their kids behave like Americans—freely, without anybody threatening, without anything to fear. And the important thing for those parents was to realize that their kids were no different from anybody else in America; no better, no worse—but the same. That is what those people had trekked across Europe for—to find that.

"At the same time America was in the economic doldrums, the exploitation of labor was fearful and my father was having a terrible time. He was just getting by making a living working twelve to fourteen hours a day. And he was suffering like a coal miner suffers, because in the sweatshops, at that time, instead of coal dust what you got was lint. Lint got down the throat and into the lungs and caused the same coughing, the same diseases, the same sickness as dust. And in the end it killed you. And in the end it probably was what killed him.

"I remember, at that time, I used to come home from school with books from the little library around the corner, it was really a beautiful library. I would come home with a volume of Dickens or Jules Verne and I would have to fight my father, tired though he was from the sweatshop, for who should read the book first. On his way to America he had stopped in England in order to get the boat from Liverpool as so many immigrants did. It was there that he had learned about English writers. But he still wanted to live in America. He never became rich, he never became successful—and he never became bitter. There was never any disillusion with America in him; even though he took the worst the country had to hand him, he knew that he was better off than he would have been in Poland. Remember, he had come from a place where, if you were Jewish, you didn't count as a human being and you had no rights, you had no rights at all. In America they gave my father the vote, they allowed him a place to live, and they let his children grow up as Americans. Because of that he could never feel bitter or disillusioned.

"Later on when my father saw me go into the union, and become a union organizer and a union leader and then, finally, the editor of the union paper, I knew I had made him proud of me. From time to time I'd hear him use phrases like, 'my son the writer,' 'my son the editor.' He never said much about it and, to this day, my mother has never said much about it. But I know they're both proud of me. But what I also know is that I have achieved their immigrant ambition for me. I am all American and wholly conscious of my immigrant origins. What more could they hope for, what more could any immigrant to this country want?"

Leon Stein did well at school but not so well that he could stay at school. By the time he was old enough to work his parents' marriage had broken up and his mother was struggling to keep Leon and his sister. Leon Stein went out to work, he wanted to, there was no question of anything else. He, too, went into the rag trade. He wanted to become a cutter, one of the most talented of the craftsmen in any garment shop. He wanted, as well, to join the union. Shortly after he entered his first garment factory, the union organized the shop and brought them out on strike. Leon Stein was in the union; out of work—but in the union. By the time the shop went back to work he was already a passionate and active union member. At work, just before the strike, he met Miriam, courted her during the strike, and married her when they were back at work. Her parents had come to America from Poland at their own expense, comparatively wealthy middle-class immigrants. They felt that Leon Stein was perhaps too common and uppity for their daughter. Leon Stein was certainly uppity, and wouldn't take no for an answer. He won.

He became a union organizer, studied nights at City College in New York (and in time received his Bachelor of Science degree). In those days —the late '20s and early '30s—organizing a union was a sometimes dangerous, some would say foolhardy, business. Pickets would be clubbed by rowdies hired by angry employers, there were no funds to pay striking workers, little sympathy from the rest of America. The garment workers were harder to organize, in one sense, than shipbuilding or auto workers or the miners. It was largely an immigrant industry, using an immensely high proportion of female labor. And many employers were immigrants too.

In the early days Leon Stein traveled hundreds of miles from New York speaking, organizing, signing up union members. On occasion they were

Leon and his mother—she came through Ellis Island.

chased out of town. Eventually Leon was offered a job on the union newspaper, *Justice.* In time, he became its editor. Today he is the first editor emeritus. The paper and its staff have won a fistful of awards for campaigning journalism, for design and layout. It has become respected and influential. It is not unusual for the paper to solicit, and achieve, signed articles from leaders of the nation—even the President. Kennedy once wrote an article for them. By making Leon Stein editor emeritus both sides of the arrangement have indicated that they don't want to part company. It gives Leon more time to write and edit the books which have been increasingly filling his life for the past ten or fifteen years; books on work, labor, race, immigrant life. His latest book, *Out of the Sweatshop,* is a chronicle of union battles, from before his time. But he himself remembers selling the union paper on the streets and in the commuter trains. In the days when he was first made editor it was printed in one language only, English. Now *Justice* is printed in Chinese, Spanish, Portuguese, and all the languages of all the new immigrants, laboring in the rag trade and swelling the ranks of the International Ladies Garment Workers Union.

The aim of the ILGWU is to protect its members, secure proper working conditions and wages, and further the best interests of the industry— including, they say, employers. They are not motivated, says Leon Stein, as are trade unions in Great Britain and Europe, to bring about the public ownership of industry—a workers' takeover. Leon says: "In the ILGWU we expect employers to behave like employers. We don't squeal about their prerogatives but we expect our rights. We don't tell them how to run their business and we hope that they have the good sense to run a prosperous business, so that we can get decent wages out of them.

"But in this country the situation is quite unambiguous. You can only have collective bargaining if you have management *and* labor. We are labor and we don't want to be management. In this industry, there has been some ambiguity. But it isn't a problem because we all understand it. A man who was a worker on a machine one day could become an employer the next. But usually with a little, two-by-four, peanut kind of establishment with just six machines and a cutting table. And good luck to the man. But usually he was broke the year after he started and back at the machines, as a worker. We would welcome him back into the union. We would have welcomed him when he was an employer and bargained with him for conditions and he would be just as useful to us back in the union, as a worker. After all, this has got to be a unique union in one way.

"Take the situations where we bargain with the employers for wages. Invariably you have Jews on one side of the table who are the employers, and Jews on the other side of the table, who are the union. They're all speaking the same language, they all understand the same industry. I'm still proud of the fact that I was one of the best cutters in the business

He started as a cutter.

He joined the union "with joy."

before I became the union man. I don't know any union man who wouldn't joyfully go back to his craft if he had the opportunity."

These days the ILGWU is fighting the sweatshops again—foreign sweatshops. Fearful for the future of the industry which supports its members, they are moving to protect domestically made clothing against imports from the East, from where—because of very much lower wages—a price-cutting war could even drive the American rag trade out of business. But on Seventh Avenue—recently renamed Fashion Avenue—the skyscrapers are still devoted to the rag trade; a vertical industry with a different factory on nearly every floor, threatened, now, by fashion wear from Asia.

In fighting back, the union started its own campaign of radio and TV commercials—"Look for the union label." This catchy jingle and its amateur but energetic presentation captured the attention of the American public. All the singers were union workers. All the results were good for the bosses as well as the workers. "Look for the union label" has become a catch phrase. Leon told me: "We have surveys which have corroborated that this has been a splendid campaign. We're now doing it for a second year. People have told us how much they love the jingle and the people who do it on television. We think there's a very special reason for that. All the singers are members of this union, workers straight out of the shops, and they're really singing from their hearts and I think that sincerity communicates itself. They're singing for their jobs too, singing for their families. The important thing to remember about it all is that when you look at that commercial on television you see black people or Spanish people, Chinese people, Jewish people, European people—all the members of the ILGWU, all immigrants. It's this union of ours that has taken more immigrants than any other organization in America has and molded them into good Americans.

Leon Stein's enthusiasm was even matched by the trade press. When the jingle was first released it was reviewed as follows: "So how's business? —Don't ask. So if business is bad? —Write a jingle." And: "Union label is boffo on Tin Pan Alley." The jingle is even going to be published in a new book, *Great American Songs of Madison Avenue.*

It may be top-of-the-charts time for the ILGWU these days, but it wasn't always that way. When the International Ladies Garment Workers Union was first formed they found it an almost impossible struggle to get any real support and enthusiasm from the workers and a more-than-impossible task to persuade the employers and city authorities that better wages and working conditions were a minimal necessity—not a greedy demand. It took a tragedy—a disaster which shocked the conscience of the nation— to bring about a real change in the face of the whole industry. That tragedy became known as the Triangle Fire. There can hardly be a single worker in the rag trade who hasn't heard of it. Certainly Leon Stein had, but he hadn't paid it enough attention until, some years ago, he became obsessed with searching out and interviewing any survivors from that disaster. For years he researched, and listened, and then, eventually, published *The Triangle Fire.*

I went back with him to the corner of Washington Square and Green Street, where the disaster took place. He told me: "It happened on Saturday, March twenty-fifth, nineteen eleven. A Saturday was just another working day for people in sweatshops. Although for most people in sweatshops it was the Sabbath, that didn't matter, it was another day at the machines. The Triangle Shirtwaist Company—they made those rather attractive blouse-type garments that hang down over the hip and which have become so fashionable again recently—occupied the top three floors, the eighth, ninth, and tenth floors of a new building. It was only ten years old, it had been completed in nineteen hundred one and was advertised as being fireproof. On this particular Saturday the work day was nearly over, it was about five o'clock and the whistles and bells had rung to mark the end of the day. Five hundred or so workers, most of them women, were getting their things together and just about to leave when fire broke out.

"The fire began on the eighth floor and it burned for what the firemen say is some considerable time—that's actually just a matter of minutes. But the fire didn't then go to the ninth floor, it leaped to the tenth floor so that in a matter of minutes the people on the ninth floor were encased with fire below them, and fire above them. Now the doors to the fire escapes of this building were locked. It had been the practice of the employers to keep the doors locked in order to stop workers knocking off a few minutes early and sneaking away—and also because the union had come banging on these doors trying to unionize the shop and recruit members. Nearly all of the people trapped by the fire, which within a few minutes was an inferno, were women and girls. There were some men there. There was one particular foreman there, I'll swear he must be the bravest son of a gun that ever lived. He was called Bronstein and apparently he stood at the door pushing and shoving women through while the flames were coming closer and closer. On the eighth floor some tried to get out and did. On the tenth floor some tried to get out and did. But on the ninth floor there was no exit—except through the windows or down a rear escape. Eventually they kicked the exit door open and crowded onto the fire escape. It collapsed. Then, there was no exit at all. And the flames got worse. The crowds gathered below as the fire brigade and firemen arrived with the very latest equipment and the latest ladders. But even the longest ladder the firemen had still stopped three or four floors short of that ninth floor.

"And the women and the girls began to jump. At first nobody knew quite what was happening. They thought bundles of clothing, rags with

sparks coming out of them, were hurtling to the ground below. The sidewalk around the building was composed of glass deadlights. The bodies hit those glass deadlights with such force that they crashed right through to the basement. (Days later relatives were still trying to identify some of the victims.) Some of the girls tried to jump for the ladders—and missed. Some tried to jump into outstretched arms below—and missed. They came smashing down through the deadlights, with their hair on fire, with their dresses on fire.

"And, in the end, a hundred and forty-six died by jumping, by asphyxiation, some even by drowning from the hoses.

"I became deeply interested, almost obsessed, with the story in nineteen fifty, when I was preparing a documentary history for the union. So I worked for four and a half years and interviewed all the survivors that I could find. It took me weeks sometimes to check out an individual name. I managed to speak to twenty-six who were still alive. Some of them wanted to forget. But for most of them who had survived, there was the feeling that they could never forget it. One old woman told me that she had dreamed about it every night of her life since then. So I wrote it all down. And then I had to find a publisher and that took time as well. But eventually I did and it was published. I don't suppose it's sold in vast numbers. But I found it necessary to write it and I think it is important that someone did. And somehow it made all those early days, in Baltimore and Virginia, when Miriam was pregnant with our son Walter, and we were trying to organize the union in towns like Hancock and Baltimore, when we would get run out of town, or refused a place in motels, or threatened, and menaced, seem worthwhile. Somehow writing that book about the Triangle fire put all of my own experiences into perspective—made them seem nothing."

Leon continued: "What this tragedy did was to dramatize—at a terrible cost to the whole country, indeed the whole world—what government has a responsibility for. It made certain that no city authority, or government, dare turn away from factory working conditions in the future. It brought into being a debate about the length of the working day, about the use of children in heavy industry, about positioning of fire escapes, about proper conditions. The death of those girls made the future of the union more secure."

I asked him if it was difficult to persuade new immigrants, in those early days, to join the union. Didn't they sometimes feel that they were being invited to cooperate in a militant organization, against the country that had welcomed them as immigrants? Leon said: "My dear friend, no trade unionist, not even a new one, sees joining a union and building its strength as an attack upon the country in which he lives. Indeed, it's quite the opposite. He sees it as improving the country. And as for persuading young girls and women to join, they were among the first to come in and

239

they came in with an enthusiasm and with an energy that could sometimes have a greater impact than the men. The men were frequently exhausted at the end of the day, unable to make good union material. But the women had almost limitless energy. For the men in the sweatshop it was as Dante described the entrance to hell, you forsook all hope when you entered. The men went into sweatshops and—sometimes—came out horizontal, because it was a place of disease and exploitation, it sucked the blood, almost literally, out of their bodies. But when a young woman went in she had hope. It was a kind of hope that kept her going. She would hope that somewhere there would be a Prince Charming, there would be some handsome fellow who would come along and rescue her and take her away from this thing. No girl entering a sweatshop visualized herself as staying in that shop forever, the way a man, the breadwinner, had to. Ironically, though, many of the women remained in the shop very often for a long time—even a lifetime. They became what we call in the trade *alten mädchen,* old maids, very lovely people. Prince Charming never came along for them."

These days, members of the ILGWU are more likely to be Chinese or Spanish than Jewish or European. Leon Stein is frequently asked to speak to new groups or to fresh members, newly arrived as immigrants and newly joined as garment workers. I went with him when, through an interpreter, he addressed a roomful of Chinese men and women. He said to them: "You have become part of a family, a family composed of all kinds of people who came to America to make a better life for themselves. And what I want to say to you is remember your own heritage, remember your heritage is Chinese because it's very precious and you must hang on to it and maintain it. But, at the same time, make every effort, through this union, through the educational system of this country, to make yourselves better Americans. I am now in my fiftieth year as a union member and I've done service for the union for forty years. Between the time when my parents came here, some seventy years ago, and now when you're coming into the union, people have come from every country in Europe, from Asia, from Africa. And in this union we all become one family.

"Work has no color. Pay has no national origin. So in this union we are all equal and we fight for the same thing, we fight for a better life and we do it through the union. So, I say to you as new members, remember, first of all, your heritage is Chinese, which is precious to you; but then, through this union, help make a better America for yourselves and for your children and for all of America."

Afterward he explained to me why he speaks as he does to new union members: "This union is a product of immigrant hope, immigrant idealism, the belief and faith that what we can't win for ourselves today, we will achieve for our children tomorrow. It is a basic faith in this country that

New immigrants today are likely to be Chinese.

exists nowhere else except in a trade union such as the ILGWU. This union is building better human beings, better Americans. If you think about it carefully you'll realize that this is the only institution in which many of them can learn to say no. They come from countries where all they've ever been allowed to say was yes, yes. In this country at union meetings they've learned the word no. They've learned the power of the vote, which many of them have never had in their lives before. We teach them, here, how to vote; not who to vote for, but how. Hours are spent in these headquarters teaching newcomers the meaning of a ballot, something some of them haven't even known about in the past. This is the Americanizing process, this is where immigrants are turned into Americans—and allowed never to forget their immigrant origins."

I wondered if, as a young, still unmarried man, Leon had thought only in terms of marrying a Jewish girl. He said: "I suppose all my instincts were pointed that way. If for no other reason than comfort. There is an inherited, a transmitted, Jewish milieu, made up of attitudes and routines, and speech, which makes you feel comfortable. It would be difficult and very uncomfortable to marry somebody who hadn't been brought up in that atmosphere and didn't have those patterns, so I suppose you're right to believe that I thought in traditional Jewish terms about marrying 'a nice Jewish girl.' "

Miriam is more positive about being a Jew. She told me: "I've never kept a particularly orthodox home, certainly not a kosher one. But I was always frightened to let my parents know and if I heard my father coming up the garden path to visit us, at the weekend, I would quickly rush around the kitchen and take all the bacon out of the fridge and throw it in the garbage can. And with the children I was very concerned that they should go to synagogue and Sunday school. I wanted them brought up Jewish, I wanted them to know the history of the Jews and to identify strongly with it. I certainly wanted them both to marry Jews and to have Jewish children. I think it is to do with the Second World War and what happened to the Jews. I somehow felt that if the Jews in America started assimilating too much they would disintegrate as a race and then it would be almost as though Hitler had succeeded in annihilating the Jews by assimilation rather than slaughter. And when the question of Israel as a nation came up I thought we should all support it, become Zionists, even.

"I brought the children up to believe this very strongly. So when Barbara started going out with a gentile, I was really very worried indeed. And when she assured me that Scott wanted to convert she told me, 'Never mind, Mother, you're not losing a daughter, but the tribe is gaining a Jew.' And remember, being Jewish isn't an evangelistic thing, it's very difficult for somebody to convert. Yet I have to say that I accepted it very quickly because I knew, as a Jewish mother, I would feel happier if my daughter was married to a Jew, even a recently converted one. I've never really talked to him about why he converted, perhaps it's because I would be frightened to discover that he only did it as a way of marrying Barbara. Well, of course he did it as a way of marrying Barbara—I'd be a fool to think anything else. But somehow now I like to think that he might have wanted to become Jewish as well; however foolish that thought is I like to think it. He says he enjoys it."

Leon and Miriam Stein traveled to Israel and returned impressed and moved by what they found there. For Leon, working on his books, and for Miriam, studying in night classes for her sociology degree, being Jewish has become increasingly more important in their lives. But Leon worries that he is unable with logic to accept a faith which, like most religious beliefs, requires some suspension of logic. He would like to, but he can't. He told me: "The humanist strain in me is so strong that I used not to worry at all about not being what some people are pleased to call a practicing Jew, not to worry about my failure to practice the rituals and the ceremonials and the regular attendance at a place of worship. But now I do worry that I find it difficult to make what has been called a leap of faith. Many people urge religion upon me and tell me that I have to believe. And when I tell them I cannot understand why I have to believe they reply that it is because I cannot understand that I should believe, that the act of belief is beyond the question of understanding. It would, therefore, seem impossible to achieve heaven through logic. But logic has been the most important thing in my life and if I cannot get there that way I'll have to find some other route, because I really cannot subscribe to ritual or to magic."

Nevertheless, Leon admits to what he calls "close scrapes." In Israel, he and Miriam visited "the Wall." The atmosphere nearly overwhelmed them. "As I stood there a young rabbi came over to me and said, 'Do you want to pray?' And I told him I didn't know how. So he said, 'I'll show you how,' and he took me close to the Wall and he put on the phylacteries for me, which he wound around my arm and which ended up with the little box on my forehead. Now I'd seen medieval pictures of this thing but I had never thought the day would come when I would stand at the Wall like that. The rabbi put his arm around me and made me put one hand on the Wall and I felt the coldness, the spirit in that Wall and I started to shake and when he said the first few words I couldn't repeat them, I was shaking so hard. And I just got through the prayer with him—and for those few minutes I was a member of the tribe, I was right in there with the most religious of them. Four or five minutes later I was able to step back from myself and say, 'For God's sake, Stein, what is happening to you here? That's not you, that's silly . . .' But you know what did happen was important and fundamental. A few days later I would say to myself, well, I'd better go back and read William James on *The Variety of Religious Experience,* there must be some explanation for this thing, the atmosphere, the mumbo-jumbo, the hocus-pocus, I can explain it as an anthropologist or a sociologist. But the experience was genuine and moving.

"And being Jewish is important to me. I'm not sure I could ever make myself part of one of those extremely orthodox Jewish communities who are steeped in the Talmud, although I have tremendous respect for them. But I do believe that being Jewish is the answer to many of the questions that Jews in America might have. If I ask myself sometimes how it was possible for a wandering people—who only occasionally sat down in one country or put their bedrolls down in another country—to survive for two thousand years of history without a place, a physical place, that they could call their own, then I open up an inquiry for myself about Jewishness. And I've come to the conclusion—I don't suppose it's an original conclusion at all—that the real country of the Jews is the country of the mind. They have taken the basic legal structure provided by the Old Testament and through generations of wise men and teachers they have elaborated a tremendously complicated structure of directives, blessings, bindings, ethical goals—a whole little universe of the mind, a mental universe that is self-contained and portable. Never mind whether you are in Yugoslavia or Spain, what you carry with you, what all Jews subscribe to is the belief that you're natives of that same country—the country of the mind. You know and understand that all Jews have suffered and that you have suf-

A Jewish family meal for Leon Stein.

fered with them and you've endured, in whatever country has played host to you, the privation and the afflictions of the ghetto, the anger and the hostile attitudes but, still, you've carried with you the teachings of the wise fathers. It is the boundaries of that country in your mind that protect you and look after you.

"Just think of the Talmud and those teachings. When I look into that area, when I think about it, I find all sorts of wonderful things in there. Those teachings will tell you how to open an egg, how to buy a chicken, how to get a divorce, how to live your daily life. But the teachings will also tell you what it means to be a righteous man, how to pursue justice, how to behave in the treatment of animals, how to employ servants and how to respect those who labor for you.

"You know, years after I first read the Talmud, I examined a document called 'The Protocol of Peace,' which settled the heartbreaking strike of the cloakmakers in nineteen hundred ten, and I found elements of those ethical teachings embedded in the first collective agreement of the garment industry. It said, in effect, there are things which you mustn't do to a human being because you reduce him to animal status, reason must prevail and humanitarian attitudes must be paramount. In The Protocol of Peace all of this was written down exactly as it had been in the Talmud. As a Jew, if you couldn't settle a dispute reason must prevail, so you took it—in the old days—to the rabbi. In The Protocol of Peace, within the industrial frame of reference, you took it to an impartial chairman.

"You know, that damned agreement was promulgated—the first of its kind—by Jews sitting on both sides of the table, ten on one side, bosses; and ten on the other side, union men; all of them raised in the same spirit of the Talmud.

"I think when I retire I'll take time out to try and explore that little country of the mind. To try and be a better Jew."

THE FILM STAR

JODIE FOSTER

At fifteen she looks like many other California teenage girls, freckled, a little on the plump side, smiling. She is accomplished on the skateboard and spends hours listening to pop music. But she is also an international film star, able to earn a million dollars a year as an experienced actress. Jodie Foster may be following in the footsteps of Shirley Temple, Judy Garland, Jackie Cooper, Mickey Rooney, Margaret O'Brien, Elizabeth Taylor—and scores of other precocious and glamorous child-star wonders—but she's doing it in her own way, yet still measuring up to the more demanding and critical standards that exist today.

Hollywood, perhaps more than any other place, has been responsible for celebrating American archetypes; I wonder how well known American cowboys, Indians, soldiers, or detectives would have become without the movie industry. And in the fifty years or so since the movie industry really began to flourish, Hollywood has not only perpetuated the archetypes of the country, but it has created one of its own—the film star. The public has always paid money to see stars. Their names become household words; their lives, their loves, their salaries are objects of fascination and envy for millions.

Hollywood also created the child star. And for many of the youngsters who were catapulted, emotionally unprepared, into the limelight, it became a place that exploited and destroyed, twisted and hardened. Few child stars made it beyond the gooey and sentimental roles in which they were cast to elicit easy laughter and easier tears from movie audiences. Some did, but just a handful who were able to leave their child-size handprints in the wet cement in front of Grauman's Chinese Theatre and then return as adults—still successful, still stars. Today the same risks apply, little has really changed. Many try and are forgotten but a few make it to the top and stay there.

Like their adult counterparts, the child stars of today have to face audiences that have become more discerning; the "Jodie Fosters" of this world have to be better at their craft than their forebears. If they work hard, the rewards are proportionally no less glittering than they ever have been in Hollywood—and the pressures just as tough. Avaricious and propulsive parents, greedy and demanding agents, insensitive and ambitious directors, uncaring, money-conscious producers, are just a few of the Hollywood-jungle creatures that—far too often—may be found gathered around the glamorized, and money-making, talents of child stars.

Jodie Foster may manage to avoid all these things. Her mother may be propulsive, but she is also protective. And Jodie herself is probably more expert at summing up, and dealing sharply with, agents, producers, directors, writers, and the whole noisy, grasping carousel of Hollywood hangers-on than many actors three times her age. At fifteen she has already won an Academy Award nomination for Best Supporting Actress for her role as a twelve-year-old New York street prostitute in *Taxi Driver;* has won acclaim in *Bugsy Malone,* a film about gangsters acted entirely by children; has starred in *The Little Girl Who Lives Down the Lane,* in which she plays a child murderer. Between times she has continued to perform in the slightly sugary Disney films which first brought her to the attention of the moviegoing public. She has also appeared on most of the top late-night television talk shows—and actually hosted one of them. She has received two British Academy Awards; picked up other awards in France and Italy; secured the admiration of directors and fellow actors; even captured the hearts of a toughened group of French journalists by conducting a press conference in their language. Now she wants to learn to drive.

Interviewing Jodie can be an alarming experience. It is hardly just talking to a teenager—she is a highly intelligent girl, clearly observing the Hollywood around her. But at the same time, she *is* a teenager—so what part do teenage things play in her life? It is possible, too, that Jodie Foster has already been interviewed many more times than most interviewers dare consider. "You must have heard all the questions before?" I suggested. "Yes, I have," she demolished me and added, with the perfect timing that has become a characteristic of her acting performances, "Well, only most of them." She grinned and pushed her straight blond hair back from her forehead, a gesture she repeats constantly.

It is reassuring, at least, that her favorite words are "gross" and "dumb," part of the familiar slang of teenagers. But then she upsets

She could be any Californian teenager.

type-casting by using them with a shrewd perception beyond her years. She is, very probably, the most talented newcomer in the film-acting world at the moment. Helen Hayes and David Niven believe that she may be a genius. Jodie herself doesn't accept that at all. All she will concede is: "You shouldn't act unless you have gigantic talent and you want to."

She accepts her own talent as casually—she has never had an acting lesson in her life—as she accepts her own looks. She has blue eyes, straight hair, a gap between her teeth, and she reveals a small teenage vanity by worrying that her nose is too big. But when I told her I thought she looked pretty anyway, she made another concession to her youth—she blushed. She never has any trouble learning lines, she speaks French like a native and attends the Lycée Français in Los Angeles, in between tutoring on location and at the studio. She seldom looks in the mirror before going on the set, scorns the use of any makeup unless it is specifically called for in the script, and fights off her mother's constant injunctions to lose weight and get more sleep. She is, therefore, rounded and does have light purple circles beneath her eyes. Her screen career has climbed steadily, almost a parody of the child-star success story.

Her discovery is a Hollywood classic. At the age of eight, her older brother was auditioning for a commercial when Jodie, then three, followed him into an interview—and got the job instead. It was a Coppertone commercial and Jodie's face—and half-naked bottom—launched her toward a whole series of commercials; by the time she was six she had made fifty. Her mother, whose real name is Evelyn but who calls herself "Brandy" (just as Jodie's real name is Elisia, "but she looked more like a Jodie"), was a Hollywood publicist. Her marriage broke up a few months before Jodie was born, leaving her with the task of supporting four children. She used her knowledge of Hollywood and the good looks and talents of her children—and she used both well. These days she is quickly, and unnecessarily, defensive, anticipating the criticism that she exploited her children and that she is making money from Jodie. This kind of charge is, in any case, something of a tabloid cliché these days and certainly doesn't stand close examination as far as the Foster family is concerned. To meet Jodie is to become aware of a very cool and level-headed young lady, certainly not a high-strung, exploited teenager who may be suffering emotional damage. I suspect that, more often than not, it is Jodie who is the steadying influence in her mother's life, Jodie who probably comes up with the mature advice and cautionary injunctions.

Nowadays Jodie works around the world, in multilingual films, and travels with her mother as companion and manager and—invariably during the school year—with a tutor. At the Lycée Français her quick mind and phenomenal memory enable her speedily to catch up on lessons missed, all of which are conducted in French. Next year she sits for the

Brandy Foster, guardian of Jodie's interests

baccalauréat, an examination that strikes terror in all French teenagers. She and her mother live with a pet Yorkshire terrier and a collection of noisy pop music in a small, unpretentious house in North Hollywood. Both of them resist the Bel Air and Beverly Hills life-style that Jodie's acting fees could provide, if they wished. Her money is held for her and administered by her mother, who is fiercely unresponsive to questions about it. But, equally obvious, nobody seems to have "leeched" on to Jodie Foster's earnings. It is also not possible to find a critic of Jodie. Her talents may be precocious but her manner is not. She is engaging, simple, refreshing—and attractive. She doesn't play the little girl. "I don't like to wear dresses very often unless a part calls for it," she told me. "I prefer to be in jeans, sweaters, and jackets. I have a huge collection of tee shirts which is my particular pride. I don't worry about the future, I just like acting."

"I don't think of myself as a star. I certainly don't think of myself as a child star. I'm just an actress playing child parts. And then, when I'm older, I'll be an actress playing other parts. I think I want, eventually, to be a writer—even a director. But I think I would like to do that and act too. The most stimulating man I have ever worked with has been Martin Scorcese, who cast me in *Taxi Driver* as the child prostitute. He is a quite amazing man. He chews his fingernails, scratches his head, pulls his shirt

She wants to be a director and make her own film.

252

out, worries and worries and worries. But he does let you work out the part yourself; he's an actor too, you know. He worries so much about moviemaking that at the end of every movie he winds up in the hospital with ulcers. But I've enjoyed working for him more than anybody else. Actually, I don't think I've had a director that I haven't enjoyed working for. Alan Parker, who chose me for *Bugsy Malone*, was marvelous. He was fun to be with every moment on the set, he was just crazy."

She advanced on a criticism before it was voiced. "People who worried about me playing a prostitute are just dumb. It's gross to think that playing that part would have harmed me. There was a lot of stuff printed in the newspapers and a lot of journalists came around trying to make my mother and me say that playing a prostitute would affect my stability as a teenager. But, after all, we live just several blocks from Hollywood Boulevard and what do you think I see every time I go downtown with my mother to visit a drugstore, or go shopping, or buy a meal? There are many child prostitutes in this city and child prostitutes in New York, too. That is a fact of life. And playing the part of a prostitute doesn't mean that I run the risk of becoming one or I am exposing myself to danger and damage. But everybody made a dumb fuss about it all. The Board of Education lady here in Los Angeles made my mother take me to a psychiatrist to see if playing the part would affect me. And of course the psychiatrist said it would not. So finally they let me play the part." Then she disarmingly revealed one of the behind-the-scenes secrets of filming *Taxi Driver.* "In the scenes which were really sexy they made my older sister Connie stand in for me. She's got a sexier body than me. And, if you want to know, it's her body that is seen from the back naked in *The Little Girl Who Lives Down the Lane.* Mind you, I didn't like that. I could have played the part myself. But I can understand that they would want to get my older sister to do it so that no one could attack the film or the filmmakers for exploiting me." She paused. "Anyway, Connie is much sexier-looking than me."

Faced with such rapid-fire and clear-cut demolition of overprotective adult fears, it is difficult to imagine *anybody* being able to exploit Jodie.

Jodie's unpretentious room at the top of the modest house in North Hollywood contains an almost standard collection of teenage memorabilia —glossy cushions, dolls, dart-board games—together with film posters bearing her name as star, scripts waiting for her attention and approval, and awards from various film festivals—already more awards than most actresses could expect to receive in a lifetime. If she recognizes that she has talent, even genius, she doesn't reveal it in conversation. She talks about work, and luck, and instinct. She makes learning lines, remembering moves, and working out the correct timing seem a simple game. She concedes little, or nothing, by way of personal effort. She won't even

Babysitting at a dollar an hour for her sister Connie's child, Christian.

acknowledge pain or depression: "There's no excuse for lots of things. You can always keep misery and depression inside you. Letting everybody know how you feel is just big-headed—it's gross."

Jodie is refreshingly tight-fisted with money. When she babysits for sister Connie's child, Christian, she receives a dollar an hour—and hangs on to it. This probably goes to prove that in a world of artificial and inflated values the movie industry has not only not corrupted her but failed even to dent her. She earns as much for a single film as many workingmen will receive in a lifetime. She hasn't been spoiled by it. The money sits in the bank, waiting for her. In the meantime, she is acquiring a sense of thrift that would earn the approval of the most parsimonious accountant. She

In her bedroom with awards and posters

doesn't lack friends of her own age but on location she also strikes up instant friendships with movie technicians. She understands and enjoys the technicalities that fill the world of cameramen and sound recordists. Critics have speculated that the combination of precocity and a startlingly early maturity might have deprived her of an ordinary childhood—an adolescent period of learning and discovering. Jodie dismisses the idea as "dumb" and her mother insists: "She is an ordinary child. Off the set, the things she does (even the things she doesn't do—like not doing her share of the chores in the house) are exactly the things you would expect from any teenager. I find it difficult to realize that she is such an ordinary teenager. Because as well as being her mother, I am also her number-one fan. Jodie is just a very, very nice person to be with. She really is very good company indeed. She's witty and generous and imaginative. Just watching her and being with her is fascinating.

"Don't ask me how it happened, it just did, and I'm truly grateful." Does she miss the company of her father? "No, I don't think so. It mattered very much more to the other three because they had known him before he left home. But he abandoned us before she was born and so she never really knew him."

As for "father figures" in Jodie's life, there has been no shortage of men who have taken a genuine and affectionate interest in Jodie. Although the Hollywood movie industry has more than a fair share of the phony and insincere, the kind of men Jodie herself would describe as "creeps," she has been lucky—and her mother has been wise with guidance—in the choice of directors and producers with whom she has worked.

There is no doubt that Brandy Foster, a petite, dark-haired lady with a rather overrevealed figure, and something of Elizabeth Taylor in the shape of her face and her violet eyes, sacrificed a great deal of her private life—perhaps opportunities to marry again—in order to devote herself to her daughter's career. All the Foster children—Jodie's two sisters, Connie and Lucinda, and her older brother, Buddy—worked as models in commercials and in movies.

Buddy was a star in a Disney-style television series called *Mayberry RFD*, and while he remained blond-haired, pink-faced, and appealingly cheeky, in the great tradition of Hollywood performers in sugar-and-spice soap operas about children, he remained employed, the star of the Foster family. But then, Buddy's voice began to break, inevitable pimples appeared on his chin, the roundness went from his face. Maturity, or at least puberty, overtook and wiped out Buddy Foster's child-star qualities. He's nineteen now and works parking cars for the Beverly Hills Hotel. He's married, the father of a small baby, and is restless, unsettled. He still talks about himself as an actor "between jobs"—although it has been some years, now, "between jobs." Buddy is perhaps an example—even a warn-

Left to right: Jodie, Buddy's wife Diana, Brother Buddy, Sister Connie, Mother Brandy

ing—of what can happen to a child star not properly prepared for adult life—or adult life without stardom. He talks constantly about finding scripts that would be suitable for him, or of parts that he would like to play. But the reality seems obvious to everybody, except Buddy.

While Buddy's career has dwindled and expired, Jodie's has flowered and developed. Brandy Foster has also learned a lesson. Now she supervises Jodie with intense care and thought for the future. She reads every script, carefully choosing movies that will guard Jodie as she faces the gap between playing child roles in Disney productions and working as a mature actress. But Jodie is confident about the gap and will tell you: "I can't remember when I wasn't an actress. All this isn't sudden, you know. I've been working for this for ten years; it takes a long time and you have to build it very slowly. Even for children there still isn't that overnight discovery that you read about in the magazines—that's dumb." By the time she

With Madame Kabaz, principal of Lycée Français, Los Angeles

was six she had made fifty commercials, by twelve she had acted with Oscar-winning Ellen Burstyn in *Alice Doesn't Live Here Anymore,* before her mother started pointing her alternately at Disney propositions and new "adult" areas with films like *Taxi Driver* and *The Little Girl Who Lives Down the Lane.* She has been described by critics as having a voice like a velvet fog—and she uses it for good comedy effect. She has also been called a thirty-year-old woman inside the body of a fifteen-year-old girl—and it might be true. But it is only as a pupil that Jodie attends the demanding and disciplined Lycée Français, which includes in its student body the children of other film stars. The school is not just a fashionable learning academy for the offspring of the rich and famous in the movie industry. The principal, Madame Kabaz, makes sure of that.

Madame Kabaz, tall, immaculately groomed, jingling with exactly the right kind of jewelry, is an impressive educator. Her admiration of Jodie is obvious and genuine. She told me: "Jodie is an excellent student, she's very happy here in school, very good at her work, gets on well with all the other pupils." Madame Kabaz has even traveled with Jodie to Europe on film locations for a recent production. California law requires that a tutor, or qualified teacher, be present (during the school term) on the set both as chaperone and teacher for all children under sixteen. And the law, on this point, is fiercely applied in Los Angeles. (There have been, in the past history of the movie industry, outrageous examples of exploitation.) But Madame Kabaz insists that, "I went as a friend, not as a tutor—although I served the purpose of a tutor. Normally Jodie has a tutor supplied by the Los Angeles education authority and paid for by the film company when she is away on location during school time. But she is such a quick learner, such a bright girl, that this represents no problem for her when she returns here to the school. She quickly catches up with all the work that she has missed and has never failed to be placed well in her class. She is a person who loves school and school life, she also loves the film industry and loves being in the studios or on a set. She is one of the most balanced human beings I've met in a long time and that includes most of the adults I know here in California." Madame Kabaz shuddered at her memories of California life-styles. "Do you know," she told me, "that a few years ago, when this so-called hippie movement was going on, I had actors come here to try and enlist their children in the Lycée and not only were they wearing jeans and open-necked shirts and long hair, but sometimes they didn't have shoes on. I wouldn't even see them, let alone consider registering their children for this school.

"The Lycée is, of course, French; it is a European school with French discipline. We lay great stress on the discipline. In this, Jodie is no problem at all. She wears her uniform, behaves herself, understands the rules." I asked Madame Kabaz if she was ever worried that Jodie's full and precociously adult life might be interfering with her capacity to enjoy her own teenage years. She told me: "I don't think so. I think she is such an intelligent person and so enjoys what she is doing, both in school and with acting that this, for her, is still a teenage time. I've also noticed that she is quite well able to insulate herself against the artificial values of the film business. When she's been on the set, and I've observed her, she has been interested in the direction, the camera, the lighting, and the sound. She certainly doesn't subscribe to the idea of being a star—actually, she just likes to make people laugh by clowning around. Also, you must remember that when she makes films for people like Disney, it is still a child's world, although it is an adult business, because the actors and actresses are nearly all children. They may be acting in strongly imaginative plots, with other children, but that is exactly how teenage children play with each other anyway."

At the Lycée, Jodie's friends, like Marlon Brando's son and Peter Sellers' daughter, are more concerned with the task of preparing for the baccalauréat than reflecting on the comparative star status of their parents —or of Jodie. Only once did Jodie make the mistake of "coming on strong" as a star. She had been cast, by Alan Parker, as the lead, Tallulah, in *Bugsy Malone.* Nearly every other child in the film was an amateur and Jodie was not just the only professional among them, but she was already the veteran of ten years in the film business, a long time even by Hollywood standards and three-quarters of Jodie's lifetime. When she arrived on the set in England, she made fun of the mistakes of her amateur English North Country fellow actors. They retaliated by turning the fire hose on her. She cheerfully admits the incident—and was certainly better behaved on the set of *Bugsy Malone* after that.

Charles Champlin is film critic for the *Los Angeles Times.* In his latest book, *Flicks,* subtitled, "Whatever Happened to Andy Hardy?," he tackles the problem of Hollywood's exploitation of the very young, and the very innocent. Champlin is a thoughtful, sensitive man who for years has observed, accurately and without cynicism, the vicissitudes of the movie world. At his home in Bel Air he told me: "I knew Jackie Cooper as a child star and Roddy McDowall and many, many others and I've managed to talk to most of them since they grew up. But so few of them made it from childhood to adult status as actors. Those who did make it are rare and few made it without suffering some damage, paying some emotional price. I remember talking to Natalie Wood, who is very articulate on the perils and pains of being a child star. There was some little Oriental girl who was making a splash at that time on the Jack Paar show and Natalie told me that when she saw this kid, who was only four years old, getting adult treatment on a national television show her response was to yell at the television screen, 'Turn back, turn back before it's too late.' You see, it struck horror into Natalie's heart because she could see ahead of the child all the frustrations, all the pain, and all the emotional savaging which she herself had experienced. I think that Natalie found her youth a most particularly painful time notwithstanding all the financial and artistic rewards. She got good roles but she does believe that she was deprived of anything like a normal childhood."

He went on: "I remember once talking to Shirley Temple, later in her life. We were standing beside a large cardboard cutout of Shirley Temple at the age of five or six—we had been at some show commemorating her early days—and while we were talking she put her arm around the cardboard cutout and said to me, 'This person is a total stranger to me.' She looked at it almost with hatred and I had the feeling that Shirley Temple had buried that part of her life and had just chosen not to remember it at all. I sensed that there must have been an awful lot of strain in it.

Paramount Pictures in the twenties

"Jackie Cooper is particularly fascinating on this subject because he was thrown into very emotional roles and I know at the end of *The Champ,* which he made with Wallace Beery, he had to cry for two days' worth of takes. He found afterward that he couldn't stop crying. He was, I think, nine years old at the time and it really alarmed the psychiatrist that they brought in to deal with him. It must have been the most amazing and traumatic filmmaking and I asked the director of that film how they had made Jackie Cooper cry for two days. He told me, 'Oh, we told him his dog had been run over and then he finally stopped crying about that, so we told him that a favorite friend of his on the crew had just been fired from the movie, and later we even staged a fight on the set and let him think that another friend of his had been badly hurt and taken to the hospital. That's the way we kept him going.' So those are the kind of things that used to happen in order to get the right return from the children as actors and stars. I don't think that any of that is acceptable treatment at all. If Jackie Cooper had not gone into the navy as a young man I doubt very much if he would have been able to make sense of his adult life.

"Now, it is true that today the child stars are better protected, not by the studios, who still like to get all the hours and all the value they can out of these children, but by law. You see, you must remember that this doesn't happen because producers and directors are cruel, but because producers and directors are under pressure themselves. If they have a huge team of as many as a hundred or two hundred standing by on the set or on location to shoot a scene and they are about to get the take they want, they are bound to care less about whether the child has been working for six, or eight, or ten hours, or needs a session with the school tutor, so they try to break the rules. As a result the protection now comes from a division of the Los Angeles Department of Labor which was brought into being when it became apparent just how bad some of the exploitation was in the thirties and forties. This is a very efficient department, run very fiercely, and any studio crosses swords with it at its peril. The life of a child star is better now, in any case, because parents and lawyers and agents have become more knowledgable about the whole business. I think the parents of those earlier children, of Jackie Cooper, Natalie Wood, and Judy Garland, were much more easily persuaded and knew much less about what to look out for.

"Actually, I think the whole use of child actors is tampering with nature, bringing forward the adult process. It must be horrifying to be treated as an adult when you're only three or five, when you're at an age that particularly needs adult protection. So instead of receiving it you're put into competition with adults, required to undergo adult emotions in adult situations. I think it is probably less damaging than it was in the older days and I think that Jodie may not be so affected by this because she has a very smart mother and a very normal family life and goes to school and appears to be able to take in her stride a great deal that would affect many other children. Nevertheless there is a considerable risk. A child has only to go through a depressed period, and, after all, adolescence is a period of great emotional vulnerability for children in any case, to become much more vulnerable.

"We do, these days, seem to be going through a renaissance in the use of child stars and I worry sometimes about what the movie industry is doing to them. Linda Blair is a fascinating example; she was thrust into *The Exorcist* at a crucial age, the turning point in her life from young girl to woman, and God knows how she survived all that she was asked to do in that film. What concerns me most about many of the films I see children in these days, is that I think the children are in jeopardy because they are being asked to act out adult fantasies. It seems to me that when children are asked to act out children's fantasies, as in the Disney films, then that is a demand upon them which is not likely to destroy them. But putting them in films where the fantasies and the horrors are those of an adult is to produce real problems, in my opinion.

"Scott Jacoby is perhaps the nearest male equivalent to Jodie presently in the child-star business, and both he and Jodie are being asked to play more sophisticated and more adult roles. In one way it is more difficult for them but in another way it may be the saving of them; it may help them grow up and pass through the awkward middle stage to become adult actors and actresses. In the old days a studio would have no use for a child star when he, or she, had passed beyond the capacity to play sugary and tearful roles. So, the pressure from the children's parents, agents, and others was to remain looking young; they used to tape down Judy Garland's breasts, keep Shirley Temple's hair in ringlets, and all sorts of other devices to extend childhood.

"Now I think there is a better possibility for the good child actor and actress to become an adult actor and actress. But there is a very difficult and probably damaging period of playing in adult-type films before they do it. When Jodie played in *Taxi Driver* they sent for a psychiatrist to see if it would damage her and he finally ruled, much to the studio's relief, that it would not. Her mother was triumphant about it. But I think her mother should have been more cautious. I don't believe it did damage Jodie but nevertheless I like to think that everybody around her was concerned not with how fast they could force her ahead, and what strange new role they could make her play, but how gently and how carefully they might let her travel along this awkward and unknown road. I also think whatever anybody says, whatever even Jodie says about herself, that when these children reflect back in later life to their beginnings, they will see that they were in some sense deprived of a normal childhood. It may be that the

childhood they had on the set, making friends with the members of the crew, understanding directors and cameramen rather than playing cowboys and Indians, will provide a kind of childhood, but what they have they will only have in common with other members of the film industry and this means we are breeding a type of person, exclusive to this industry—and that has always been one of the horrible capacities of Hollywood. But Jodie has special strengths and I know she'll survive. But survive is what she'll have to do and I think it is a telling comment on our movie industry that it should be that way around. Perhaps there's no alternative but that doesn't mean to say I have to approve of it."

Zev Braun is the producer of *The Little Girl Who Lives Down the Lane.* There is no doubting the success of the movie, or of Jodie's starring role in it—nor, particularly, Zev Braun's deep, personal affection for Jodie. He worked with her before, when she made a film for him called *The Smell of Onions,* a Western for children. In *The Little Girl Who Lives Down the Lane* Jodie plays a teenage murderer, has an affair with another teenager, and fends off the advances of a neighboring child molester. The role would be demanding for an actor several years Jodie's senior in both age and experience. But Zev Braun says: "She has multipersonality both on the screen and off the screen. She's child, she's adult, she's consummate performer, and now she's becoming a woman as well. Very often when I've been talking to her on the set I've wondered which one I'm talking to. Am I talking to the star? Am I talking to the girl I would like to have as a daughter?—which I certainly would—or is this just a little woman who is growing up and has become complex and fascinating?

"I don't think that she's even terribly aware of these changes in herself. On the set she is entirely professional. One of the charming things about her is that she never exploits herself in that precocious way that some child performers do. I am sure that she will make the transition from child star to adult star. She already has all the qualities of survival that it takes to do that, and certainly more than enough acting experience." I wondered, since Zev Braun felt affectionate enough about Jodie to describe her as the daughter he would have liked to have himself, if he, therefore, had any hesitation before casting her in this role. He said: "I think the answer is if I had a daughter I would want her to become aware of all the aspects of life, including the seamy aspects of life, and if my daughter, at the age of thirteen (which is the age of the girl Jodie played in the film) was to have an affair then I would like to think that it was as gentle and as loving as the one in the film. I wouldn't actually want her to have an affair at thirteen but if it were to happen then I'd want it to happen that way. I think Jodie

---

Will she pass from child star to adult successfully?

understood all of that and also understood about how to deal with the scenes about natural sex and even unnatural sex. It's because of her strength in this way that I didn't hesitate when asking her to play the role. When she grows up I think that she will become a leading lady of great distinction. Not a leading lady in the glamorous Elizabeth Taylor sense, beautiful flowing furs and jewels, but a leading lady of the sort that audiences queue to see acting. I've watched her, now, from a child, first playing in Disney pictures and a few television parts, and I've watched her emerge clearly as one of the big stars in the United States and in Europe and she hasn't changed a bit during all that. She is just a very lovely girl and I hope she remains like that."

It is obvious also that Zev Braun would like Jodie to act, again, in one of his productions, because these days Jodie Foster is becoming a box-office guarantee. Already her price for each film has mounted to the "star" bracket and the hard-headed men who make the front-office cash assessments very seldom make mistakes—because of affection or sentiment.

Helen Hayes, one of the most distinguished ladies of the American stage and still working in her seventy-seventh year, has just finished a film with David Niven—and Jodie Foster. Helen Hayes was herself a child star who "made it," and has continued to make it for several generations since. But Helen Hayes usually dislikes working with child stars. In the case of Jodie, she was won over. "I adored her, I really loved her. I haven't always loved the children I've worked with on the set, although I've never really detested them, like W.C. Fields—he used to kick them in the stomach and that sort of thing. But nevertheless, I don't think the usual child actress is very lovable. They're either good at their job, or not, but as personalities they are very unchildlike and difficult creatures to deal with. Jodie is quite the opposite, she is really very lovable in every respect." She went on: "I know what I'm talking about, you know, young man. Fred Astaire and I were, for a long time, the only two successful adult stars who had begun as child actors. I am quite sure this girl Jodie will go on and make that transition without any trouble at all.

"For me being a child actress was a wonderful childhood. I know how horrible it was for many people but I suppose I must have been very, very fortunate. I wouldn't have swapped it for anything. I played with some of the finest actors and they were all intelligent and beautiful people and they were kind and good to me and I wouldn't have changed my childhood a bit. I think it must be more difficult today, because it's a harsher world and the competition is so terribly strong that I don't believe people have time for the quiet leisurely pursuits that they had in those days. What is the difference, what is the quality that makes one child star grow up into an adult star and another vanish? Well, I think the difference is the parent. I had a good, wise mother who didn't push me, who didn't make me obnoxious to people. And I think Jodie's mother is realistic and wise in her selection about what is good for Jodie. Jodie's mother has a very healthy respect for Jodie's own intelligence. But Jodie's mother must be careful at all times to protect her. Fred Astaire also had a strongly protective mother. I think that is the difference and I think it is the essential difference."

Martin Scorcese, the talented and internationally known director, not only works with Jodie, he counts her a friend. He told me: "She is extremely easy to direct. I first used her in *Alice Doesn't Live Here Anymore* and I fell for that deep husky voice. When she came to the audition I thought she was a boy, of course. When we used her in *Taxi Driver* the script had to be approved by the Department of Labor's Child Welfare section, and they were frightened of the effect it would have on Jodie, but I never had any doubts. She's always very fresh and very clear in her personality. When we were shooting in some of the rougher areas of New York on location for *Taxi Driver,* I was more worried about the effect it was going to have on some of my more adult performers, than on her. She takes direction extremely well and has a natural craft, a natural capacity when acting, which is a delight. In one scene she plays with Robert De Niro, they're in a cafe together and she has to pour sugar on top of jam on her toast and she does it in such a way that it is not only childish and natural but it is also sophisticated and sensual. She was the master of that scene."

Alan Parker, who directed her in *Bugsy Malone,* was stunned by Jodie's capacity to learn lines. "One morning she was in makeup and I went in with three very complicated pages of script which I had written only the night before. I went to tell Jodie that I had rewritten the scene and to take her time learning the script and let me know when she was ready. She took the script from me, read it through once, and said, 'I'm ready now.' I didn't believe her and told her so. She said, 'Try me,' so I read the lines to her and she came back word perfect. Now that's total photographic recall. It's phenomenal, and she has it all the time. What's more, she takes such an intelligent interest in the way the film is being made that, if I had been run over by a bus, I think she was probably the only person on the set able to take over as director. Her sense of timing, her knowledge about how to read a line, is the greatest."

Jodie says her closest friend, her "best friend," is Christopher Connelly, who played Ryan O'Neal's younger brother for five years in the TV version of *Peyton Place* and played Jodie's temporary father in the thirteen-part television series of *Paper Moon.* Jodie became very close to Chris. He taught her to drive, although she is still not old enough to take out a license. If anybody at any time came close to becoming the father figure in her life, it was probably Chris.

However, at home, Jodie and her mother make a formidable team when

Jodie in Disneyland. "Don't spoil the illusion," she said.

considering Jodie's future. All the scripts submitted—sometimes dozens each week—are read first by Brandy Foster and then by Jodie, who always has the final say about whether or not she will do a film. In their small Spanish-style bungalow the alcove in the stairs is full of scripts, waiting to be read; alongside is a much larger pile of scripts, waiting to be sent back. Recently, together, they made another significant decision, designed to help Jodie through the emotional minefield which exists between child and adult roles. They decided to do a two-language picture, in French and English. In it Jodie has her first real love affair, with a young French poet. The film, called *Moi Fleur Bleu*, was shot mostly on location in Paris side streets.

I visited the set, where Jodie was happily at home with the French technicians and the Vietnamese director. Her co-star, Sydne Rome, seemed, in fact, less French in the French version than Jodie herself. Each scene was shot several times, first in English and then in French. At moments like this there is no room for sentiment or affection. Everybody is a professional—and what they expect is professionalism from everybody else. Jodie knew it and remained professional.

But weeks later, I was with her in Disneyland, which she visits as often as she can. There, she delighted, as any child might, in getting in as many free rides as she could from the Disneyland publicity lady. To any observer she would have been just another girl enjoying herself. But people did recognize her and stopped her and asked for her autograph or to pose for photographs. She coped with it all calmly, without apparent self-consciousness. At one point she stopped to pose with several of the giant Disney "creatures," like Baloo the Bear, for the benefit of visitors with cameras. She knew, and I knew, that inside the "skin" of those animals were performers, sometimes out-of-work actors. I asked her, as she was snapped by the crowd, if she'd talked to the actor inside the skin. She leaned forward quickly and put her hand over my mouth. "Don't do that," she whispered urgently. "*We* may know there is an actor in there but the children here don't—and you mustn't spoil the illusion for them."

Jodie Foster, film star, was right. At her own craft—and at understanding it—I think she always will be.

THE RANCHER

EARL HARDEMAN

They dug the grave under a tree in the little cemetery on a hill at the end of the valley. Standing alongside it you could see all the way across the valley to the mountains beyond. From that point, it still looked exactly as it had when the man in the grave had first brought his team through the Rockies and into the valley.

Gerritt Hardeman was one of the first to open up the valley known as Jackson Hole. He was eighty-six when he died and, in nearly seventy years in the valley, he had seen many changes. His son Earl stood by the grave, tall, leathery, weather-beaten, Stetson in hand. He wondered if *he* would be one of the last, in the old pioneer style.

Earl Hardeman, at fifty-two, is a rancher, as his father, Gerritt, was before him. His son Robbie is fifteen, and Earl hopes that eventually he will be able to run the ranch, in Jackson Hole, Wyoming, in the heart of the Rockies, exactly as he has done, and his father did. But things are changing and the old ways are dying out; and as Earl and his son walked from the grave the flowers were already beginning to wilt in the heat of Jackson's brief summer. In July 1977, when Gerritt Hardeman was buried, they finished a chapter in American history.

Of all the characters in America's landscape there can hardly be one whose way of life is better known anywhere in the world than that of the rancher—and the cowboy. Together, they have become the basis of the biggest of all American mythologies—the Western. In movies and on television screens, on dude ranches for vacationers, in rodeos and old-time saloons, armies of people work hard to keep the legends of the West alive. All the while they do so, the real life that they are celebrating is dying out; the genuine working rancher, using horses and cowboys, is becoming rarer. Men like Earl Hardeman are finding it harder to survive the pressures from developers and tourists than their forebears did to win the country from the wild in the first place.

The Hardeman ranch is at an elevation of six thousand feet in the heart of the Rockies, just off the tourist track. Earl Hardeman, his wife Pat, his son Robbie, and daughter Heidi still run the place much as Earl's father did when he first settled it. Earl and his brother Howard own, between them, one thousand acres of Jackson Hole, and run their thoroughbred Hereford cattle across a further one thousand square miles of mountain country. They like ranching in the old tradition. They are determined to keep it that way, but they may not succeed.

Earl leaned against his pickup outside the little cemetery on the hill and told me: "My father was one of the first into this valley. It was settled late in frontier history. Up until the early 1800s it was pretty well just hunting country for roaming bands of Indians and then the Mountain Men crossed, and recrossed it, trapping and hunting. Toward the end of the century ranchers, like my father, came in over the Teton Pass, struggling with horses to get across at more than eight thousand feet, freighting in everything they needed. These days there is a superhighway and you can speed at fifty miles per hour out of the valley. My father was a Dutchmans." Earl used the old Western term for a Dutchman. In the early days of the West the Dutch settlers were invariably referred to as "Dutchmans," rather than "Dutchmen" or "the Dutch." "He came here as a very young man and he watched all the changes in this valley; that's why there were so many people at his funeral, there were plenty here who had come to pay their last respects. You know, toward the end of his life he knew things were changing, he knew the valley would never be the same again. He always had faith in people and he was interested in the changes but in his heart, I think he regretted it. He picked this plot out himself. It's one of the oldest cemeteries in the valley. I think this little piece of ground probably hasn't changed at all. It's just the same as when the Mountain Men came through here and the first settlers followed them."

Jackson Hole is an oasis, at an altitude which varies between six and seven thousand feet, encompassed on all sides by mountain barriers. The valley is nearly fifty miles long, seldom more than six miles wide. Through the center of it the Snake River flows through the flatlands and roars through the canyons. The Hole was named by William Sublette, a partner of David Jackson who, with Jedediah Smith, Jim Bridger, and others, opened up the region for what became known as "the fur trade era."

They buried Earl's father in a cemetery on a hill.
Earl and Robin, his son.

272

Further south another "Hole" became famous, later, as the refuge and headquarters for the "Hole in the Wall Gang" and its leader Butch Cassidy; an incident in American frontier history comparatively little known until the exaggerations of Hollywood turned it into legend.

Gerritt Hardeman came into the valley when he was nineteen. Earl, who had heard the story many times, told me: "It was 1911 and he was nineteen years old. Everybody wanted to come to America to make their fortune and it was wide open spaces that they were looking for, when they came. So he came to Iowa, because he knew some Dutchmans there and he worked there for about a year and a half before he heard, from somebody, about the West, about how they had all this free ground and wide open spaces which—providing you were tough enough—you could have for the asking. He finally came on out here with a horse and wagon and a few supplies and he started working around the area until he found a plot of land of his own and built up a ranch. It was still a big, wide-open country then and the land was all free. He was a young man, full of challenge and for him the words 'Go West, young man,' were new and had a real meaning. Now they've just become corny words used in Hollywood movies. But then it was true. There were hardships in those days but they were the real pioneers, the guys with real guts.

"There was nowhere to buy your stores, no grocery or post office or anything like that, you had to go plumb over to Idaho to get your groceries and supplies and then you had to buy them for a year at a time. A horse was the only means of transport and to get into the valley you had to go over the pass up there—eight thousand feet."

Even when Earl Hardeman was growing up in the twenties and thirties, life in Jackson Hole was hardly cushioned and comfortable. He went on: "Yes, it was a tough life. I was raised in Kelly—there was no electricity or phone and although the mail came in every day, it came in with horses and in winter with a horse-drawn sleigh. We ourselves couldn't go to town more than once all winter and going to school, three or four of us would all ride the same horse, three miles each way, whatever the storms or the weather was doing. Our clothing was old-fashioned and we didn't have refrigeration so we couldn't have salad or green stuff from the refrigerator in winter, we just ate meat, eggs, potatoes, and stuff off the ranch. It didn't seem to make any difference to us. I know my own kids take a lot of different vitamin pills and they have their salads every day, but we grew up without all that and it doesn't seem to have hurt us.

"But I often think that the work must have been toughest for the women. It always was a man's world in the West and it was all right being a boy growing up, because you knew you were going to be a man and you knew that you were going to be tough to be able to stand with other men out here. But frontier life is a life that can break women, it sucks the energy out of them, leaves them dried up and worn out. My mother worked harder than any other person I've known. Mind you, she was always happy and smiling and good to look at. But I never knew a woman who made a successful wife in the West who *did* complain. But now I think about it, they must have had a pretty tough life because they had to do all the chores and work alongside the men, as partners, help with the cattle and the horses, bring up the kids, be doctor, nurse, psychiatrist, and teacher to the whole family. As well, they were frequently left on their own for long periods of time while the men went off in the mountains herding the cattle, or hunting for elk to bring back for meat. It's a way of life that's gone now. I suppose there may still be a few odd places in the United States where there are pockets left over—and it's still this way. But I doubt it. Things have changed. In the old days we went out to town on Saturday nights and we all had a dance, we all had a drink—several drinks—and sometimes we had a fight. And once in a while we'd meet a girl. No, I never did wear a gun. My dad always told me it was better to be a live coward than a dead hero. Anyway, the six-gun is a much overrated weapon, you don't need one. You need a rifle to hunt and that's it.

"I was brought up strict because my father when he came to this country wanted to be a good citizen and I was always conscious of the fact that he wanted us to be good Americans. He made us work hard and accept responsibility and understand why we were doing it. He didn't want us to be lazy, or mean, or crooked, or violent. He thought that this was the greatest country in the world and that, since we were born in it, we must be proud of it. And I'm glad that I've inherited, with my brother Howard, his ranch here in Jackson Hole. But you know I've inherited very much more than that. I've inherited all his love of the West, of wide open spaces, of mountains—the Frontier Life. It's a shrinking life, not much left. I suppose there's only a handful of us here still struggling in the old way. But it's the way I like. It's the way my dad taught me. It's the way this country was built."

Just before Earl Hardeman's father died he "got mad" at his family and at the County authority. He liked to drive his car and at eighty-six his eyesight wasn't all it had been, though his natural stubbornness hadn't dimmed at all. Consequently he refused to admit to any visual handicap. He was involved in an accident. Nobody was hurt, but cars were damaged and they took his license away. Earl said: "The trouble was that he learned to drive around here when there weren't too many cars, practically none. He wouldn't get over the fact that there were thousands of cars now and he would still drive as fast as he wanted and always down the middle of every road. It was bound to happen and I'm glad he wasn't hurt. His first car was a model-T Ford—I think that was in 1934. But after the County took his license away from him I think he began to go downhill. He'd do

WANTED

YOUNG, SKINNY

Wiry fellows not over 18.

Must be expert riders, willing to risk death daily. Orphans preferred.

Wages $25.00 per week

some gardening, fix the plants, and once in a while do a little fishing or walk around the ranch. But he'd already made the ranch over to my brother and me and there wasn't really a great deal for him to do. In the days when he had his car he would drive over to his friends in another part of the valley, but it was too far to walk and he was too old to ride a horse.

"But he was still a tough old guy. When they took him into the hospital, just before he died, it was because he'd said that he'd been a little sick and had a headache; it didn't seem to be anything very much or any great problem. So we took him to see a doctor and when a nurse came up with a wheelchair he said, 'No, I'll walk. I won't ride in that thing.' She put her arm around him and took his hand and started leading him down the hall to the room where he was going to be examined and he was walking pretty good so she let go of him and went ahead of him, but he stopped and said, 'No, by damn, I'm not going to run, either.' He was an independent man. But he was a good man and he made friends throughout the valley. Just about everybody turned up at his funeral. He dug his ranch, and his life, out of the wilderness. And they buried him in one of the prettiest parts of it. That's the way he would have wanted it."

Each spring Earl Hardeman, with other ranchers in the valley, drives his cattle into the high mountain and forest land of the National Park, where they have grazing rights. It is then that ranching life takes on its original style, even seems to conform to the Hollywood mythologies. It is then, too, that the ranchers use cowboys—hired hands—to help them with the drive. In fact, all the ranchers of Jackson Hole together still manage to employ only a few cowboys, solitary "lonely cowpokes"—to stay up in the mountains during the long summer weeks, watching the herds. Each cowboy lives in an old cabin or a trailer which has been hauled up there. He has to work as rancher, guard dog, veterinarian, and farmer to several thousand head of Hereford cattle roaming over miles of mountain pasture and forest land.

Earl likes cowboy films, Westerns. "I think they're pretty good," he told me. "Mind you, nobody runs a horse the way the heroes do in the Western films. You just couldn't run a horse forever and ever. The thing the public never seem to realize about a cowboy's life and a rancher's life is that it's a slow life. You can't move cattle fast or else all the feed you've put into them gets run off and they get frightened and fall into holes and damage themselves. You can't run a horse fast or else you'll lather it and sweat it and kill it. Therefore, the whole pace of Western life is represented wrong in the movies and on the TV. But, apart from that, everything else is right. And I guess they have to compress it. But it's a shame if people believe that the frontier life was something that took place in a hurry, always urgent. The frontier life was all about open spaces and big skies and man alone. And that is a slow, thoughtful process."

Another familiar feature of Western mythology is the posse. In fact, Earl Hardeman once rode as part of a posse: "Some years ago one of my neighbors called me and said, 'Have you got an extra horse?' and I said, 'Yes, we do,' and she said, 'Well look, we've got a man who lives in this section and he's stabbed another man real bad and now he's driven right through my ranch and left his car and he's loose in the mountains and the Sheriff's Department has said that we should all saddle up and go into the mountains and look for him.' The runaway had left shells in his car so we figured he was armed and that's one time when I did take a gun. But we never did get to find that man. So I never did shoot a gun while riding as part of a posse. In fact he was captured by some guys on the other side of the mountain who had gone in there bear-hunting. But I like the memory—it's kind of Western.

"What really makes me feel pretty proud is that I feel that I'm very American, typically American. I know you've come here to visit me because you think I'm an archetype. Well, I agree. I also think I'm an archetype. It was the cattle that really made this country, that brought people West, people like my father, out to the frontier. They came here to raise cattle or to trap for fur, but they opened up a country so beautiful that I think about it every day. Even though it's getting pretty filled up with visitors and tourists, it's still terrific country. And I can't blame people for wanting to visit it. If I think it's beautiful it's likely that they will too."

Winter in Jackson Hole is a different prospect. It can last as long as six months, with deep snow and temperatures as low as 40 degrees below zero. This is the part of the cowboy's life that people don't see in the Westerns, or the tourists on the dude-ranch vacations don't have to be bothered with. But for Earl Hardeman and his family, winter is a matter of survival, survival for the family—and the herd. But then the whole pattern of a cowboy's life, the daily routine of the ranch, is about survival; about the battle just to be able to continue with this American way of life.

In winter Earl Hardeman wakes in the dark, at 5:30 A.M. Then, in felt-lined boots and quilted parka, with his pipe showering sparks in the crisp, predawn air, he stomps across the snow to the barn, where he and his son Robbie, grumbling and sleepy, tie up and milk the family cow. Then together, working silently but efficiently, they harness the two heavy-shouldered and stately farm work horses to a huge sledge, loaded high with winter hay for the young Hereford cattle already standing stomach-deep in snow in the home meadows. As the thin wintry sun breaks over the Teton Rockies the sledge snakes its way backward and forward, the horses' breath steaming, while Earl and Robbie pitchfork hay among the cattle. Whatever the weather, this daily feeding has to take place. Earl's wife Pat collects the eggs, strains the milk, and starts the breakfast. Earl and Robbie return to the ranch at about 7 A.M. for breakfast, a big break-

Winter in Jackson.

fast. They will already have put in an hour, or two, of back-breaking farm work. Then, during the school year, Robbie and his sister Heidi go to school and Earl and Pat go back to work on the ranch. It is at times like this that the rancher's life may seem hard to endure—particularly for a man who is fifty-two years old. And the idea that may be even more difficult to endure is the fact that Earl Hardeman knows very well that—at least on paper—he is a millionaire. He lives like a poor man, in fact he is a poor man, but paradoxically, he's still worth $10 million.

Land in Jackson Hole has increased in value in direct proportion to the tourist trade. The skiers come in winter, the hunters in autumn, and tourists at all other times of the year. The land is being swallowed up by hotels, restaurants, cabin homes, weekend cottages, and ski developments. Earl Hardeman and his brother inherited, from their pioneering father, nearly one thousand acres. With current prices standing at $10,000 an acre, that makes them worth $10 million. But only if they sell. On those cold winter mornings, harnessing his work horses or butting the milk cow

Earl and Pat work as partners.

with his head as he sits on a two-legged stool in the dark, Earl Hardeman must surely reflect on the uncomfortable economic trap in which he now finds himself. Because of the short summer it is not possible to raise any other crop in Jackson Hole, just grass and cattle. But it takes one acre to support each cow, one acre worth $10,000. A cow may, after two years of rearing and grazing, fetch a few hundred dollars. The economic pressure is inevitable and remorseless. Most of Earl Hardeman's neighbors have already sold all, or part, of their ranches, particularly the older ones who began to find that the toughness of their daily existence was in harsh, and tempting, contrast to the comfort they could so easily achieve just by picking up the telephone and responding to the developers, the local Realtors, and the bank.

But so far, Earl and his brother have held on to their frontier style. They have leased a few acres to a restaurant development and that has just enabled them to keep their heads above water financially. But Earl drives an eight-year-old pickup truck with an unhealthy cough in its engine and Pat Hardeman can't remember when she last had a new dress. She laughs and declares she wouldn't want one anyway. Their ranch house is a modest, wood-frame building. The only thing for which the family really yearns is a new piano. The one they gather around on winter evenings has keys that stick. So it is possible that the money from the land that they have leased to the restaurant developers will bring, if not wealth, music into the life of the Hardeman family. As Earl says: "It's difficult to sell out. I often think about it but so far I've managed to resist it. You see, you never actually starve here. There's always beef—we slaughter a cow about twice a year to provide both our families with enough good meat every day. And if you fancy some other kind of meat there's the game which we're allowed to shoot. Elk meat is pretty good and as a boy I was practically raised on it. Then there's fish in the river and Pat has a little vegetable garden just outside the house and we put loads of vegetables into the freezer, so, with the occasional chicken and pig, we're pretty well self-sufficient.

"And I like the idea of looking after ourselves and living off our own resources. If I sell my land I'll have nothing to pass on to my son and no feeling that I am able to rely only on myself. I will become somehow dependent on the rest of America. It will mean that I will have to have money and need supermarkets and I will know that those big trailer trucks will just have to get through that mountain pass in winter to bring me the food and goods that I need to live on. Now, at the moment I can live like my father did, when he first came into this valley with his wagon and horses. I needn't see anybody for a good twelve months because we can look after ourselves.

"But it is dying out and I know I can't hold forever. It wouldn't be fair to Pat. But I am determined to pass on this ranch to my boy and not to sell it off before. He's going to be a good rancher one day and, although it may not be possible to live the frontier life that we have done, he may find some way to stay on. That's why I use work horses instead of tractors. In fact, horses are very much better in winter in Jackson Hole than tractors. A tractor would stick in drifts and it wouldn't know instinctively where to avoid the potholes. A horse is a sensible creature, and a friend as well as a farm tool. So I hang onto them for practical, as well as romantic, reasons. After all, it was the horse that first brought the trappers over to this valley when they came in with their pack animals looking for beaver."

Beavers have become a considerable problem in the valley and the lives of the ranchers. In order to irrigate his fields properly in the summer, Earl makes dams of canvas and poles across the tributary streams of the Snake River, spilling the water out into the meadows. But the beavers have other ideas. They make their own dams, not always in the places most convenient to the farmer. So, a distasteful part of Earl's life is breaking up the dams and an irritating part of his life is that the beavers rebuild them overnight. National Park game rangers are brought in two or three times every spring and summer to trap the beaver and take them, alive, to other parts of the park. None of the ranchers like the idea of trapping the animals, as in the old days, for their fur. The elk, too, has become one of the natural enemies of man in Jackson Hole. The herd that comes down from the mountains into Jackson Valley in winter is now the largest herd in the United States, sometimes as many as 15,000 elk, protected by law, milling around the outskirts of the town of Jackson. They are fed regularly by tractor-drawn sleighs which also tow camera-clicking tourists into the middle of the herd. But still the elk will jump any normal-sized fence to get at unprotected hay or into an open-sided barn. As a result, elk fences and walled-in barns have become a matter of routine for the ranchers in Jackson Hole.

In winter these days the ranchers and their families continue the cowboy tradition of roping. Both Earl and his son Robbie enter all local competitions for calf-roping. In winter, they maintain their skill in a huge, cold, local barn, owned by a dude rancher and used by the ranchers for indoor rodeos. Earl explained: "You may think that we're just keeping up with the old Western way of life and showing off for the sake of it. But in fact we use a rope a lot. Even though when we brand a calf these days we usually bring them into the corral by the barn and put them on a board which clamps them and holds them while we apply the brand, we some-

The Hardeman Ranch.
He prefers to use horses.

times do have to brand out in the open and then we use the old method of roping and pulling down. We also have to rope calves and cows who have come into contact with porcupines (it takes a pair of pliers to pull out porcupine quills) and we need a rope to pull out three trunks and broken sections of fencing. A rope is the most essential part of a rancher's or a cowboy's life—not the six-gun. The six-gun is a Hollywood fiction. The rope is the cowboy's true trademark."

The Hardeman children, Robbie and Heidi, belong to the 4-H program dedicated to encouraging young people to take an interest in farm management and rearing livestock. Each year Robbie and Heidi are given a cow to raise. Each year they feed, groom, and care for one calf from the herd. And when the cow is ready to be sold, either for slaughter as meat or for fattening on another ranch, they must learn to accept that fact of farming life. It is part of the plan that the children become fond of the animals they raise so devotedly and then learn to face the reality of a farmer's life. The money from the sale of the cow is paid directly into the children's bank accounts and set against the cost of foodstuffs and various other bills. So they also face the economic realities of farming. Last year Robbie lost money when the time came to sell his calf. Earl told me: "There is no question that his mother or I would make that money up for him. He had a little left over in the 4-H bank account from the two previous years, when he had made a profit on his cows, so the debt wiped that out. This way, when the time comes for him to take over from me, he'll know what he's up against. The program teaches him not to be false and sentimental about the animals on the farm. You must treat your animals kindly and look after them good; it isn't any part of a rancher's life to neglect his crop, but sentiment doesn't come into it. It's a difficult concept for parents and children who live in towns to accept. They think we are heartless and without feeling. It is just that, living here on the land with the animals, we understand the ways of nature better."

The Hardemans, twice a year, kill one of their herd to provide meat for both families. It becomes something of a family occasion. Brother Howard will join Earl on the ranch (Howard does not live on the ranch and farms elsewhere in the valley) to help with the slaughter and the carving up. Earl kills the steer, from a distance of three or four yards, with a .22 rifle. "I use a .22 because it hasn't so much percussion in it and doesn't kill the animal quite so fast as a big game rifle and this gives you better meat. The animal doesn't feel anything. It's unconscious from the moment the bullet hits it between its eyes but the body actually dies more slowly and then the calf bleeds out a lot more. I know this is another aspect of our life

Daughter, Heidi.

where people probably think we are being cruel. The average tourist probably doesn't think about killing meat much. But he should do so. He eats it in the restaurants all the time. The trouble with most people is that they want what we provide for them but they don't want to face some of the realities of the system. They don't want to acknowledge that ranching involves killing animals. They also don't want to be bothered with the fact that the price of beef is now so low that the average rancher is economically worse off than he would be on welfare. He may have his land and his stock but, unless he sells both, he would be hard put to find the price of a pair of pants, or a new hat. There have been some years, when I've sold my beef, that I've hardly dared count up what all the months of hard work have produced—practically nothing."

Earl Hardeman's operation differs from those of many other ranchers because he specializes in thoroughbred cattle as well as the ordinary steers which are usually purchased by a middleman and then taken to the Midwest and fattened in grassland pastures for an additional year before butchering. He also raises breeding bulls which fetch a high price and have a deservedly high reputation. His ranch is, in fact, not far from the tourist track, just three miles down a side road from a route that runs between the Teton skiing village and the town of Jackson itself. His house, barn, and fields are tucked under the spur of a mountain which, like all of the Tetons, rises dramatically, almost straight up from the valley floor. It would be an idyllic setting for a hotel, a restaurant, or a luxury retirement home. But for the time being, Earl Hardeman and Pat can still ride their own acres ignoring the tourists, the campers, and the coach parties—but only just. The town of Jackson used to be the central point for the farming and ranching community. Now Earl can't even buy farm machinery there. He has to drive ninety miles to find replacement parts.

The town itself is an attractive but overcrowded and untidy collection of pseudo-Western shops, souvenir stores, restaurants, and other tourist attractions. Every afternoon at four o'clock the "stagecoach" is driven into the main square and members of one of the local theater groups stage "The Jackson Shoot-out," a mock gun battle with an intensely complicated plot which involves several arrangements of "goodies" and "baddies," some standing on the roofs of local stores. There is much firing of blank ammunition from pistols and it ends with everyone getting up and walking away—to applause from the tourists, just as in most Western stories. Nearly every store sells Indian jewelry, boots, Stetsons, spurs, and Levi's. Around the town and outside it, the motels, the swimming pools, the guided fishing parties, the "white water" trips down the Snake River, the dude ranches—all vie with each other for tourist attention—and money. You can fish, hunt, canoe, or just drive around. And millions of Americans do.

The Hardeman ranch has two brands: spear-two-spear 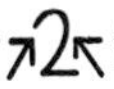 for pure-bred Herefords and quarter-circle-two-bar 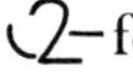 for other cattle. Once a year, with brother Howard and family, the Hardemans round up and brand their cattle. Tourists sometimes think branding is cruel and unnecessary. But Earl points out: "Ear tags may seem a fine alternative, or even putting paint on their horns. But tags can be pulled out, or substituted, and paint can come off. The only identification that is accepted as legal in this country is if the hide is burnt. It does look bad, at the time, because the calf yells a bit and you can smell burning hair. But it isn't actually as bad as it looks and it is the only effective way. There's not much rustling these days. Mostly I think it is the occasional visitor who may drive through and get greedy and has no sense of honesty, who will kill and take a calf in the back of his pickup. But the old days of having large numbers of your herd cut out by rustlers are gone. But it used to happen, my dad could remember it." We were talking on the cattle drive, near the abandoned "homesteads" the moviemakers chose as a background for the classic Western *Shane.* The empty buildings were a reminder of the real past.

The Jackson cowboy I met, one of the only "real live cowboys" left in Jackson, works for an association of ranchers, which includes Earl Hardeman. The year I met him, on the cattle drive to the high pastures, Dean Crisp looked every inch the traditional cowboy—except for Polaroid sunglasses. He had already spent two days in the mountains scattering salt and preparing for the arrival of the huge herd of five thousand. About himself, he told me: "I came originally from Nebraska but I prefer to do my cowboying down here. I've cowboyed all the way from the north to south, from Dakota and Montana to Mexico. But I really enjoy Wyoming, I find the high mountain country very challenging. I've been a cowboy and a farmer all my life. I had my own ranch for twenty years, but cattle prices went bad—and I went bust. So I started cowboying. My marriage broke up because I was away for weeks on end—now I'm just a cowboy. There aren't too many of us left today. I like the life. I spend sixteen weeks up in the mountains, on my own, being mother, father, and caretaker to the cows. No, I don't read much. I'm one of the worst readers in the world. But I've got plenty of things to keep myself busy and I get visitors from time to time when the hikers and back-packers come through. They all want to stop and have a cup of coffee with the real cowboy. I keep a gun out there in the cabin, too. I need it to shoot game and occasionally I might have to deal with a predator threatening the herd. I like to think that as long as there are cattle there'll always be cowboys. It will always take a man, a horse, a rope. That's my life and it will see me out. But I just hope it continues for others."

For busy ranchers there isn't much time to sit round campfires and sing

cowboy songs, to keep alive the legends of the West. But there is a little. Earl Hardeman is passionate about rodeos. He brushes aside the arguments that rage about cruelty, because the horses and bulls are made to buck by tightening a deliberately placed cinch. He points out: "The rodeo is really the cowboy's traditional recreation. It came about from his desire to demonstrate his everyday ranching skills; his skill with horses, with cattle, with ropes. It combined that with a chance to show strength and bravery. These days the rodeo may be a big tourist attraction and it has become more organized with its own following of pretty professional riders, competing for the prize money. But it's still a very genuine Western event."

Earl Hardeman is a Westerner who enjoys talking. He takes the microphone at the local rodeo grounds to do the commentaries. He makes them slick, punchy, peppered with jokes. He also acts as a local auctioneer and will sell a yard full of furniture, a barn full of machinery, or a herd of cattle, with speed and patter to match. He thinks it a skill worth having. He was encouraged to take it up by his wife Pat—he even went on an auctioneering course while he was on his honeymoon.

Earl and Pat first met when she came from Pasadena, California, to work as a nurse at the local hospital. At the time Earl was thirty-five and something of a hell-raiser in the town. He told me: "I was having a pretty good time living on the ranch and going into town most evenings and having a few drinks. I never had thought of settling down. Pat and I were introduced by a friend. Then, one day, I saw her pick up a fifty-pound bag of dog food and put it in the back of the car and I thought, 'That's a good strong girl. She'd make a rancher's wife.' And we started courting. We courted in the old-fashioned way. Pat didn't like me drinking and going out raising hell in the town. So we just sat on the porch and and I'd take her out for a walk. I guess I was ready to settle down and I guess that I was looking for someone who would want to work with me on the ranch. You know, it wasn't just the fact that she picked up a fifty-pound bag, but it takes something special to be a rancher's wife.

"We've got on better and better ever since we've met and she's as good a rancher now as I am. We work together on everything and that's a nice thing about being a rancher. Your wife can be your partner and your time can be your own. There are things that have to be done but if you want to stop for an hour and talk to a neighbor or take half an hour to have coffee with your wife then you can do that. You know that you have to make up that time but you can set your own pace. When we were first married I was still living at what we call the 'old place.' We didn't even

Branding and marking time with brother, Howard.

291

Earl is the rodeo commentator.

have an electric stove, we were using the old wood stove and oil lamps. This was quite a shock to a girl brought up in California, with all the modern conveniences. But she took to it fine.''

I asked Pat if she thought Earl was a romantic man. ''At first, you would think not,'' she replied. ''But he is deeply attached to this way of life and all that it stands for. He also feels very strongly about family life. When you work together, as we have, over the years, there are many things that you tend not to talk about very much. But they're there all the same—and you know it. Do I miss any of the comforts of life? Oh, I suppose I do. I'd like a carpet in the bedroom and I'd certainly like a new piano. But I don't yearn for jewelry or dresses or a new coat. And I don't mind that we don't have a new car, although our pickup is getting old. But there's plenty to keep me occupied. I don't mind it being hard but it's when it's hard and you still don't know if you're going to make enough money to live properly at the end of the year that it really gets at you. But I wouldn't change it.''

Pat works alongside Earl whenever she can. They work without exchanging words, in perfect harmony. They are a strong team. But their way of life is under threat. Raising beef shows little reward for much hard work. Selling land is becoming the only way to survive. Earl is part of a committee which, with the Teton National Park Service (the park itself started as a massive bequest from the Rockefeller family) is exploring a scheme to protect ranching land in Jackson Hole by bringing it under the wing of the National Park regulations. This would allow existing farming to continue, on protected land, leased by the farmers and their heirs after they had sold it to the park. Whether they will succeed against pressure from developers and entrepreneurs is, perhaps, doubtful. Certainly it seems that some form of control will have to be brought in before one of the last valleys of the old Western frontier turns into a high-altitude Jones Beach. But Earl is not resentful. He told me: ''There has to be development in this valley. Tourists come through here and I can understand them wanting to see it. Somebody has to fill their cars with gasoline, give them a place to sleep—somebody had to cook your breakfast for you this morning. And the people who do that have to have some life of their own.''

Many of Earl's ranching neighbors have turned to dude ranching, as a compromise. Betty and Roy Chambers switched some years ago. Roy was brought up, like Earl, in Jackson when the population consisted only of cattlemen. He chewed tobacco as he told me: ''The change was so gradual that you really would have to look back very carefully to understand how it happened. I think it must have been in 1935 or so when the first outside people came into the valley and bought themselves a few acres and built some pretty log cabins, as places to live. They weren't ranchers, they hadn't come here to work the land or to raise stock. They were wealthy people who wanted somewhere to retire. Some were doctors, or dentists, or lawyers. We were happy to have them live quietly among us. Sometimes their friends would come to visit them and their friends would need somewhere to stay. And so a motel was built—the first in the valley. But the 'cabin fever' started. Lots of people began to come in and they didn't want a few acres, they wanted half an acre. They didn't want to build a solid log house, they wanted a quick wooden house that they could put up and visit only on the weekends. And they wanted, most of all, a brand of their own. We called them 'the Belt-Buckle Ranchers' because they used to go into town and register a brand and have it made up as a belt buckle, or a door knocker, and have it burned on their gatepost. They probably didn't own a dog or a cat, let alone a cow. But they had a brand and they had a little shack up here and they thought they were part of the West. After that it all started to develop very quickly.

"We found trying to raise beef in the middle of all that just too much. So, because we had always been interested in horse-riding and we got on well with people, we started a dude ranch."

The "Flying V" $\bigvee$ is a very successful dude ranch. Betty, plump and jolly, cooks—with very little help—two or three meals a day for as many as thirty people at a time. Roy runs a string of twenty or thirty horses, guiding the experienced and inexperienced in the ways of Western saddles and bridles on the valley's beautiful trails. They work hard during the summer season and are able to relax more during the winter than when they ran a cattle ranch. Roy said: "I don't feel I sold out. I preferred the old way. But the old way wasn't going to last. If you want to stay on the land you've got to go along with the changes that have taken place. Take Earl Hardeman and Pat. I'm surprised they've managed to hold out as long as they have. But think of the sacrifice, think of the muscle, the work, the sweat, and the worry it takes them to keep running cattle; particularly when you can sell just four acres of ground and live in luxury for the rest of your life. And it gets harder. When you're thirty or forty you feel tough and you feel you can fight against the world. But when you're over fifty you're not the man you were and you can't keep fighting. Earl Hardeman is one of the last, but he's over fifty now."

Earl, still working his ranch, says: "It does get hard when you get past fifty. You're still fit, you're still healthy, and you still love the life. But whether you like it or not, you creak a bit and get tired, your bones ache a little more when you get into bed at night. The cold bites deeper every winter. But I don't mind that, it's part of growing old. It happened to my father. I know it's the pattern of this way of life, it's what being a rancher's all about. I still hope I may be able to pass the ranch on to my children."

Does Earl feel part of a vanishing breed? "I do feel it," he told me. "I feel there'll always be cattle in America and there will always be people to raise them. But in this part of Wyoming we are getting more and more crowded, so perhaps people like me, and our cattle, may have to be pushed into some other part of America—if there's anyplace left for us to go. There are too many fences here. They're fencing in the cowboys, and the ranchers, like they did when they put the Indians in the reservations.

"Now, maybe they'll have to build a reservation for old cowboys—like me."

THE FOOTBALL COACH

WOODY HAYES

They won the first game of the season. He always said winning is what it's all about. Nevertheless, after the game, he climbed high up among the seats in the deserted stadium, where the wind was swirling paper and rattling cans. He sat and reflected that the afternoon hadn't been good enough. There was a whole season ahead of them, a frenetic, intense, competitive season of just twelve games. At the end of it all there was the big match, the Michigan game. He wondered if this year was going to be a loser.

Woody Hayes, at sixty-four, didn't feel tired, or particularly depressed. After twenty-seven years as coach to the Ohio State University football team, the Buckeyes, he felt like a general who has survived a skirmish, and needs to win the battle but is determined to win the war.

Twenty-four hours later, in the same stadium, with the rubbish cleared away and the artificial turf watered for practice, all ninety-four members of his football squad sweated, strained, and groaned as the Coach pushed, bullied, lashed, and cursed, driving them harder and harder: "I'm going to knock the ——— out of you, I'm going to push some ——— sense into your goddamned heads. I'm going to have a better offensive side than this. I've had all I want of this, you ———s. I've had to apologize to the defense every goddamned game, for you ——— heads. The defense have carried us every ——— time, they carried us during the game and they carried us today. It's a goddam crime. During that last game we didn't generate a pint of ——— during that second half and we're supposed to be in god-dam ——— shape. Well, I tell you fellers that's going to be the ——— end of that."

The giant young athletes strained and sweated, thudded into the heavy machines, pounded—as a punishment for moving too slowly—to the top of the spectators' bleachers and back again; up again and back again and up again. For four unrelenting hours ninety-four men, studying to be lawyers, doctors, farmers, engineers, journalists, and teachers, but all of them *working* their way through college as football players, kept up a pace as fierce and crippling as that of any Olympic training squad. And Wayne Woodrow Hayes, their head coach, was still not a happy man.

Their victory over Miami had been 10–0. But that had not been good enough for the Coach. As his exhausted players slumped in the locker room afterward, he had called the huge football squad to gather close around him. "Let us pray," he murmured, with a faint but distinctive suggestion of a lisp in his voice. The heads of his players were already bowed. "Our Heavenly Father, we're grateful for the victory. We're sorry we didn't play better but we're grateful that no one was seriously injured on either team. We pray that, in the future, we shall use our strength and ability better than we used it in this game. Particularly our offense needs your help, Heavenly Father. These are the things we say in Thy name, Amen." With exhausted endorsement, nearly one hundred voices echoed: "Amen."

College football, in the United States today, has become more than just a game played between university students needing an outlet for their youthful spirits, athletic ability, and competitive energies. It is now big business and has become one of the most important, certainly one of the most dramatic, aspects of the whole American sporting scene. Top teams, like Ohio State University, pack stadiums wherever they play and are followed by millions on television. The ninety-four players in the Buckeyes, ninety of them on football scholarships, would actually rather die than lose; particularly in the home stadium in front of a crowd of 87,000. And the key figure in these contests between twentieth-century American gladiators has become the coach, the man who—in order to survive himself—must drive his team to victory each year. Athletic purists may argue that "the game's the thing," that playing to win destroys the spirit of friendly rivalry—but in college football, these days, winning has become the only important thing. And for close to thirty years, Ohio State's coach Woody Hayes has been among the most successful, the most colorful, of all winning coaches. Hayes has become a national figure, a legend in his own lifetime, famous for his fierce training methods, his tyrannical rages, his single-minded, obsessive dedication to football—and winning. Supporters have come to expect only one thing from the Buckeyes and Woody —a win. And he knows it. He knows that is why, when he leads his team from buses into the stadium locker room just before a game, the handshakes, the shoulder pats, the thumbs-up signs from the crowds of sup-

Nearly
one hundred
football
scholarships
at Ohio State.

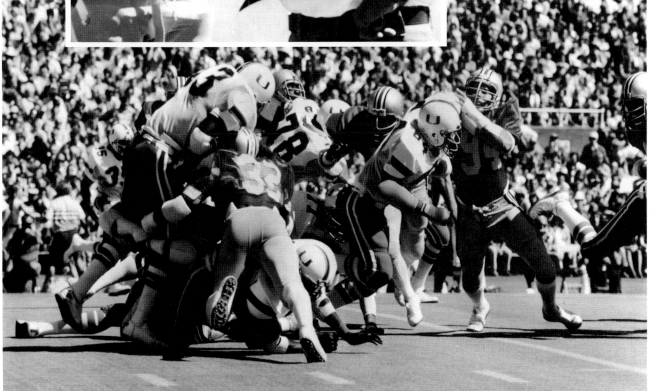

porters are always directed at him, the Coach. "Good luck, Woody," "Give us a win, Woody," "Play them hard today, Woody."

His background is Columbus, Ohio, site of Ohio State, the largest campus university in the United States, where 55,000 students can choose from 8,000 courses for degree credit. James Thurber came from Columbus and Ohio State University, but fewer Americans will remember that fact than those who know that Woody Hayes is still there. But Woody, because he is that kind of man, will always be the first to remind you that James Thurber came from Columbus. Nevertheless, if there is an O.S.U. fable, it is about Woody Hayes. It goes: "Once there was a man who went to Heaven, where he was met by Saint Peter and taken to a gigantic football stadium to watch a game. Down in the field by the sidelines was a fat old man in a baseball cap, running back and forth, jumping up and down, and gesturing hysterically. 'Who is that man?' the new arrival asked of Saint Peter. 'That's God,' said Saint Peter. 'But He thinks He's Woody Hayes.' "

He was born on St. Valentine's Day 1913. He told me: "I had an enormously happy childhood, I had great parents and—I'm not saying it boastfully—I had the greatest teachers that anyone ever, ever had. When I look back on them now, I realize I loved every one of them. I think they liked me pretty much, too. I was a good student, a little lazy like all kids, but I really did like to learn. My father was a school superintendent, a totally self-educated man. He never went to high school until he went to one to be principal of one. At the end of his life I would have to say that he was the best-educated man that I ever saw and a great teacher himself. That's why I like to teach—and I'm a pretty good teacher. It came from watching him and copying him, I guess. I suppose all good teachers are really disappointed thespians, we're all a little bit hammy.

"My father didn't live to see me become head coach at Ohio State, he died almost forty years ago, when I was coaching high school football. He never did say what he wanted me to be. He never insisted on any particular career. But he did insist that I go to college and take tough courses. As a matter of fact, at that time I had planned to be a lawyer and he wasn't against that at all. I got into coaching because of law. I was going to coach for a few years, in order to save some money and get into law school, but the war came along and I went into the service and the first job that came my way when I came out was football coaching. I still would like to have been a lawyer. Mind you, I'm not saying that I'm dissatisfied with my life and I wouldn't have had it any other way, but it might have been interesting to be a lawyer." I asked Woody what happened when his own son came of college age—did he hope to see him follow his father's footsteps into football coaching? "No, not at all. Actually, I'm afraid I was the sort of disappointed father who managed to persuade his own son to live out his father's ambitions. Perhaps because I didn't become a lawyer I pushed my son pretty hard in that direction. I had to be awfully careful that I didn't push him in a direction he didn't want to go. But as it happened he was quite interested in law and I was quite pleased to be able to shove him along that path. He is a lawyer today, and a pretty good one. I hope eventually that he will become a judge. I have that feeling that he will go all the way."

Woody Hayes served in the Navy for five years during the war, in both the Atlantic and the Pacific. Among the many pictures of college football heroes in his office at the Ohio State stadium, is an aging photograph of a naval ship under full steam, a reminder of the past. "I enjoyed the Navy very much. It is an enormously good organization, it takes care of its men and here at Ohio State we still use ideas from the Navy's communication system." Woody doesn't volunteer the fact that by the time he was discharged he had risen to the rank of lieutenant-commander, in charge of a patrol chaser and a destroyer escort in the Pacific. One of his Navy friends told me that, in the service, Woody was a tough disciplinarian, very straight-laced, who was seldom seen to unwind, never drank, smoked, played cards, or "fooled around" in port.

When he left the Navy in the spring of 1946 he took over as coach at Denison. He has been with football ever since. After a stupendously bad first season Denison went on to win nineteen games straight. Woody had discovered one of the natural laws of college football: there is a direct and mathematical relation between victories and alumni donations. In 1947 the Denison team finished the season undefeated for the first time in fifty-eight years; suddenly the previously tight fists of the alumni began to loosen up; within a few months $100,000 had been collected toward a new field house. In 1949 he accepted an offer to coach at Miami University, a larger college at Oxford, thirty-five miles northwest of Cincinnati. Once again the first year was poor but the second brought eight wins out of nine, a near-perfect season which also brought Woody to the attention of the press for the first time. In 1951 he decided to go after the often vacant position of head coach at Ohio State University. He got the job.

He has short gray hair swept back from his forehead, wears glasses, has a little paunch. During matches he's invariably seen on the field wearing slacks, a jacket, and—always—a tie (during training he wears a scarlet training shirt and gray trousers like his other coaches). At first he seems softly spoken, with that touch of a lisp. He talks constantly about his passion, the study of military history and strategy. But on the field he can, and does, turn into a raving, cursing maniac who physically assaults play-

Punishment running.

ers, rips up and smashes line markers and telephones, takes off his wristwatch and jumps on it, smashes his spectacles, punches news cameramen and reporters, blacks his own eyes—and drives his team to win.

Has Woody Hayes ever wanted to be a top player himself? "I would like to have been. I had a brother who was a much better football player than I was but, frankly, I wasn't good enough. Actually you will find, when it comes to coaching, that the top coaches have seldom been top players. You'll find that the qualities needed in a coach, to look back and analyze what went wrong, are different from the qualities needed in a top player."

For America's best-known college football coach, Woody Hayes draws a very low salary, $38,000 a year, and clearly does not care much for money. He told me: "I don't know whether I'm the best or not. I've had good players so, honestly, I can't tell how good a coach I am. I've never particularly cared how good a coach I am. I've just done my best. I think I'm a terribly lucky coach. Yes, that's it—I'm lucky. If you give me the same material as anyone else then I think I'll beat him on my luck, if nothing else. And there is one other thing, of course. I have experience and I am devoted to the game and I have learned a trick or two in my time. As for money, it doesn't concern me at all. The reason I've never worried about money is because I am afraid that money might spoil me. If I started to think about how my investments were coming, or about whether I should switch my money from one stock to another, then the first thing you know is that I wouldn't be thinking about coaching; I wouldn't be single-minded; I wouldn't be successful—I wouldn't be winning. I want to stay in coaching, it's in coaching that I feel I can do the best I can. I've seen money spoil so many people that I think it would spoil me as a coach. As it is, I don't worry about what size my car is, what size my house is, or whether there's a new suit of clothes hanging in the wardrobe. The whole of my family has always lived well above what I call the Vanity Level. My dad was a very humble man, although I believe he was a truly great man. He taught me, because he never wanted or needed anything himself, to live by the principles of Socrates, who used to walk through the marketplace and say, 'Look at all the things I don't need.' Well, I'm American enough not to agree totally with that philosophy but, frankly, I go along with most of it. So many people try to get money and then, when they do, it turns to ashes in their hands. It spoils them. That's why I've never been interested in it."

What about his histrionic displays, the one-man "fight-ins" staged by Woody Hayes? "Well, I've always been a highly strung individual and perhaps it's my artistic temperament." He said it without a glimmer of a smile, so he may even have meant it. "I've never had much artistic ability in a general way so maybe it comes out this way. At least I can console myself that I put the worst side of my temperament in front of everybody

and don't attempt to conceal it from them. Mind you, I don't do it just for color, just for effect, just to show off in front of the crowd. I'm just so darn disgusted when my team blows a play on which I've worked hard with them. I put too much into training and preparing my players and I just get disgusted when they blow a good one, which they frequently do. Also there are many times when I can see what officials can't see. Remember that I look at as many as fifty plays, for every one that they see. And then I see them on films all week, I play them backward and forward with my players. That's why I can see better than the officials. My eyesight may not be as good but I have that peripheral vision which enables me to see whether a tackle moved ahead of a ball. After all, I've been doing this job for forty-five years and most of the officials out there have only been on a football field for half that time."

Woody Hayes expounded a favorite theory of his: "I believe we should use television to test the decisions of the officials. If a coach objects to a decision, and the instant television playback shows that the coach was wrong, then the team should be penalized by a loss of fifteen yards. That would soon put a stop to frivolous objections, that hold up the game, but it would at least allow experienced coaches like me an opportunity to demonstrate that we see the details of the game better than the officials."

For a man who speaks passionately on all matters it is a surprise when Woody Hayes tells you that he is an introvert, a shy person, who finds it difficult to talk to strangers, to make friends, or to engage in conversation at parties. Millions of Americans who have witnessed his tantrums and his outbursts of temper may find it unbelievable. But Woody says: "I actually spend an awful lot of time alone, thinking. I have always known that there are many people in the world who are smarter than I am and I've found that the only way to cope with that is to sit back and think things over. I can't rush a decision, I can't rush at a fundamental proposition and decide instantly what to do about it. On the football field I am more experienced than anybody else I know, so there I can decide quickly. But I've found that to make up my mind on a new idea I have to consider it for a long time. It means that I find it difficult to strike up new friendships and respond in the area of small talk. I don't have any small talk. I don't think it's a failing—it's just a condition in me."

Woody Hayes takes his holidays separately from his wife. He usually goes climbing, or walking in the country; he spends most of his evenings alone, playing and replaying the training films taken during games and practices. Before the season starts he moves into the same dormitory as his team. His wife seldom sees him but understands and certainly doesn't begrudge the fact that her husband's passion turns her into a "football widow."

Woody Hayes *is* a good teacher, and he goes out of his way to demonstrate it. Each year he gives vocabulary classes to the freshmen on the team. He uses a simple increase-your-word-power paperback. The freshmen attend these Sunday morning classes reluctantly at first, and then with increasing enthusiasm. Woody's teaching is interspersed with homespun homilies and morality tales. He takes, for instance, the word "apathy" and it enables him to condemn, at length, apathetic students, apathetic teachers, apathetic athletes. That leads, naturally, to a homily on drug-taking, "copping out," lack of discipline. If it is astonishing that young men already in college need to be taught a basic vocabulary, does it mean that the myth of the dumb-as-an-ox football player, being crammed for examinations in order to maintain his place on the team, is fact? "Not so," says Woody Hayes. But he concedes his horror at the lack of word power in most freshmen. "I think this thing is getting worse and my attitude on it is quite simple. I am tired of talking about it. You know Mark Twain, our great humorist, said that everybody talks about the weather but never does anything about it. Well, we talk about this lack of vocabulary in our students and what a great problem it is and nobody does anything about it. Well, I'm doing something about it. If I can get them interested in broadening their vocabulary then I've done a good job. Most youngsters still like to learn. That's why I resent the kids who are on drugs, who don't want to learn, who just want to sit and do nothing. I always tell my squad that if they use drugs then they're out—immediately.

The college football season is short. Eleven, at most twelve, games between early September and late November. But, for many years now, for Ohio State University, and the city of Columbus, there has only been the one game, the match against Michigan, a team Woody refuses to call anything but "that team up north." He explained: "It's really part of a rivalry between two great universities which goes right back to Andy Jackson's administration, in the 1830s, when both universities fought fiercely over a piece of land that we Ohioans finally acquired, north of Toledo. It would seem that some competitive spirit has continued from that time. I believe the game between Ohio and Michigan is still the greatest college game there is. Forgive me if I boast a bit but, when I first came here, we had not beaten Michigan in eight years. So I trained and trained the squad and we changed that thing around and beat Michigan. Actually they're a great team and their coach is a great man. I admire them both. But football is about winning—and I'm about winning.

"I am not prepared to listen to the man who tells me that the spirit of the game is the thing and that winning isn't important. God damn that man to hell. He doesn't understand the purpose of the game. The will to win does not detract from team effort. The only thing for a team to want is to win. They've got to feel that they'd rather die than lose. I want them out there killing themselves to win. I want them to play with every bone broken and with their heads kicked in. As far as I'm concerned the spirit to win *is* a team spirit and it is indoctrinated into every member of my team."

For all his record of success and years of achievement, Woody Hayes still knows that if he started to fail, those who pay his salary would look elsewhere for a coach. "Sure, that's true," he told me. "I'd deserve to be fired. That's the way I feel about it, too. You don't get along on mediocrity in football. As a matter of fact, this whole civilization has been built on winning—and a civilization wouldn't be worth considering if you didn't want to go on winning. I think the worse thing that can happen to a civilization, and the worse thing that can happen to a football coach, is to feel too secure. If you feel too secure then you're in trouble. When things go wrong I give my team a little lecture, from history, you've probably noticed. Some of them may occasionally look as if they're getting too much of it but, actually, they can't get enough of it. Take the boy who tells me how he is, when I ask him, by saying, 'Oh, I'm fine, Coach, my legs are fine, my ankles are fine, I'm good.' I worry about that boy. He's too

The Yale–Princeton game at the Berkeley Oval in New York City, in 1889.

confident, too secure. In a game he's going to contribute to losing. I'm not interested in losing, losing isn't part of my philosophy or anything I teach these boys. You want to call me a dictator?—then call me a dictator. I am a dictator. You want to say that I indoctrinate the team?—then say I indoctrinate the team. You bet, I indoctrinate the team. You're doggone right, I indoctrinate the team. But, I've studied the dictators of the world and they're among the stupidest people in world history. And that is because they forgot communication. They had the power, they had the authority, they had the capacity, they had the will and the attention of the people. But the difference between them and me is that, although I dictate as much as they did, I remember communication. I communicate with my team, share my thoughts, and therefore my team wins. And that means I win."

Woody has set many precedents during his years at Ohio State. He was among the first to give chances to black players, among the first to employ black coaches. Out of the public eye, he also encourages a considerable amount of criticism from his assistant coaches. "They give it to me pretty good after a game sometimes," he told me. "They let me know pretty well if they think I've been calling the wrong damn plays. And they're right. I picked them because they're good and so there's no point in telling them to shut up. I picked them for what they are, for what they can become." George Hill, defense coach, has been working for Woody for seven years. He told me: "This is one of the great traditional football schools in the country. As a youngster I always followed Ohio State and it was my dream that, one day, I would meet Woody Hayes. Then I came here to work for him and my dream was achieved. The particular thing that he brings to the game of football is that he cares for people. He cares for people very much, he cares for his players and I think that is his greatest strength."

The coaches who work for Woody also help him spot talent and recruit players. They collect films from high schools and watch the playing of likely prospects, personally. They'll be tipped off by stringers and other alumni coaches around the country. They wind up with about a hundred students on football scholarships, all between eighteen and twenty-two.

Some of the academics at Ohio State worry that, because of the passion that surrounds the football team (and Woody Hayes), the value of the university, as a place of higher learning, is diminished. They are quick to point out that there are seventeen different colleges in which the 55,000 students can choose among courses which include agriculture, engineering, medicine, and the humanities. Although they know that the first to boast about the academic standards of Ohio State University is always Woody Hayes himself, they still don't want the football "tail" wagging the university "dog." They particularly don't like the sort of locker-room jibes that greet them at conferences and conventions and they certainly don't like reading about "Woody Hayes' University" in the papers. Woody answers these criticisms: "Saying that football is taking over the image of the university is too easy. I won't buy it. I won't buy it at all. For instance, we had the top man in pre-med playing on our football squad. For four years, he played football while he studied medicine. For the next thirty or forty years he'll be a physician or perhaps a surgeon. We gave him that, football gave him that. Many of these boys would not be able to get an education if they did not come here on football scholarships. And the first thing I make sure they get is an education. Sure I want them to play football. Sure I want them to win. Sure I want them to be the best team in the United States. But they're no goddam good to me if they don't get good grades in college. The only satisfaction I get, as a football coach, is knowing that football is helping these kids get an education.

"I've heard these criticisms from the academics around here before and, frankly, my response isn't printable. If they can teach football one-tenth as well as I know I could do their own jobs, I'd pay more attention to their criticisms. You know, the older I get the less I care about what the critics say. I'm sorry, but I have to level with Woody Hayes. I don't have to level with critics. As long as I, personally, feel that I am treating these youngsters right and that I am honestly helping them to get an education, then I don't care what they say about me, because I'll step into their classroom and I'll do a better job, there, than they'll ever do on a football field.''

He paused and then revealed a great deal of himself, as he went on: "Actually, you know, I wouldn't have minded being a professor, a teacher myself. It's a job I think I would have done well. But by the time I am ready to retire from public service there'll be no place for me as a teacher.''

Football is big business for Ohio State University. Even with an expenditure of $1.6 million a year, the Buckeyes still produce an overall annual profit of more than $2 million for the university. And that represents 98 percent of the cost of the entire athletic program for the whole of the university. The statistics for phone calls, recruiting trips, training and transport are impressive—and all dwarfed by the fact that the team's box-office draw has given Ohio State the biggest athletic budget in the country. When Dr. Enarson, the president of the university, first moved into his office, he found the walls were covered with pictures of the football team and the Rose Bowl game. He took them down. In a cupboard, where they had been neglected for years, he found the original Thurber cartoons owned by the university. Now, these decorate his office walls. But that doesn't make him anti-football, just anti-fanatic. As for Woody Hayes, he says:

"I like the man. As is often the case with public figures, there is an extremely complex and complicated human being lurking beneath the clownlike veneer that has been painted over him for years, more by the media than by himself. In fact, he's rather a creature of the media, in one sense. The media—television and radio particularly—manage to magnify any quirks that he has, but in fact he is an immensely shrewd man, who says and does things very carefully and in a very calculated manner. He is also an authentic human being. His virtues, like his defects, are as large as life. And, in an otherwise dull age, that is extremely refreshing.

"I do not, as so many fine-talking academics may do, believe that our winning football team, and Coach Hayes, detract from the reputation and capacity of this university. A number of our faculty indulge in this kind of nonsense and I am forced to remind them that if we lost every single game this year and every single game next year it wouldn't put one more book in the library, it wouldn't buy us a new electron microscope, nor would it increase faculty salaries one bit. The fact is, as I am sure you know by now, our excellent overall athletics program is self-financing and there's not a dollar that goes into it that is extracted from the academic enterprise. I know, and I think it fair to say, that there may be a small psychic damage;

310

a feeling on the part of the academic faculty that it is impossible to have a first-rate football team and be first-rate academically. But this is outrageously bad logic and they ought to be sent back to first-year philosophy and told to take the course all over again. I also think that we have become a nation of softies. We're not alone in this of course, but if football can introduce a competitive concept and a tougher attitude into the minds of our young people, then I think it's a very good thing and I think that what Woody Hayes is doing is a fine thing. I also like to see the team win. Don't we all?"

The alumni of Ohio State University, like those of other universities, not only like their alma mater to win at football, they like to make sure of the fact. And if it takes money, that is what they would like to provide. But Woody Hayes will never endorse or allow any deceit or underhanded practices. He insists that the strict rules about finance and incentives be followed. However, there are some "practices" to which he cannot really object. Students frequently need, and invariably search for, vacation jobs. So, in this area, the alumni take care to see that star players are not without worthwhile and remunerative occupations during vacation. It is said that one summer it was arranged for a player to be paid $1,000 a month as a lifeguard at a beach resort. At the end of the summer it was discovered that he couldn't swim. It is also said that one alumni committee man sold his two-year-old Cadillac to a Buckeye quarterback—for five dollars. Hayes always denies any knowledge of things like this but the players themselves have told me that the practice is so widespread that he *must* know about it. In any case, it is not illegal and Woody's very efficient spy network throughout the university is certain to bring to his attention anything that is. He likes to know, immediately, everything that his players are doing and he is invariably in full possession of information about their off-duty activities, their girlfriends, trouble at home and the way they spend their money and how much money they have. He, himself, so disapproves of the effect of money on college football that he will not hesitate to blow the whistle on any other team that he believes may be allowing the corruption of illegal bribes and incentives. He once blew the whistle on the Michigan team: "Yes, I did. They were clear out of line and it was proven so. I did it for the sake of the whole league, not to damage a rival team. I would say that, about now, our league is as clean as any league in the country. There might be some minor infractions but that's because it's a bit like traffic offenses; there are so many rules it is difficult to keep up with them all. But as far as going out and buying athletes, outright bribery, I'd say that the majority of schools do not do it. These days there are enough coaches, like me, who are prepared to see the game won by skill, effort, and training—not by waving dollars."

Woody regularly visits the local hospital, to check on the condition of injured players. While he tries to limit injuries on the team as much as possible, a walk round the locker room while the players are being taped up for a training session will reveal more knees and ankles with terrifyingly large surgical scars than most people will see in a lifetime. Many of the top players have suffered serious damage at one time or another; quite a few have been hospitalized for serious operations. One boy, Norman Burrows, went to the hospital for major knee surgery before he had even run so much as a single yard for the Buckeyes. He had been recruited from high school and was injured in his last game before going to Ohio State. Nevertheless, the terms of his football scholarship still applied. As a member of the Buckeyes team, he was entitled to be given the best medical and surgical treatment that could be provided in Columbus. Visiting him, Woody asked how he was getting along, reassured him about his future, talked with the boy's mother, signed an autograph for his father. Woody told me: "That boy, I'm afraid, will certainly not be able to play for us this season, but maybe he'll be able to turn out for the squad next season. It doesn't matter. I don't want the boy to feel that he's let us down or that he's lost his chance here. We've had players recruited and signed, who were then in accidents and unable to play for the whole of their college career. That doesn't matter, it only matters to me that they get the education that their talent qualified them to receive in the first place. That boy is studying to be an engineer and, even if he never runs a yard for Ohio State, his football scholarship will allow him to qualify as an engineer. That's the important thing for me."

Knee injuries are among the most common suffered by football players. The playing field of Ohio State's stadium is not covered by grass, but by "astroturf," a plastic and durable manmade surface. It has a disadvantage. Players are more likely to damage tendons, cartilage, and muscles when the turf is dry. So paradoxically, in a nation with a water shortage, for all practices and scrimmages, Woody has the turf watered. And you can see, on all dry days, giant sprinklers depositing tons of water on plastic grass that never grows and doesn't wear out.

Students on the Woody Hayes team put in more hours than most university students. They have to. In order to allow time for training and to achieve the requisite grades, they get up earlier and work more intensely than other students. But the Buckeyes look after their own. They provide "brain coaches," academics hired to push, stretch, and develop the minds of the Saturday stadium heroes, in the same way as Woody Hayes trains their muscles. Most of the players on football scholarships at Ohio State will have been approached when in high school by at least a hundred universities, before choosing Ohio State. The competition between college teams for top players is fierce. Doug Mackie, who is studying industrial arts, and weighs 252 pounds and strikes terror into

Practice.

opposition teams, was approached by 120 colleges with the offer of a football scholarship. He chose Ohio State because "it suits my kind of playing."

Although the players are studying diverse subjects, nearly all of the players I spoke to confessed that, before trying to start a career, they would like to play pro football. But the life of a pro football player is very short; three or five or, very occasionally, eight years. The players know it's no way to make a living but it is, as they say, a certain way to make a killing. To be "drafted"—which is the term used to describe the transaction when college players are signed on by professional teams—it is usually necessary for a player to be named "All American." This sportswriters' list of the best football players of the year, drawn from all the universities in America, men who will never play together as one team and who may never meet each other on the field, is the annual assessment by which players are rated and has become almost the guidebook of pro football teams, when they go recruiting.

Chris Ward, four years on the Ohio State squad and this year captain of the team, is heavily tipped to be named All American this year. At 270 pounds (by no means the heaviest on the team) Chris, who is studying finance, told me: "I'd like to use my finance degree, if I get it, by starting a little business somewhere. But in order to start a little business I need some capital so I'd like to play pro football and make some money that way. I'm not worried about getting hurt. I know it happens to some guys but now I reckon I've learned to take care of myself." Gazing up at Chris Ward it was impossible not to believe him.

Geoff Logan, star quarterback of the Ohio State Buckeyes, who damaged his ankle during the first game of the season, is also playing in his fourth year. He told me: "I probably started to think about football scholarships when I was seventeen years old in high school and coaches would come to visit the school and they would take good care to speak to me after the game and say, 'Remember the name of our university.' It was then that I realized that I was probably good enough to get a place on one of the big teams, like the Buckeyes. It was actually George Hill, the defense coach, who signed me for the team. I thought about it very carefully before I came to Ohio State. I know they're a winning team, but they also have a reputation for playing heavy, defensive, blocking play and I wanted to develop as a runner, as a quarterback. The thing that persuaded me, in the end, is the reputation of Coach Hayes. His name is magic throughout the world of football. I am majoring in public relations and I hope to get into business. But if I was offered a place on a pro football team I think I'd play a few years before going into public relations. I would like to play pro football for as long as I could, but being a running back and the guy who carries the ball, you take a lot more physical abuse than most of the other players. The life expectancy of a running back in pro football is very much less than five years, so I wouldn't say that there was much security in a professional football career."

Woody Hayes is firmly against the idea that a team like the Buckeyes is mainly preparing players for pro football. "Many of them may go into it, and we have a good record in this field. But that isn't the aim. We're here to give the youngsters a college education and let them earn that education by playing football. I am not training them to become pro football players, I am training them to become educated. I am more interested in their education than I am in their subsequent football career."

Joe Robinson, six-foot-five and 250 pounds, is getting an education. It is particularly important to him. He is black. He has been playing for the Buckeyes for three years. He was a star football player with his high school team. Eighty-nine universities approached him with offers, including schools in Mississippi and Arkansas. Why did he choose Ohio? "I thought it was a good opportunity to come here and play in a big-town atmosphere. I come from a really small town which is predominantly Caucasian. I belonged to the black minority in that town and a lot of people thought I was too big and too cocky—and black. My father had a mental illness and because of that, and because I was black, everybody in the town thought I was big for my boots even to dream of playing for such a team as Ohio State. They all told me to go to a small school. 'Joe,' they used to say, 'go to a small school where you can be the big fish in the little pond.' And I used to listen to them and say nothing. Because man, if you're black in a town that is mostly white, it doesn't matter how big you are, you still do a lot of listening—and you don't do a lot of talking back. But I said to myself, I've got enough self-respect to go to a school large enough to find the competition I need so that I can test myself against the best in the country and see how I make out. That was always a dream of mine, it was also a dream of mine to go on and play pro football. If you've played for a team like Ohio State then you stand a very good chance of being drafted into pro football.

"How is it now? Well, when I go home I discover just how two-faced people are because, now, they all slap me on the back and put their arms around me and they say, 'Hey, Joe, I knew you could make it all along,' and then they come and say, 'Hey, Joe, that was a great game. When do I get tickets for the next game?' and things like that. It doesn't teach me anything I didn't already know. Look at the color of my skin, man, and you'll know that I learned that lesson as soon as I could see that my skin wasn't the same as everyone else. But out there on the field you have a helmet on and a guard over your face and padding on, and if you're big and if you're strong you can win. On the field, they're not going to see the color of your skin, they're just going to see the way you play football." Joe Robinson plays guitar, sings in local folk music groups, and is popular with the rest of the team. Every home game finds his father and younger brothers sitting excitedly in seats provided by Joe. Joe Robinson has competed, on the terms he wanted, and won. But he is about to take on another battle. He has a white girlfriend. They want to marry, and it's clear that they would make a splendid couple, but the situation has left Joe's family bewildered and the girl's family frightened. Nevertheless, Joe is calm about the future. "I feel the same way about this as I did about playing football. It's the big one. I want to tackle it; and I want to do it on my own terms; and I want to win." I think he will.

Woody Hayes' wife, Anne, sees very little of her husband during the season. She goes to all the games, discusses them with him afterward, but because of his absences from home either traveling to "away" games or living with his players during training, she has developed a life of her own

Woody's wife, Anne.

and has become an accomplished lecturer, much in demand by luncheon clubs and ladies' societies. But Woody Hayes has never heard his wife speak, even though she makes more speeches than he does. "We have an agreement about it," he told me. "I think she must be awfully good because, if she wanted, she could make three speeches in a day. But I think that if I went to listen to her I might get critical of what she was saying, I might even be tempted to criticize her and I don't want to do that. I think it's much better not to listen to her. When I write a book now, I don't take the chapters for her to read so that we don't have a row or an argument if she criticizes it. We tend to take separate vacations too, although down in the southern part of the state I've got a few acres of land and I'm building a log cabin there and she kids me and says I'm only building it so that when I retire I can use it as a power base to run for President."

Anne is devoted to her husband and understands his obsessive passion for football, even shares it. She puts up with middle-of-the-night phone calls from disgruntled fans; she'll travel with Woody when he's recruiting players, talk to a boy's parents who may be undecided which college to choose; she keeps in touch with Woody's and her son and the grandchildren and generally orders the coach's life. During the football season she says: "I know that football comes first and so I behave like a good obedient coach's wife. When the season's over I know that I can get in a little nagging, get a little house-painting done, and talk about holidays with him. But it's been a good life, the best. I worry about what he will do when he retires because football has been his life and his passion all these years and I think it might be very difficult indeed for him to replace it."

Woody Hayes holds a weekly press conference in which he fiercely defends his players from any criticism from sportswriters, and discusses the next game with television and radio reporters. He also runs his own Saturday night television show, just called *Woody,* in which he discusses football. His own players appear regularly on it with him and are these days interviewed only by him, since he was, in the past, provoked to anger by questions, from sports reporters, that he thought less than fair to his players. But not only does he interview his players, he'll usually answer for them as well. It all makes good television and it doesn't surprise anyone who knows about Woody or his reputation. Even the academics who speak disparagingly of the Buckeyes tend to find themselves in front of a television set when Woody's program is on.

On the day of a game the city prepares. In hotels, even the menu cards have been changed, listing dishes such as Coach's Pick, Band's Delight, The Tackle, The Line Backer, The Full Back, The Referee, The Quarterback and Cheerleaders' Choice. Postcards of the team—and Woody— appear everywhere. For Columbus, a game means business. But the night before a home game Woody Hayes takes his team away from the university, registers them all in a motel on the edge of town. "I do this because I don't want them interfered with, I don't want them to worry unnecessarily, and I want to keep them together." That night he always takes the team to a movie, carefully selected by one of the coaches as suitable for the players. Woody told me: "If you get the wrong kind of movie it doesn't relax them or put them in the right mood. We like old Westerns, we like war movies, we like wholesome movies, but we don't like too much comedy or too much laughter. The reason for that is you never see a man make a tackle with a smile on his face. You don't laugh your way to victory, you fight your way to victory. Then, there are movies that are disaster. We made a mistake some years ago and took them all to see *Easy Rider.* When they came out of the movie I took one look at them and it was obvious that something was wrong. So I spent over two hours talking to some of the kids that night because what it had done to them, watching that movie, was to challenge their sense of values to the extent that they were beginning to doubt the things that were worthwhile. I spent a lot of time with them, that night, getting them back into the mood to win. We find that if we can get our team into a quiet and serious mood then they invariably play the best games. If they're talking loud, at dinner after the movie, then I know that something's gone wrong and I have to quiet them down."

After the movie part of the process of "quieting them down" come more football training films, and a final pregame briefing and indoctrination from Woody and the coaches. Then those who have difficulty sleeping or need pills for their bruises and strained muscles are handed their medication and by 9 P.M. the whole team is in bed. Just to make sure, Woody Hayes does the rounds of every room. It's a bizarre, muscular, "kiss-me-goodnight-sergeant-major" routine that is taken with utmost seriousness, by both players and coaches. Father-figure Hayes opens every door, greets every player, turns off television sets and lights, admonishes those who have forgotten to bring their word-power vocabulary books, makes sure they don't have the heating turned too high, then says goodnight and shuts the door. The players accept it, even seem to need it.

On the morning of the game the team eats breakfast together, after a passionate Grace, in which Woody invariably calls upon the Lord to put spirit into his players—and make them win. All dressed in their best clothes, he leads them in a fast walk once round the motel before loading them into the buses. They are taped up by the trainers at the motel and all that remains for the locker room at the stadium is to finish putting on their armor, their uniforms and their helmets. Up until the very last moment the coaches have the offensive and defensive teams grouped around blackboards on which they are still sketching, rubbing out and resketching moves and strategies. Woody takes over, just before they run out onto the field. He reminds them of the lessons they've learned, urges them to remember the weakness of the opposition, and to win. Then he prays again, briefly, just for victory. He sends them out with a shout and, roaring, slapping, knocking each other on the helmets, the Buckeyes run toward the crowd.

During the game, in a tower above the stadium, the coaches will work out and phone each play down to the coaches on the line. Woody may spend as much as half a game with a telephone to his ear. The film cameras record every move, for later analysis and inquest. As each play is called, as ground is won or lost, as the single replacement player is sent running on each time, to give the number of the new play to the team, so the tension builds. The offensive team is replaced by the defensive team and vice versa, in a complicated and intricate arrangement that, nevertheless, is clearly understood by millions.

Tactics and deceit.

In the game against Miami, at halftime, the Buckeyes were winning but not, for Woody Hayes, by enough. In the locker room he lashed into the players, tearing their skill, their capacity, even their enthusiasm apart, calling upon God to witness how thick-headed, how useless they all were. He sent them out for the second half. They won, but only by 10–0 and it was still not good enough for Woody Hayes. Afterward in the locker room, surrounded by press men, tape recorders, and cameras, he admitted that he would have liked to win by a bigger margin. Later he told me: "It isn't that I wanted to win by a massacre, just that, in this first game of the season, I wanted to give as many players on the squad a chance to play, particularly the freshmen. But to do that we would have had to build up a truly convincing lead. Without that I couldn't afford to take chances. The defense team played brilliantly today. It's the offense that I've got to rip into. Next week we're going to teach, and teach, and teach again."

Woody Hayes has written three books on football and football methods. He will probably write more. He had a mild heart attack three years ago, hardly surprising in view of the energy he generates. But he did exactly what his doctor told him to and within six months he was back at work,

After the game with the press.

as noisy and energetic as ever. For the moment, football is still his life. But in a few years he will have to face retirement. How will he tackle it?

"It's something I just don't want to think about. I'll probably do some more writing, I'd like to do some more teaching—but I suppose they'll say that I'm too old for that. But it's true to say that this stadium has been pretty well the whole of my life, for more than a quarter of a century now, so it's difficult to say what I'll do without it. I know I'm getting older, even though I feel as strong as ever I did, but sometimes I do get a little absentminded. I find myself remembering faces and forgetting names, even telling the same story twice. Why, I think I've told you the same stories more than once." He had but, at the time, there was no way that I could even begin to consider suggesting to Woody Hayes that I'd already heard the story. He knows that, too. "Goddammit, why do you make me think of retirement. It isn't fair." A flash of the Woody Hayes whose colorful rages have entranced crowds for years returned. "I won't let you make me think of it. No, doggone it, I'm not ready to think of it.

"This is my life, right here in the stadium. I'm not through yet. I haven't finished winning . . ."

They won.

THE FIRST LADY
ROSALYNN CARTER

As the Air Force jet climbed steeply from Andrews Air Force Base, the pain behind her eyes increased. Isolated in the No. 1 seat of the Presidential plane, she rubbed her temples to ease the headache. She had told me that she nearly always suffered when flying, but she didn't complain; long ago she had learned to accept physical discomfort, even pain, as part of the daily life she and her husband chose to lead.

So, she thought of other things: wondered if her nine-year-old daughter, left at home, would behave and remember her violin practice; she made a note on the pad in front of her about a question that she must ask her husband, when she phoned him that night. She considered what was ahead of her, all the things that she most feared: foreign dignitaries; greetings to be responded to in another language; a thousand, perhaps even two thousand, handshakes; newspaper and magazine photographers and television cameras; reporters' questions; the constant smiling and the attentive manner—and the speeches, the dreaded speeches.

Rosalynn Carter is not normally an extrovert. But she has learned to do very much more than just stand at her husband's side. She acts as his ambassador and emissary and willingly accepts the grave responsibility of extending their "partnership-in-marriage" at the most important and sensitive levels in international relations, and political dealing, in the world today. Rosalynn Carter, as First Lady of the United States, is also the President's Partner—and the rest of the world is becoming aware of it.

The plane with its distinctive pale blue livery, with only the words "United States of America" on its side, turned south for Puerto Rico, a self-governing commonwealth in union with the U.S., where political differences have become particularly sensitive and sometimes violent, and where the issue of nationalistic separatism has raised its head. The First Lady's job? To meet newspaper editors at a convention and, also, to talk to the leaders of the commonwealth which seems likely, despite the separatist rumblings, to become the fifty-first state of America. A tough assignment which would result in unflattering headlines if she made a mistake. But she was not likely to. She has been toughened and forged in many political battles. Nevertheless, Rosalynn Carter doesn't like the label which newspaper columnists and political reporters used to describe her during the long, strenuous campaign for the Presidency—"The Steel Magnolia." She doesn't think it fair or accurate. It may not have occurred to her that it is beginning to be used with affection and admiration. Certainly, after three weeks traveling with her constantly I would hand her that title as a badge of office to be worn with honor. She has earned it and continues to do so. The First Lady was away from the White House— "doing a job for Jimmy."

The White House must, by now, rate as one of the world's best-known settings for dramas of power. As the executive headquarters for the President of the richest and most powerful country the world has ever known, it has become a symbol that characterizes both the weaknesses and strengths of the United States. It is also, of course, a Presidential home, to be "presided over"—by the First Lady. Unlike their husbands, First Ladies tend to emerge as public figures and personalities only after they've arrived in the White House. There have been many famous ones, some who have almost matched their Presidential husbands in both reputation and achievement. First Ladies like Jackie Kennedy, "Lady Bird" Johnson, and, of course, Eleanor Roosevelt, have become perhaps even better remembered than many Presidents. First Ladies have been of all types, come in all shapes and sizes, from high-born ladies and society beauties—to plain Janes and teetotaling puritans. But the farmer's wife who came to Washington from Plains, Georgia, when they elected Jimmy Carter President, is determined to be a First Lady remembered for her own style.

As a title, First Lady is comparatively new. It began appearing in print in the 1880s when a correspondent used it in reporting President Cleveland's marriage to Miss Frances Folsom. An advertisement of the day even claimed that the First Lady owed her complexion to a preparation which contained arsenic. In 1911 a comedy, *The First Lady of the Land,* re-emphasized the label—the heroine of the comedy was Dolly Madison. The first President, George Washington, was partnered by his wife, "Dear Patsy," but she was not generally known as the First Lady. In fact, visiting dignitaries, foreign ambassadors, and political figures in the days of the first Presidency didn't know how to address Mrs. Washington on formal occasions and at receptions. They thought plain "Mrs." not dignified enough,

The first First Lady,
Martha Washington.

Dolly Madison was a very
popular hostess during her
husband's Presidency.

so many of them took to calling her "Lady Washington." It may be that this uncorrected misnomer led, eventually, to the title "First Lady." Certainly it seems that only in America today could the wife of a President, elected by the people, become as significant and as important as the First Lady. The wives of Russian, Chinese, French, English premiers and presidents have, for the most part, remained supportive but somewhat anonymous figures in their husbands' backgrounds. That would never have been considered a possibility by Rosalynn Carter.

But not all First Ladies have found the role even bearable. Martha Washington wrote, in one of the few letters still left from the time of her husband's Presidency: "I think that I am more like a State prisoner than anything else, there are certain bounds set for me which I must not depart from . . . ." In the same letter she confided that she "would much rather be at home" and, in that respect, her feelings are shared by Rosalynn Carter. Mrs. Carter told me: "Oh, when it's over—and I know it will be over—I just want to go home; to go home to my things." In that sentence the attractive, intelligent Southern farmer's wife captured the essence of a need for familiar surroundings and domestic stability that many women will recognize and share.

She was born Rosalynn Smith, in Plains, Georgia, a town of fewer than 600 people, where later she was to meet, fall in love with, and then marry Midshipman Jimmy Carter, a young man who, everybody in the small town knew, was sure of a successful career—in the Navy. She was born poor and became poorer. Her father, Edgar, was a garage mechanic, a sensitive and good man who loved and cared for his family. When Rosalynn, the eldest of four children, was only thirteen years old, her father died of leukemia. It was only years later that Rosalynn, her sister, and two brothers, learned how deeply their father had actually disliked his job, which left him greasy and grimy every night, and how much he had yearned to earn his living in a more "respectable" way.

Rosalynn's mother, Allie Smith ("Miz Allie" to the whole town), left as a widow to bring up four children, took in sewing. She made bridal trousseaux, distinguished for their fine needlework, for most of the families in the area. Later, when her youngest child was old enough to go to school, she worked at the post office. Rosalynn used to come home from school and take over the "little mother" role until Miz Allie returned from the post office. Scrimping, saving, and going without became a normal part of young Rosalynn's life, but it was not a puritanical or Calvinistic imposition. She still remembers a great deal of laughter, happiness, and fun from her childhood. She knows, like the whole town, that she owes that to her mother's strength of character. Rosalynn told me: "My mother was only thirty-four when my father died and she took over the complete responsibility for the family and never asked for any help from a charity or relatives, or anyone in the town. She grew into an extremely strong and independent person and even at that age it made a deep impression on me and has been a permanent influence on my life. She never complained and never demanded support or help from any of us. In fact, I've frequently felt very guilty about not helping out enough as a teenager. But like all teenagers, I suppose, I was selfish and unaware because I see now that I could have been far more helpful in looking after the rest of the children and the house. But it tells you what kind of woman she was that she never once suggested to me that I wasn't doing enough and has never since talked about it with me."

The Smith family are Methodists and Miz Allie insisted that all her children go to Sunday School and church and study the Bible every day. Church became an essential activity in their lives. Rosalynn's brother Murray is a Methodist lay speaker and—like his famous brother-in-law Jimmy Carter—he regularly teaches Sunday School. Rosalynn's mother never remarried although, as a pretty widow in her thirties, she did not lack for suitors. She told people it was because she remained in love with the memory of her husband, whom she met while she was in the ninth grade and he was the driver of the school bus. At the time of his death Rosalynn was thirteen; Gerry, eleven; Murray, eight; and Althea, three. Rosalynn was a good student at the local school and she worked in the evenings and on weekends in a local hairdresser's, shampooing and setting. She was the valedictorian of her high school class and then went on to a local college. But she never graduated. She left to marry Jimmy Carter.

Rosalynn had always known Jimmy Carter; she was his sister Ruth's best friend, and frequently Ruth would stay with the Smiths or Rosalynn would weekend with the Carters. But for young Rosalynn, Jimmy was the most distant and unobtainable person. He was three years older. Romantically speaking, for fifteen-year-old Rosalynn, Jimmy Carter at eighteen might just as well have lived on another planet. But then, Jimmy Carter, after a year at Georgia Technical College, achieved his most burning ambition by entering the Naval Academy at Annapolis.

Rosalynn's crush on Jimmy began during the next two years when Jimmy would visit home and look so smart and heroic in his white uniform. According to Rosalynn, he didn't notice her. Then, in the last summer before the war in Europe ended, Jimmy Carter came home again to Plains, Georgia. Two days before he was due to return for his senior year at Annapolis he asked Rosalynn to go to a movie with him, their first date. After that they dated constantly. She recalls that when he returned to the Naval Academy she was already in love with him and he had told his mother, Miz Lillian, that Rosalynn was the girl he intended to marry.

Miz Lillian is a formidable lady, clearly an awesome prospect for any girl

to face as a mother-in-law. There have been many stories about her disapproval of Jimmy's prospective bride, her general disapproval of the poor and hard-working Smith family, and about her strong belief that he should wait until his career was underway until he married anyone. But not one of these stories has been given real foundation by Rosalynn, Jimmy, or Miz Lillian herself.

Even at eighteen, Rosalynn was a girl with a spirit and will of her own. Jimmy Carter knew that he was in love with more than just a pretty face. Rosalynn told me: "Once Jimmy and I decided to marry I never thought about another boy. That was it. We were going to do it and nothing was going to stop us. I'm like that. He's like that. We are both still that way and," she laughed, "thank heavens we still feel the same way about each other after all these years." As soon as Jimmy Carter graduated from Annapolis they were married, on July 7, 1946, in Rosalynn's church, the Plains Methodist Church. But since then Rosalynn Carter has been, like her husband, a Baptist.

They became a Navy couple. Their first son, Jack (christened John William), was born while Jimmy was stationed in Portsmouth, Virginia. After that Jimmy was ordered to submarine school in New London, Connecticut, and a little later he and his new family were posted to Honolulu, where he served on submarines. It was in Honolulu that their second son, Chip (James Earl III), was born. From Honolulu they were sent to San Diego and then back to New London where their third son, Jeff (Jeffrey), was born in 1952.

For Rosalynn the life of a Navy wife was hard, demanding, frequently lonely—but always exciting. She told me: "I loved it, I really, really loved it. We traveled to so many places, we made so many friends, we saw so many things, that every morning I would wake up all excited about the day ahead. We were enjoying our life together doing absolutely everything together and having an amazingly good time. I didn't like the separations from Jimmy, when he was at sea, but I knew it was part of the price we had to pay for his Navy career and the life we led. I didn't mind having to raise three children, on my own a lot of the time, because when Jimmy was at home he was a marvelous father and would pitch in and help enormously. We were very, very happy."

And then it changed. In 1953 Jimmy Carter's father died of cancer, leaving the Carter family peanut business, in Plains, in need of leadership. Jimmy decided to resign his commission in the Navy and return home to his family responsibilities. It was a hard decision to make. By then young Lieutenant Carter had already been noted for senior promotion and was

Rosalynn's mother, Miz Allie (Mrs. Allethea Smith).

expected to go to the top. He had been selected by the famous Admiral Rickover for a senior job in the nuclear submarine program. Jimmy Carter had been marked for success only to turn his back on it to face family duties—and Rosalynn Carter didn't like it.

"I couldn't bear it when Jimmy told me that he was going to resign and go back to Plains. By that time, Plains seemed such a small life, and so far away and so unexciting, that I felt physically ill at the thought of returning to it. Mind you, I loved all our friends and relatives in Plains but, remember, I was having a marvelous time in the Navy and I didn't want to give it up. I also thought that Jimmy was sacrificing everything that he had worked and slaved for, over the years, by abandoning his Naval career just as he was about to become really successful. It was the first big row in our married life. It was more than an argument, it was a battle and it went on for days and days. I screamed, yelled, and argued, and did everything I could to make him change his mind, but once Jimmy"—her soft Georgia accent always turns her husband's name into *Jimmuh*—"has made up his mind that something is right, then there is no way that anybody will persuade him differently. And I couldn't.

"So we packed up and we went home to Plains. And we were poor, oh golly, we were poor. In those first years we had hardly any money. We even had to apply for minimum-rent public housing, a small apartment on the edge of Plains. And we worked, and we worked and we worked."

In 1954, at the end of their first year out of the Navy and back in Plains, the family peanut business made a total profit of just $200. Jimmy, in blue jeans, boots, and plaid shirt, would get up at 5 or 6 A.M. and do the manual labor. Rosalynn, still looking after three young children, would get up with him and keep the books, organize the office—she worked. Or *wukked,* as she pronounces the word. "We wukked. That's about all I remember about that time. But we were doing it together, side by side, and on weekends, and after school, our boys would join us and help. We also began to build up a fertilizer and seed business as well as the peanut business, and gradually we turned the corner."

"Turning the corner" allowed Jimmy Carter time to look around and, looking around, he "caught" politics. He was already used to political life from the time when his father had been a member of the Georgia State Legislature. The elder Carter had been active in local state politics. So, Jimmy ran for the Georgia State Senate and won; but only after a long-drawn-out legal battle, in which he exposed his political opponent and a corrupt aspect of local voting procedures. The lawyer who helped him to investigate and then win a reverse of the poll which had put Jimmy's opponent into office was Charles Kirbo, who is now a close Presidential adviser. For Jimmy Carter, political ambition had set in. In 1966 the Carter team—Jimmy and Rosalynn—ran for the Governorship of Georgia. They lost to Lester Maddox, a dedicated segregationist. The Carters, in debt and depressed, went back to Plains. Four years later they ran again and Jimmy became Governor of Georgia. During this period their daughter Amy was born, the girl that Jimmy had always told Rosalynn he wanted. In 1977 Jimmy Carter and his wife Rosalynn stepped into the history books, as he became the thirty-ninth President of the United States and she took on the role of First Lady.

Now she runs the White House and its large staff and serves alongside her husband, constantly in the public eye. Historically speaking, perhaps the most significant of all her predecessors was Eleanor Roosevelt, who, because of her husband's paralysis and confinement to a wheelchair, acted not only throughout the White House, but throughout the country, as his eyes and ears: she traveled, investigated, and questioned constantly, always reporting back to him. Although Rosalynn Carter vigorously denies that she has studied Eleanor Roosevelt or modeled herself on her behavior, she is also the first to admit that some conditions in her life are similar. Jimmy is tied to the White House, where he is constantly needed for decisions that only he can make. So, she has taken on the role of his agent, investigating on his behalf and reporting back—acting as the President's emissary. She told me: "I didn't study previous First Ladies. I don't think I particularly thought about the job in that way. During the campaigning, when I worked out just how much we all wanted Jimmy to be President and the fact that that would make me First Lady, I thought about how I would do the job and what I would like to achieve when Jimmy was in office —if he made it. But it's a long step from campaigning to winning, and you have to put one foot in front of the other and not think too far ahead. It was only when reporters, during the campaign, started asking what I would do if I became First Lady and what other First Ladies I admired, that I, then, thought about the job in more detail. I had always, until that time, thought that I would do many things the same way as I had when Jimmy was Governor of Georgia and I was the Governor's wife.

"It was then that I realized that people like me were in a position to achieve a great deal, have an influence on many things. I realized if I used this influence wisely and honestly and to good purpose then it would all be worthwhile. Of course, one is always approached by the kind of people who wish to use your name in causes or campaigns, even for commercial interests. I know there have been people who have succumbed to this temptation and done just that. But that, in my opinion, is wrong and it couldn't happen to me, or Jimmy; it is just not the way we could live. But as to whether or not I'm like Eleanor Roosevelt or any of the other First Ladies, I really cannot say. Other people must draw that comparison, I don't think of it in that way.

"Certainly, you know, I don't think of myself as the wife of a President,

Checking arrangements for a state dinner.

confined only to the domestic planning, the entertaining and hospitality
—the hostess with the mostest. But that's because, as Rosalynn Carter,
I've always been in partnership with Jimmy Carter. During those first
seven years of our marriage when he was in the Navy, he was gone so much
that I had to take care of everything. And I learned, then, that I could do
many things that I'd never done before, like run the house and take care
of the children, look after emergencies and medical crises by myself. And
after our row about him leaving the Navy to run the peanut business, I
worked alongside him as a partner. I always worked and helped with the
business even though I was also running the home. It never occurred to
me that I should do anything else and it would have seemed unnatural to
Jimmy not to have me work alongside him. Then when Jimmy ran for
Governor, I went out and campaigned with him. He knew that I had
particular projects that I was interested in—mental health, the care of old

people, and various social problems—so he encouraged me to develop my interest in those and campaign alongside him, with those in the forefront.

"Now, in the White House, it's true that I do have a social secretary and a good many social commitments and we have to entertain on a vast, even rather frightening, scale. But you must remember that although it is quite true that I came from humble little Plains, Georgia, there were those years in the Governor's Mansion in Atlanta. As Governor, Jimmy set a style that was very international indeed and we entertained many foreign Heads of State, so I became used to it. Nevertheless, I would not like supervising the entertaining and hospitality, and the domestic running of the White House, to become my main priority. I am not like Jacqueline Kennedy, for instance. I appreciate fine things and I love good furniture and paintings, but I couldn't devote the whole of my time as First Lady to restoring a fine antique atmosphere into the White House or specialize only in patronizing the arts.

But Rosalynn Carter has, nevertheless, taken over the domestic running of the White House with a firm hand. She and her President husband both admit, cheerfully, to being more than just frugal—they call themselves "tight." Politically, a President determined to cut indulgence and extravagance out of the nation's housekeeping is an excellent one, at least on the face of it, according to most of the nation. The Carters serve no hard liquor in the White House, only wine. And there have been other savings. "I discovered when we got here," she said, "that there were between three and four hundred TV sets in the White House. Imagine that, nearly four hundred TV sets. It's ridiculous. It really is, isn't it? I didn't need to be told that something had to be done about it. I did it." I caught a flash of that resolve and sense of purpose that probably caused reporters to invent the "Steel Magnolia" label. "Now there are just a handful of TV sets. If I find any other indulgences and crazy situations then I shall put those right, too. Jimmy will expect me to. Mind you, I always discuss everything with him in advance and when we have an argument I listen to his point of view and, if he's right, then I agree to do it his way—and if I'm right then we'll do it my way."

The President agrees. So much does he have to discuss with his partner wife that now he has an official weekly lunch with her (served on trays in the Oval Office). It is the same arrangement that he has with the Vice-President and the Secretary of State, and other key advisers. And it is obvious, despite those who may raise their hands in horror at the exaggerated prospect of Rosalynn Carter as a kind of second President, that his wife rates at least as high on the team as his other advisers. In an exclusive interview about his domestic life and his relationship with Rosalynn he told me: "I see her role as a really wonderful opportunity. Of course the role of First Lady is to support me, and be a partner to me, in major projects that we undertake for the American people both here and around the world. But she can also exert her own individual personality in areas where I couldn't possibly address the issues with adequate attention. So, she is an extension of me in many ways. She has already traveled to eight or ten countries since I have been in the White House, to meet with Heads of State and discuss matters that are important to them. They know that she'll relay their ideas to me and give my ideas to them, and they've accepted her. In addition she's taken on an individual role recently in dealing with the mentally ill and the elderly, and their problems. She also works very closely with the rest of our family. My daughters-in-law or my mother (she's having a fine old time in Ireland right now) relate, through Rosalynn, to me and manage therefore to stay in touch with me domestically so that we remain a family.

"And of course, she's my wife, and a housewife, and a loved one, and a partner in many personal ways. We've been married for thirty-one years and the personal partnership has been there all the time, but she was quite reluctant in the beginning to get involved in the political realm when I ran for Governor of Georgia, in 1966. I had already run, before that time, for the State Senate, but she didn't play a major role in that campaign. She helped plan strategy but was not an active campaigner. But when I ran for Governor of Georgia in 1966, and again in 1970, she—on her own initiative—campaigned separately from me in order to increase and magnify our presence. She took our children and campaigned on the streets; she began to make speeches. Again, this was reluctantly because it's something she's frightened of and hates to do, but she did it with increasing effectiveness. And then, back in 1972 when we began to plan the Presidential campaign, she was one of that very small group around me who planned the tactics and strategy, analyzed what our chances were, and gave me good advice. During the Presidential campaign Rosalynn was able to represent me in public, before the news media and at large gatherings, as well as making individual contacts with the American people. She was able to let me know, in a much more accurate way, the sense of Americans and what their concerns were, the more personal aspects of their yearnings and problems."

I asked if the wife of a President so strongly a partner in all matters was allowed to criticize in matters of Presidential judgment. "Oh yes," he said, and grinned. "She certainly does criticize me and I encourage it. We have a completely unconstrained and natural ability to communicate with each other. We don't let barriers arise between us personally. I think she sees

---

Partners.
With the President in the Oval Office.

336

that if she and I ever disagree publicly, even on an issue of relative insignificance, then the disagreement would be magnified out of all proportion. So she tries, I think, on her own initiative to let our disagreements be resolved and discussed more privately. But she has a mind of her own, a strong mind and a good mind. And I would say that when we do have disagreements, particularly on matters where her knowledge is equal to mine, then she prevails, most of the time."

He went on: "During the campaign we didn't specifically discuss her role as First Lady but I know she thought about it and the way other First Ladies had behaved, just as I thought about the role of President and the lives of other Presidents, in order to learn from their mistakes and capitalize on their accomplishments and experience. I think that when we have completed our service in the White House Rosalynn will be recognized, accurately, for her own individual self. Her worth and contribution, both as a partner to me and in her own right, will be seen for what they are. It is, in fact, an unwarranted constraint on her ability, and talent, to make her just be a mirror of me, or subservient to me, or always working in lockstep with me, because she has so much to contribute that I couldn't possibly do.

"This weekend, for instance, we had a catastrophe in the mountain area of the south in Georgia where a dam works broke and thirty-seven people were killed. We both learned about it while we were at church and we told the Secret Service to order a plane at once. Rosalynn flew down there and she was able to be my spokesman on the spot. She also was able to bring all the compassion and understanding to the bereaved people, in a way that I couldn't possibly have done. So there she was acting for me in one way—but acting for herself in her own way. Does she still surprise me? Oh yes, she does. She surprised me, for instance, when she made her Latin American trip, with the fervency with which she studied and learned the detailed issues that are important in those countries; and she surprised me also in her rapid learning of Spanish and her ability to use it effectively. She also surprised me very much when, after her visit, I discovered the impact she had made on the foreign leaders she met there. I've seen most of them since she returned and, almost without exception, they have been effusive and, I think, quite genuine in their praise of her representation of our country. You know, all my surprises from Rosalynn have been pleasant ones."

The President talked about the burden of office and how, thanks to Rosalynn, it was considerably lightened. He said: "Sharing makes the strain easier and less of a burden. If I had to bear the responsibilities of a President without her it would be much more difficult for me. It is the help of having someone you love to relate to. She makes every day more pleasant than it would be otherwise."

338

Rosalynn not only criticizes and advises her husband the President, she acts as subeditor and "previewer" for his major policy speeches. While I was in the White House the President was preparing to deliver a major policy speech about energy, a preoccupation which he brought with him to office, and which has increased since. In bed, the night before he was due to deliver the speech to the nation on television, he read it to Rosalynn. She criticized it—considerably. He told me: "The sort of thing that she was able to point out was that the language and the phrases, which I took for granted, were such that the average person, a taxi driver, a farmer, wouldn't understand. I sometimes write in a way that isn't as simple as it should be. As I've said before, Rosalynn is able to see things much more clearly, from the viewpoint of the average American, than I am, so I don't mind her criticizing my speeches—even if she does start coming up with changes before I've reached the end of the first paragraph."

"White House Watchers" focus on every aspect of the Carter family life. "White House Watchers" live in the press rooms of both the West and the East Wings; those in the West Wing are more concerned with politics and Presidential style and those in the East Wing focus on the First Lady and her engagements. In previous Presidencies "First Lady Watchers" saw their role quite clearly. They were, almost without exception, women reporters writing for the women's pages or the "style" sections of newspapers and magazines, concerned with fashion, hairstyles, guest lists, menus, cocktail conversation, and jewelry. Rosalynn Carter has been a severe disappointment to them—and she proposes to go on being so. Some newspaper editors have been bruised by the brusque response they've

Spanish lessons in the White House for the First Lady.

Conference with Press Secretary Mary Hoyt in the presidential plane.

received from Mrs. Carter's press staff when they've devoted more time and attention to reporting Rosalynn's shopping trips than to her Chairmanship of the Mental Health Commission, to which she was appointed by the President. Her press secretary, Mary Hoyt, campaigned with the Carters and moved in, naturally, as Mrs. Carter's right hand. She is a lady to be reckoned with, a professional journalist and writer, now fiercely the guardian of Rosalynn Carter's image. She denies that she is in the business of image building but does not hesitate to pick up the phone and warn an editor that his writers are treading on sensitive ground. Mary Hoyt is part of a staff of seventeen who work with Rosalynn. And there is what Rosalynn calls "security," the Secret Service agents, identifiable to the public, and each other, by the badges they all wear on their lapels and the wrist microphones and plastic earpieces with which they communicate to each other (by seeming to talk into their sleeves). They may seem a cumbersome and perhaps even comic part of the paraphernalia surrounding the First Lady, but they are far from that. The small platoon which is attached to the First Lady, in order to maintain a round-the-clock watch, know that theirs is one of the most difficult and daunting protection jobs in the whole world. More U.S. Presidents have died from assassination than in any other country in the world. So, the Secret Service, heavily armed and highly trained, are always close to Mrs. Carter, though they never actually look at her. Instead, they watch us, the crowd, the windows, the roofs, passing vehicles. They carry, in neat briefcases, folding Israeli "Uzi" submachine guns. The bulletproof cars in which Rosalynn Carter travels are equipped with radio and telephones and the drivers are also Secret Service agents. Rosalynn told me: "I am used to security and so is Amy. It's been like that ever since we went to the Governor's Mansion in Atlanta. We had to have security and protection there all the time, so we got used to it. I think after a while it doesn't feel like an intrusion. And when we go to Camp David for our family weekends the Secret Service agents don't have to stick so close to us as they are able to make the whole area secure and we can wander about more."

The Secret Service also guard the Carter home back in Plains, Georgia. Plains has become a thriving tourist attraction, with a variety of guided tours taking visitors around a town so small that you can drive right through it in less than two minutes. The Secret Service have somehow become mixed up with the souvenir shops, the postcard stands, and, of course, Jimmy's brother Billy Carter and his garage and beer-boosting business. The Secret Service have taken a lease on a house near the Carter home—for ten years. And guides on the bus tours report with glee, over their loudspeakers, that the Secret Service must know something about whether Jimmy is running for a second term and is likely to get in. In the meantime, plenty of traders are just cashing in and finding that having Jimmy Carter as President is good for business at home. The largest peanut in the world stands eighteen feet high, outside a local supermarket. And, although brother Billy has outraged and scandalized the moralist matrons of the United States, he continues to amuse his own family. He drives around Plains in a pickup truck with the words "Redneck Power" written down both sides of it and "Ain't Apologizing" on the tailgate. It is difficult, in any case, to censure those who do nothing more harmful than sell postcards, souvenir pencils, and "Jimmy Won" T-shirts. But still, Rosalynn's mother, Miz Allie, regrets it. She misses her daughter and the daily visits and conversations she used to have with her. She used to sit quietly each evening in a rocking chair on her porch. Now she cannot do so. The guided tours pass her porch and every one of them points out the house—and her—as one of the sights of Plains. She has taken, now, to sitting in her living room with the blinds down. Rosalynn's brother Murray, a gregarious teacher at the local high school, recently married, for the second time, in a Plains church. He and his wife-to-be Helen invited about twenty guests to what they hoped would be a quiet wedding (he had been divorced, and in Plains that is a situation regarded with reserve). Naturally, among the guests they invited were his sister and her husband, the President. So, the twenty friends of the family, and as many Secret Service agents, turned up—and a crowd of five thousand. Now Murray and his wife have an unlisted telephone number, to avoid the 4 A.M. calls from Australian disc jockeys wanting to interview the brother-in-law of the President.

When the Carters moved into the White House they persuaded their children to move with them, as they were determined to keep the family, children and grandchildren, together as long as possible. Now, Jeff goes to college in Washington and lives "at home" with his wife and his mother and father. Chip also moved in, with his wife and child, but found the strain of White House life difficult. Now he's back in Plains working in the family peanut business (which Jimmy Carter put in blind trust when he became President) and denying rumors of a family row. Jack runs an agricultural farming business in Calhoun, Georgia, and Amy, of course, lives at the White House. About Amy, the press reported that Rosalynn, already the mother of three boys aged twenty, seventeen, and fifteen, was reluctant to add to the family, but Jimmy wanted another child, preferably a daughter. Rosalynn told me: "There was never any doubt between us. We had always wanted another child but I had a small gynecological problem which had to be cleared up before we could have one. We talked it over with the boys and told them that we were going to have another baby, and they were just as excited as Jimmy and me.

"Does she get spoiled? Well, of course she's spoiled. You must remember that Jimmy and I had been married for twenty-one years when she was born and she was the first daughter. Now she has three grown brothers who are just like fathers to her, but I think that she's become very well adjusted to that kind of attention and affection. She's had it from the whole family always, and ever since she's been born, she's been in the public eye. She is, in fact, completely nonchalant about it and I'm very proud of her." For Amy, security may well be an inevitable and essential part of her background which she has to accept, but there is no doubt that she is uncomfortably aware that much of her life is played out in public. I was in one of the corridors of the White House when she came clattering around the corner, to join a group of friends. She was unaware and uncaring—until she caught sight of us standing by the door. She immediately slowed down, stopped swinging her arms, lowered her head, and walked decorously into the room, aware of the presence of the movie camera. But I hope that, in her head, she continued to skip and run.

The stories printed about the Carter family range from speculation about Rosalynn's "face lift" to old chestnuts, like the clash of wills between Rosalynn and her mother-in-law Miz Lillian. I asked Rosalynn whether the stories ever hurt. "Yes, they do," she told me, "they always have. Jimmy tells me not to pay any attention to them. During the campaign we were watched like hawks all the time, to see if we made a mistake or made fools of ourselves. That is probably fair when you're running for office. But I still get hurt by the stories that talk about family rows or are personal about Jimmy and me, like the 'face lift.' I didn't have a face lift and I'm glad to be able to tell you, because you're the first person to come and ask me directly about it. I've always had a problem with my eyelids and just before we came to live in the White House I went and had a tiny operation on the corners of my eyes to clear it up. I would willingly have told any reporter who had asked me, even though I think it's a rather personal question. It's true, also, that there was a family argument about marijuana but it wasn't the great bustup between us all that the papers

Amy and friends in the White House.

Sunday morning after church,
in the private apartments
of the White House.

Puerto Rico.

would have you believe. Both Jimmy and I have strong feelings about pot smoking and we make sure that the children understand those feelings. And I do get cross when newspapers talk about my shopping trips, because clothes don't mean very much to me and even less to Jimmy. I buy all his clothes for him, he won't even go to the shop to have them fitted. I find it difficult to go out into the shops now without being recognized and bothered, so I have an assortment of dresses and skirts and blouses sent to the White House once in a while and I choose a few of the sort I wear and send the rest back."

I watched Rosalynn, on her trip to Puerto Rico, move easily among TV, radio, and press people in the plane, chatting to them, asking about their assignments and their personal lives. It was a relaxed atmosphere. Nevertheless, the reporters, without exception, all felt that anything Rosalynn said during those off-duty and unguarded moments was as eligible for publication as her formal speeches and interviews. Lee Thornton, a pretty and sharp-minded CBS reporter, told me: "I know it's nice that she likes to talk to us, and it might be nice to think that she could have off-the-record moments, but we journalists talked about this in the union in CBS and decided that we just couldn't allow that. Therefore, anything she says, if it's useful, we are likely to use. But I don't feel much sympathy for her because, after all, she wanted the job, she ran for office, she knew what it was all about, she didn't have to become First Lady, and she knows the rules. Actually, I think she's a very tough cookie. I honestly think that the women who get into the White House want it, and they want it more than almost anything. I watched Betty Ford knock herself out for six months on the campaign trail and this woman Rosalynn certainly did the same thing. I know Betty Ford protested that she didn't want Gerry to have the office. But in fact both of them wanted the job when they got there and all this talk about loss of privacy is just so much hooey. If they wanted to be private First Ladies they could be, but they knew perfectly well what they were going for when they started the campaign."

Helen Thomas, veteran UPI reporter and "First Lady Watcher," is based so near to the nerve center of Carter family life that in a public speech Rosalynn has referred, edgily, to the wariness she feels about Helen Thomas. Helen Thomas herself told me: "I think Mrs. Carter is a very, very tough lady indeed and I think she's aware at all times of what she is doing. Did you know, Miz Lillian said during the campaign that Rosalynn wants to be First Lady more than Jimmy wants to be President? And Miz Lillian may have had something. I don't waste my sympathy on First Ladies and the people in the White House. They know what they're getting into. They know they're going to be totally exposed—and they ask for it. Might it be a strain on her? Well, everything is a strain. It's a strain being a reporter, jumping around, carrying your bags and typewriter. But being a reporter has a sense of fulfillment and Rosalynn Carter has a sense of accomplishment about her life, too, so I put my pity elsewhere."

Talking to these intelligent and experienced lady journalists, and remembering the label "Steel Magnolia" that they pinned on the First Lady, it's not difficult to wonder if it's a simple case of projection. They certainly deserve, for themselves, the label "iron maidens." Perhaps the reporters object to the new frugal Carter regime. Now, when they travel in Presidential planes, they must pay for their beer and soft drinks—even the peanuts. I was charged $4.26. Mrs. Carter paid $11.00.

Rosalynn may dislike formality but she handles it well. When the Shah of Iran and his Queen arrived for a State reception at the White House they were greeted with riots and demonstrations by Iranian students protesting the political regime in Iran, and the welcoming procedures and speeches were marred by drifting clouds of tear gas across the White House lawn. Rosalynn Carter dabbed her eyes and carried on. She chatted briefly and informally with the Shah and his wife, staying close beside Jimmy and, inevitably, holding hands with him. Holding hands, for the Carters a marital habit which drew the eyes of the American nation on Jimmy's Inauguration Day, is certainly a matter of affection, not affectation. I believe that they don't know they're doing it most of the time and it has now become as natural, between them, as a man putting his hands in his pockets when he walks. It is also heartwarming and refreshing to witness. Rosalynn is well aware of her wifely role: "You know, I *am* a wife, and a mother, and I like that most of all. I want to be a good mother and make a good home for Jimmy, because I think that kind of background is so important to whatever Jimmy does. I like being a partner to Jimmy and I like my work in the area of mental health and all the jobs Jimmy gives me, which stretch my mind. But I feel that I've been married to this man for so many years now that he has become my life. You mustn't forget that as his wife I love him deeply and just want to look after him too."

Inevitably, the Carters must leave the White House, perhaps after one term, and four years in office but at most, after two terms, and eight years in office. What, then, does Rosalynn Carter want for herself? "Well, I want to go home and be with my friends and be in my house. You see, it's been a long time. First, Jimmy was Governor for four years; then we campaigned together for two years; then we moved to Washington. So it's been a very, very long time since I've really been in my own house. So that's what I want to do. I want to go and be with my things. Sometimes when we get tired, I tell Jimmy, 'Oh, I wish that I could go home and do nothing.'

"And then Jimmy says to me, 'You'd only be happy for about two weeks and then you'd be looking for something else to do.' And I guess that's true too. So I'll take what comes along and do the best I can. . . ."

346

ACKNOWLEDGMENTS AND SUGGESTIONS FOR FURTHER READING:

Chapter 1 The Company President
Burlingame, R. *Engines of Democracy: Inventions and Society in Mature America* (America in Two Centuries Series), Arno Press, 1976 (reprint of 1940 ed.).
Chandler, A.D., Jr. *Giant Enterprise: Ford, General Motors and the Automobile Industry,* Harcourt, Brace & World Paperbacks, 1946.
Cochran, T.C. *American Business in the 20th Century,* Harvard University Press, 1972 (orig. title *American Business Systems,* 1957).
Gustin, L.R. *Billy Durant—Creator of General Motors,* Eerdmans, 1973.
Nader, R. *Unsafe at Any Speed,* Grossman, 1965.
Rae, J.B. *The American Automobile: A Brief History* (Chicago History of American Civilization Series), University of Chicago Press, 1965.
Rayback, J.G. *History of American Labor,* Macmillan, 1959.
Sloan, A.P., Jr. *My Years with General Motors,* Doubleday, 1964 (Pan Books, 1967).

Chapter 2 The Schoolteacher
Flexner, E. *Century of Struggle: The Women's Rights Movement in the U.S.,* Atheneum, 1968; Belknap Press & Harvard University Press (paperback), 1975 (rev. ed.).
French, W.M. *America's Educational Traditions: An Interpretive History,* Heath, 1964.
Hughes, J.M. & Schultz, F.M. (eds.) *Education in America,* Harper & Row, 1976 (4th ed.).
Katz, M.B. (ed.) *Education in American History: Readings on the Social Issues,* Praeger, 1973.
Perkinson, H.J. *Imperfect Panacea: American Faith in Education (1865–1968),* Random House, 1968.
Silberman, C. *Crisis in the Classroom,* Random House, 1971.
Woody, T. *A History of Women's Education in the United States,* Science Press, 1929.

Chapter 3 The District Attorney
Blumberg, A. *Criminal Justice (Problems of American Society),* Franklin Watts, Inc., 1967.
Friedman, L.M. *A History of American Law,* Simon & Schuster, 1973.
Griswold, E.N. *Law and Lawyers in the United States,* Stevens & Sons, 1964; Harvard University Press, 1965.
Hurst, J.W. *Law and Social Process in United States History* (American Constitutional & Legal History Series), Da Capo, 1971 (reprint of 1960 ed.).
Jacob, H. *Justice in America: Courts, Lawyers and the Judicial Process,* Little, Brown, 1972 (2nd ed.).
Miller, P. *The Legal Mind in America (from Independence to the Civil War),* Cornell University Press, 1962.
Pound, R. *The Lawyer from Antiquity to Modern Times,* West Publishing Co., 1953.
Schwartz, B. & Jensen, O. *American Heritage History of the Law in America* (2 vols.), American Heritage, 1974.

Chapter 4 The Plantation Owner
Cash, W.J. *The Mind of the South,* Knopf, 1960; Random House (paperback), 1960.
Coles, R. *Farewell to the South,* Atlantic Monthly Press, 1972.
Eaton, C. *A History of the Old South,* Macmillan, 1975 (3rd ed.).
Franklin, J.H. *From Slavery to Freedom: A History of American Negroes,* Knopf, 1974 (4th ed.).
Phillips, U.B. *Life and Labor in the Old South,* Little, Brown, 1929.

Chapter 5 The Preacher
Bestic, A. *Praise the Lord and Pass the Contribution,* Cassell, 1971.
Hudson, W.S. *Religion in America,* Scribner's, 1973 (2nd ed.).
Humbard, R. *To Tell The World,* Prentice-Hall, 1975.
McLoughlin, W.G., Jr. *Modern Revivalism—C.G. Finney to Billy Graham,* Ronald, 1959.
Mead, S.E. *The Lively Experiment—The Shaping of Christian America,* Harper & Row, 1963.
Sperry, W.L. *Religion in America,* Cambridge University Press, 1945.
Weisberger, B.A. *They Gathered at the River: The Story of the Great Revivalists and Their Impact Upon Religion in America,* Little, Brown, 1958.

Chapter 6 The Indian Chief
Brandon, W. (ed.) *The American Heritage Book of Indians,* American Heritage, 1961; Eyre & Spottiswoode, 1961.
Brown, D. *Bury My Heart at Wounded Knee: An Indian History of the American West,* Holt, Rinehart & Winston, 1971.
Hagan, W.T. *American Indians* (Chicago History of American Civilization Series), University of Chicago Press, 1961.
Josephy, A.M., Jr. *The Indian Heritage of America,* Knopf, 1968; Bantam (paperback), 1969.
McNickle, D'A. *They Came Here First,* Octagon, 1975.
Pearce, R.H. *The Savages of America,* Johns Hopkins, 1953.
Washburn, W.E. *The Indian and the White Man,* New York University Press, 1964.

Chapter 7 The Private Eye
Adams, T.F. *Law Enforcement: An Introduction to the Police Role in the Criminal Justice System,* Prentice-Hall, 1973 (2nd ed.).
Chandler, R. *Raymond Chandler Speaking,* ed. by D. Gardiner and K.S. Walker, Houghton Mifflin, 1962; Hamish Hamilton, 1962.
Cooper, L. & Platt, A. *Policing America,* Prentice-Hall, 1974.

Horan, J.D. *The Pinkertons: The Detective Dynasty That Made History,* Crown Pubs. Inc. & Robert Hale, 1970.
Kefauver, E. *Crime in America,* Greenwood, 1968 (reprint of 1951 ed.).
O'Grady, J. & Davis, N. *O'Grady: The Life and Times of Hollywood's No. 1 Private Eye,* J. Tarcher Inc., 1974.
Ruehlmann, W. *Saint With a Gun,* New York University Press, 1974.

Chapter 8 The General
Ambrose, S.E. & Barber, J.A., Jr. *The Military and American Society,* Free Press, 1972.
Cunliffe, M. *Soldiers and Civilians,* Little, Brown, 1968.
Huntington, S.P. *The Soldier and the State,* Harvard University Press, 1957.
Janowitz, M. *The Professional Soldier,* Free Press, 1960.
Weighley, R.F. *History of the U.S. Army,* Macmillan, 1967.

Chapter 9 The Immigrant
Glazer, N. & Moynihan, D.P. *Beyond the Melting Pot: The Negroes, Puerto Ricans, Jews, Italians and Irish of New York City,* M.I.T. Press, 1963 and 1970.
Handlin, O. *The Uprooted,* Atlantic Monthly Press, 1951 and 1973.
Hansen, M.L. *The Atlantic Migration, 1607–1860,* Harvard University Press and OUP, 1940.
Higham, J. *Strangers in the Land, 1860–1925,* Rutgers University Press, 1955.
Kennedy, J.F. *A Nation of Immigrants,* Harper & Row, 1964.
Riis, J. *How the Other Half Lives,* Hill & Wang, 1957 (orig. publ. 1890).
Schoener, A. (ed.) *Portal to America: The Lower East Side 1870–1925,* Holt, Rinehart & Winston, 1967.
Stein, L. *The Triangle Fire,* J.B. Lippincott Co., 1962.
Wittke, C. *We Who Built America: The Saga of the Immigrant,* U.P.B.S., 1967 (rev. ed.).

Chapter 10 The Film Star
Brownlow, K. *The Parade's Gone By,* Secker & Warburg, 1968.
Champlin, C. *The Flicks,* Ward Ritchie Press, 1977.
Halliwell, L. *The Filmgoers' Companion,* Hart-Davis, 1974 (4th ed.).
Knight, A. *The Liveliest Art,* Macmillan, 1957.
Mayersberg, P. *Hollywood the Haunted House,* Penguin Books, 1967.
Ramsaye, T. *A Million and One Nights,* F. Cass, 1964.
Rosten, L. *The Movie Colony, The Movie Makers,* Harcourt, Brace, 1941.
Wright, B. *The Long View,* Secker & Warburg, 1974.
Zierold, N. *The Child Stars,* Macdonald, 1966.

Chapter 11 The Rancher
Adams, A. *The Log of a Cowboy,* Houghton Mifflin, 1931 (orig. publ. 1903).
Dobie, J.F. *The Longhorns,* Little, Brown, 1941; Grosset & Dunlap, 1957.
Frantz, J.B. & Choate, J.E., Jr. *The American Cowboy: The Myth and the Reality,* University of Oklahoma Press, 1968 (reprint of 1955 ed.).
Pelzer, L. *The Cattlemen's Frontier,* Russell, 1969 (reprint of 1936 ed.).
Roosevelt, T. *Hunting Trips of a Ranchman,* Gregg, 1970 (reprint of 1885 ed.).
Time-Life series, *The Old West,* Time-Life, 1973.
Webb, W.P. *The Great Plains,* Ginn & Co., 1931; Grosset & Dunlap (paperback), 1957.

Chapter 12 The Football Coach
Brondfield, J. *Woody Hayes and the 100-Yard War,* Random House, 1974; Berkley Publishing Corp., 1975.
Hayes, W. *You Win With People,* 1973 (2nd ed. 1975).
Nelson, D.M. *Illustrated Football Rules,* Doubleday, Dolphin Books, 1976.
Vare, R. *Buckeye,* Harper's Magazine Press, 1974; Popular Library, 1975.

Chapter 13 The First Lady
Barzman, S. *The First Ladies,* Cowles Book Co. Inc., 1970.
Bassett, M. *Profiles & Portraits of American Presidents & Their Wives,* Grosset & Dunlap, 1969.
Means, M. *The Woman in the White House,* Random House, 1963.
Steinberg, A. *Mrs. R.: The Life of Eleanor Roosevelt,* Putnam, 1958; Longmans, Green & Co., 1958.
Stroud, K. *How Jimmy Won,* William Morrow & Co., Inc., 1977.
Wolff, P.S. *Tour of the White House with Mrs. J.F. Kennedy,* Macmillan/Doubleday, 1962.

General Reading
Beard, C.A. & M.R. (rev. & ed. by Beard, W.) *The Beard's New Basic History of the U.S.,* Doubleday, 1960; Macmillan, 1960.
Boorstin, D.J. *The Americans* (3 vols.): *1. The Colonial Experience, 2. The National Experience, 3. The Democratic Experience,* Random House, 1958–73; Penguin Books, 1965.
Cooke, A. *America,* BBC Publications, 1973.
Davidson, M.B. *Life in America* (2 vols.), Houghton Mifflin, 1951 and 1974.
Freidel, F. (ed.) & Showman, R.K. *Harvard Guide to American History,* Harvard University Press, 1974 (rev. ed.).
Furnas, J.C. *The Americans—A Social History,* Putnam, 1969.
Garraty, J.A. *A Short History of the American Nation,* Harper & Row, 1974.
Nye, R.B. & Morpurgo, J.E. *A History of the United States* (2 vols.), Penguin Books, 1970 (3rd ed.).